'A uniquely Australian ride into the dark side of film censorship, pearl-clutching outrages and moral panics, Simon Miraudo's *Book of the Banned* is an essential book for film fans, cinema scholars and card-carrying perverts alike.'
Alexandra Heller-Nicholas

'This book is f***ing great. And if they put asterisks in this quote, the censors will have won again. Impeccably researched and superbly written, *Book of the Banned* is an endlessly riveting slice of film history that demands to be read.'
Chris Taylor

'Miraudo masterfully guides us through the tangled and surprisingly fascinating history of Australian censorship and takes us on a wild journey through the rule-breaking films that tested those boundaries. Anchored by a detailed account of film history and censorship policy plus interviews with leading researchers and cinephiles, *Book of the Banned* is both a lively love-letter to controversial and challenging films and a call for our censorship practices to be reviewed.'
Dr Felicity Ford

'Important, because it pulls together the exhaustive record of snipped and smothered films, lying in the wake of decisions by Australian authorities.'
John Safran

BOOK OF THE BANNED

*Devilish Movies, Dastardly Censors and the
Scenes That Made Australia Sweat*

By Simon Miraudo

First edition published in Australia in 2023 by Low Heroes Press.

Copyright © 2023 Simon Miraudo
Simon Miraudo asserts his right to be known as the author of this work.

All rights reserved.

No part of this publication may be reproduced, stored, and/or copied electronically (except for academic use as a source), nor transmitted in any form or by any means without prior written permission of the author.

Excerpt from EASY RIDER © 1969, renewed 1997 Columbia Pictures Industries, Inc. All Rights Reserved. Courtesy of Columbia Pictures.

Lyric from 'Bloodsport and Porn' by Augie March reproduced with permission by Glenn Richards. All rights reserved.

Every effort has been made to trace copyright holders and to obtain their permission for the use of copyright material. We apologise for any errors or omissions and would be grateful if notified of any corrections that should be incorporated in future reprints or editions of this book. Contact details can be found at simonmiraudo.com

ISBN 978 0 6457063 0 7 (paperback)
ISBN 978 0 6457063 1 4 (ebook)

 A catalogue record for this book is available from the National Library of Australia

Cover Design: Hannah Atcheson
Text Design: Vaughan Davies at Stage Left Design
Editing: Elena Gomez

Simon Miraudo acknowledges the Whadjuk people of the Noongar Nation as the Traditional Custodians of the land on which this book was written. Sovereignty was never ceded. The author pays respect to Noongar elders past, present and emerging.

Printed in Australia by IngramSpark.

For Jenny and Miles

CONTENT WARNING:

This book details films that have been banned in Australia. The scenes and subject matter described include explicit sex acts, violence and gore, and troubling criminal activities that could upset even the most strong-stomached of readers.

Reader discretion is advised.

'A song, and some play, a shiny violin;
in a vault in a fuckwit's mansion.'
—*Augie March, 'Bloodsport and Porn'*

'We blew it.'
—*Peter Fonda in Easy Rider*

TABLE OF CONTENTS

Author's Note	1
A Brief Timeline of Australian Classification and Censorship	3
Introduction	5
Chapter 1: How Classification Works (Or Doesn't)	13
Chapter 2: Meet the Wowsers	21
Chapter 3: The Banned Down Under	43
Chapter 4: Are You There Margaret? It's Us, The Police	53
Chapter 5: You Can't Say That	63
Chapter 6: The 10,000 Days of Sodom	73
Chapter 7: One of the Most Revolting, Disgusting Pieces of Shit David Stratton Has Ever Seen	83
Chapter 8: Festival of Filth	93
Chapter 9: 'People Are Scared of a Hard Penis'	107
Chapter 10: Raiding the State-sanctioned Spank Bank	125
Chapter 11: Think of the Children	133
Chapter 12: No Oral, Please	147
Chapter 13: In the Realm of the Censors	161
Chapter 14: Shudder to Think	183
Chapter 15: 'Netflix Classifies Manboobs as Nudity!'	201
Chapter 16: A Collective Failure of Nerve	213
Epilogue	239
Acknowledgements	243
Notes	247
Bibliography	253

AUTHOR'S NOTE

At the start of this project, it became quickly apparent how many winding alleys and dark paths this discussion of film censorship and classification in Australia could lead us down. (Censored meaning cut or banned; classified meaning 'rated' with consumer advice.) If I had also decided to follow the detours to explain British, American and other kinds of international classification systems, you'd be holding a glorified paperweight in your hands. You'd need to devote time on forearm strength training just to crack the spine. So no, I don't go deep on Australia's history of banned books here, nor the contemporary issue of censored video games. Instead, I have tried to focus my book's scope on the censored films themselves, and their cultural worth, if any. Hopefully I've kept the historical context to only what's necessary. The rest? You'll get the gist, and that'll save me having to explain, say, the intricacies of South Australia's *Places of Public Entertainment Act 1904*. (Please don't make me explain South Australia's *Places of Public Entertainment Act 1904*.) For the sake of everyone's sanity, I have especially tried to condense the political grandstanding—and the sometimes maddening back-and-forth in parliament that occurred on censorship—in favour of providing more space for critics, filmmakers, distributors and the censors themselves. If this book proves anything, it's that politicians are the last people equipped to provide a valid contribution to the debate over difficult art, so we'll avoid them as much as possible.

A BRIEF TIMELINE OF AUSTRALIAN CLASSIFICATION AND CENSORSHIP

1896: The medium of film is introduced in Australia, with states and territories relying on public health and customs legislation to censor it.
1906: *The Story of the Kelly Gang*, the world's first feature-length film, debuts in Melbourne.
1917 - 1918: The Commonwealth Film Censorship Board is established. Australia agrees to a single censorship model, with enforcement left to the states and territories.
1927 - 1929: The Royal Commission into the Moving Picture Industry in Australia calls for the establishment of a Censorship Board and Censorship Board of Appeal. The classifications 'Suitable for Universal Exhibition' (later renamed 'For General Exhibition') and 'For Adults Only' are introduced.
--- Then, several decades of absolutely brutal bans and cuts. ---
1970 - 1971: The Film Classification Board is created; classifications are replaced by four new ratings: 'G', 'NRC' (later renamed 'PG'), 'M' and 'R'.
1973: The 'Unclassified' rating is introduced (later renamed 'Refused Classification').
1984: The 'X' classification is introduced.
1988: The Film Classification Board and the Literature Classification Board are combined into the Office of Film and Literature Classification (OFLC).
1993: The 'MA15+' classification is introduced.
1995 - 1996: The Classification Act is established. The Intragovernmental Agreement on Censorship is executed, introducing the National Classification Scheme & Code.
2005: The OFLC is dissolved and the Film Classification Board (now the Australian Classification Board) is transferred to a new department. The National Classification Code and guidelines are updated.
2012: Guidelines for the Classification of Films are updated again.
2016: The Netflix Classification Tool is introduced.
2020: A review into the Classification System commences.
Today: You begin reading this book.

INTRODUCTION

Throughout history—across banana republics, despotic empires and democratic sanctuaries alike—governments have found a way to censor incendiary expressions and ideas. Books have been burned for extolling ideologies that threatened fascist powers. Artworks have been removed, defaced or similarly thrown onto the pyre for challenging moral standards of the time. And in this very century, the Australian government outlined in legislation that there shall be no porn starring men in diapers.

The origins of that particular saga can be traced to early 2000, when the junior Coalition party in Government, the National Party, hosted a screening of five to seven hardcore pornos (the number is disputed), apparently to educate themselves on the shenanigans that occur in the kinds of flicks they were seeking to ban. As a result of that unconventional—and probably quite uncomfortable—movie night in the National Party meeting room, the conservative Australian government was compelled to add a stricter list of criteria for films that deserved the X18+ classification. This is the classification category reserved for sexually explicit movies with actual sexual activity; it was already restricted to adults 18 years of age or older, and, even more restrictively, only legal to buy or rent in the Australian Capital Territory and parts of the Northern Territory. The government decided any films that include the depiction of 'fetishes such as body piercing, application of substances such as candle wax, "golden showers", bondage, spanking or fisting' should be rated X18+. The new guidelines also now forbade any sexual activity between 'persons eighteen years of age or over [portraying] minors' in X-rated pictures. This sounds like common-sense governance, until you realise that, based on what the Nationals witnessed in their party room that night, they meant for it to include footage of adult men wearing nappies too.

Australia undeniably needs a classification system for media, primarily to ensure young people aren't harmed in the production of or by the unfettered consumption of violent, degrading or sexually abusive content. But in our attempt to walk that fine line between artistic freedom and consumer protection, Australia—and its federal and state-based arms of classification—has often waddled clumsily, usually overcorrecting to the point of absurdity. And we're not just talking about the censorship of pornography here. We've proven ourselves to be quite adept at falling face-first in our attempts to halt more traditional works, too—even while utilising the common tools of tyrannical control. It's ominous enough when police are instructed to raid cinemas, confiscate

DVDs or halt theatrical productions in the name of state-sanctioned censorship, wherever in the world that may be taking place. In Australia, however, the censorship of film and art often ends up a surreal spectacle, with police storming the stage to arrest beloved TV personality Margaret Pomeranz, or, in a particularly Brechtian instance, some literal puppets. (I'll explain later.) Consider this book a mocking tribute to both the authoritarian terror and vaudevillian farce of these efforts.

Of course, other nations have their own censorious histories. From 1934 to 1968 Hollywood had the Hays Code, which tried to stem the damage of its Golden Era scandals by keeping smut and violence off the screen, necessitating the introduction of sly visual language. (Think: a train entering a tunnel to symbolise sex; a classic of the genre!) British parliament passed the *Video Recordings Act 1984* at the behest of conservative family groups to limit violent 'video nasties' from going direct-to-VHS. China and Russia have scrubbed gay and lesbian content from many international imports. And the *Monty Python* crew faced global ire with its provocative 1979 satire *Life of Brian*, though Sweden saw the light side of the situation, using the fact it was banned in Norway on advertisements to stir some local pride in contrast with their neighbouring prudes.

Sweden's northern neighbours Denmark legalised audiovisual pornography entirely in 1969, which was followed by the nation's 1970 release *Threesome*, marketed here as the first Danish film since they abolished censorship. Australia obviously banned *Threesome* before approving a heavily edited cut, but we never banned *Life of Brian*, and we didn't cut any queer content from *Rocketman*, *Bohemian Rhapsody* or *Beauty and the Beast*, as occurred elsewhere in the world. (In the instance of Disney's live-action remake of *Beauty and the Beast*, Kuwaiti censors were rankled by Josh Gad's character, LeFou, and his longing looks at Gaston; mere seconds of screen time. An Alabama drive-in similarly refused to screen this new take on an animated classic, explaining that they would not compromise on the teachings of the bible, though I'm still not sure which biblical book gives the thumbs up to the singing French candlestick.) Australia even got the uncut version of David Lynch's *Wizard of Oz* pastiche *Wild at Heart* in 1990, while Americans had to make do with a re-edit that obscures Willem Dafoe's disgusting robber Bobby Peru accidentally blowing his own head off with a shotgun. Still, we're not yet as freewheeling as the French, who initially afforded their lascivious homegrown features *Blue is the Warmest Colour* and *Double Lover* a rating that allowed unaccompanied 12-year-olds into the cinema to see those films' full-frontal escapades. Mon dieu!

Our nation self-identifies as fair and progressive, despite not having entrenched freedom of speech in our constitution. So we have to ask: what aren't we allowed to see, and why? Who sets the rules? How harshly are they being enforced? Whose moral standards are being upheld, anyway? Who suffers as a result? And what compelled writer Robert Cettl, in his book *Offensive to a Reasonable Adult,* to declare in 2011 that Australia's classification system was 'the strictest of all democratic nations in the western world'—the same year we finally freed Pier Paolo Pasolini's *Salò, or the 120 Days of Sodom* from decades of censored solitary confinement?

This book specifically digs into the history of Australian cinematic censorship, revealing a series of surprising and sometimes shocking stories, often more memorable, disturbing, morally wrenching and darkly hilarious than the censored films themselves. In each tale, there are heroes, anti-heroes, unexpected criminals and downright dastardly villains, though they're not always whom you'd expect. Even the easily-blameable Classification Board, which has consistently shapeshifted over the decades and deserves closest scrutiny of all, offers a significant public service. In 2019 it reviewed and applied the Refused Classification (RC) rating to the Facebook livestream (or 'short film' as they described it) of Brenton Tarrant's mass shooting at a Christchurch mosque, effectively banning it and introducing criminal penalties for those who try to share it. (According to Australian law at the time, no penalties could have been enforced until the board handed down the RC-rating.) The same public service cannot be claimed for past boards' reactive ratings or straight-up censorship of classics *La Dolce Vita, Blow-Up, The Texas Chain Saw Massacre, Rosemary's Baby, Gimme Shelter, A Fistful of Dollars, The Graduate, Barbarella, The Birds, Salò, Breathless* and, um, *The Human Centipede 2,* which all had their artistic merits challenged, and which all fought back against accusations of immorality with varying degrees of success.

In the case of 1960's *La Dolce Vita,* it was a shot of a woman's cleavage that was deleted from a strip act. In 1966's *Blow-Up,* it was breasts and a flash of pubic hair in need of censoring, as well as some comparatively tame lines of dialogue (of the 'get stuffed' variety), which left the slashed sequences spluttering 'like an old Charlie Chaplin comedy', as was written in *Cinema Papers.* By the end of the sixties, the board was cutting up to six minutes from the notorious Anthony Newley feature *Can Heironymus Merkin Ever Forget Mercy Humppe and Find True Happiness?*— though this was probably not Newley's biggest problem at the time, given that his soon-to-be-ex Joan Collins later blamed the movie for their divorce.

The censors snipped 12 whole minutes from director Robert Rossen's *Lilith* in 1964, including a lesbian sex scene featuring Jean Seberg's nymphomaniac main character. Seberg probably wasn't surprised, given Jean-Luc Godard's 1960 classic *Breathless (À bout de souffle)*, in which she starred, was at this point still banned in Australia. Godard was particularly unlucky here in the 1960s; the board censored nude footage of star Brigitte Bardot from his 1963 effort *Contempt (Le Mépris)*; a year later they banned *A Married Woman (Une femme mariée)*; and they banned *Masculin Féminin* in 1966 before passing a version with eight minutes deleted, including a charged racial exchange between 'two negroes and girl in train' as it was described in a Classification Board report at the time, identified in Sari Braithwaite's documentary *[CENSORED]*. Mercifully, Godard's next feature, *Week-end*, would earn an uncut Australian release in 1971, soon after our introduction of the R-rating. That was still four years after it debuted in France.

It wasn't just Godard who irked the censors. The entire filmmaking population of Sweden wound up in the crosshairs during the supposedly swinging sixties. Though 1969's *I Love, You Love (Jag älskar, du älskar)* and *Like Night and Day* became the most inflammatory examples (discussed in Chapter 2), spare a thought for the others that were trimmed to unrecognition, like actor Mai Zetterling's first effort as a director, *Loving Couples (Älskande Par)* from 1964, which wound up 20 minutes shorter after making the trip down under. Her 1966 follow-up *Night Games (Nattlek)*, about a grown man's sexual psyche and the mother who mangled it, didn't even get that courtesy; it was first banned before a 'reconstructed' version (sans 40 seconds of sex) passed. A servile, too-grateful reporter from the *Canberra Times* nonetheless wrote, 'The censor has been gentle with *Night Games*—more power to him—and thus we may watch paedophilia, a sublimated Oedipus complex, the making of a blue movie starring the mother's bored pals, all presented so credibly and so matter-of-factly that one knows instinctively that the objective of the film is to explain, never to titillate for its own sake.'

Easily the most infamous Swedish export of the era was 1967's *I Am Curious (Yellow)*, which ignited a storm of controversy in the United States for its intersection of sociopolitical commentary and explicit sex. If you're worried how it fared in Australia, don't: the distributors, aware of our reputation, didn't even bother to attempt distribution until 1973. Even that was an ambitious swing at the time: a year earlier, the board had declared an RC-rating for *Language of Love*—submitted by the Swedish Institute of Sexual Research—before passing an edited version that came with a warning, as directed by the Attorney-General, that stressed it should only be considered for sex education purposes.

In 1953, it was written in *The West Australian* that 'the average cut in a censored feature film is about ten feet.' They continued to make the point that, actually, we had it pretty good: 'In 1952, a total of 650 feet were denied us from a total 3,103,696 feet, which constituted 390 feature films. We were denied 900 feet from 400 pictures in 1949, 1,040 feet from 407 pictures in 1950, and 860 feet from 427 films in 1951. These figures do not suggest our film censorship is heavy handed.' Never mind that this meant nearly 36 minutes had been shorn unceremoniously over four years.

But the issue of censorship and inconsistent classification isn't simply a dusty old scandal from the annals of Australian history. In this book I'll regale you with the depressing fiasco of *A Serbian Film*, which was considered suitable for release in 2011 before the board suddenly reneged due to conservative pressure, forcing the small Aussie distributor Accent Films to recall all DVDs. And in a recent twist, the board has become an unlikely bedfellow in the fight against prudishness, beginning when the Australian government allowed Netflix to classify their own movies, which unintentionally resulted in a shift towards more squeamish American standards than we previously let slide here. In the 2020s, it was the board itself that raised the red flag over the Americanisation of our shifting mores. As Margaret Anderson, former director of the Classification Board, exclaimed incredulously to me during one of our lengthy conversations, 'Netflix classifies manboobs as nudity!'

Imagine all the self-censorship this has wrought; the erasure of marginalised voices and artists, established by more than a century of jackbooted stage-stormings and legal threats, visible yet invisible in the films that eventually earn release from almost any era. Speaking of stormtroopers: if you were fortunate enough to buy a ticket to George Lucas' *Star Wars* back in 1977, you were seeing a sliced and diced version courtesy of distributor 20th Century Fox, who had secured an M-rating by excising the shot of Luke Skywalker's aunt and uncle smouldering as charred skeletons on Tatooine—it remained absent in Australia until the VHS release in 1982. Further examples of self-censorship can be found everywhere, if you know where to look (and this book will point you towards those filmic wounds), in movies ranging from *Men in Black* to *Lady Bird*—let alone the movies you'll never see. No wonder a disillusioned former deputy chief censor turned to distributing adult entertainment himself. (Again, I'll explain later.) It has even culminated with nearly all major streaming services releasing unclassified films and TV shows, thus breaking the law in Australia on a near-weekly basis, because the alternative might be to face a confounding ban. The fact is, if you watched an original movie or series on Amazon Prime Video, Stan, Binge or nearly any other major streaming service in Australia, you were likely doing so in defiance of Australian law. They get away with it (and, I suppose, so do you) because the Classification Board is no longer in the business of enforcement and hasn't been for a long while. That may sound like a win for freedom, but as this book posits, many of the politicians who championed censorship and made difficult art films their raison d'être simply refocused on even greater and more damaging culture wars later. These stories of local film censorship are the kindling for the cultural dumpster fires we regularly face in Australia today.

The censoring of films has always been a means to an end, and if films are more easily accessible now than ever before, Australia as a whole has become more censorious, secretive and invasive. In May of 2022, Australia placed 39th on Reporters Without Borders' (RSF) World Press Freedom Index, just behind the Ivory Coast and Taiwan. This ranking was the culmination of sweeping legislative actions by Scott Morrison's Coalition government, including the regulation of our online spaces, which had been persistently tinkered with by preceding governments. Because of that, how we understand and legally define the concept of 'harmful online content' refers back to the National Classification Scheme. Effectively, the way we are allowed to navigate the internet today is informed by a system that was designed decades ago to rate and censor-by-suggestion movies. This is a system that originated a century earlier for a totally different medium; an arm of censorship that was spurred by Sydney police who were sweating their depiction in bushranging flicks and Salvationists worried about sinners pashing on in darkened cinemas. *Book of the Banned* aims to connect these dots explicitly. As Ina Bertrand put it in her excoriating 1978 text *Film Censorship in Australia*,

> If films were an esoteric commodity for a limited audience they would cause no more controversy than manuscripts did in the fourteenth century, before the invention of printing made possible cheap books. But films—like books—are a mass medium, so fear of their effects goes side by side with the spread of the technology that makes them possible. Out of fear grows the desire for control, a control which can—and does—take many forms.

Forty-five years later, this truth has crystallised.

As a film critic for the past 15 years—with more than 1,400 reviews contributed to Rotten Tomatoes—I've been particularly fascinated by cinematic exploits that have pushed boundaries and, specifically, censors' noses out of joint. Some may chalk it up to an oh-so-Australian disdain for authority, or delighting in contrarianism. But I truly believe discussing the movies, scenes, shots and individual lines of dialogue that were deemed too extreme for Aussie eyes and ears helps us see how far we've come in Australia as a society; and uncovering those that continue to send the wowsers to their fainting couches reminds us how far we have to go.

Yes, these wild stories you're about to read are all true. To paraphrase John Waters' *Pink Flamingos*—which was banned five times between 1976 and 1983 for 'coprophagy' among other things, and ultimately rated 'X'—I'm not shitting ya.

CHAPTER 1
HOW CLASSIFICATION WORKS (OR DOESN'T)

If you ask the average punter today, they'll insist Australia doesn't ban films. Nah. Australia? Ban films? Crikey, mate, not in this country. Now China, yeah, they'll ban films, from government-critical flicks like *Red Corner* to features with homosexual themes like *Brokeback Mountain*. They'll even ban inexplicable fringe cases like *Christopher Robin* (because images of Winnie-the-Pooh aren't allowed, apparently, due to comparisons with Chinese leader Xi Jinping) and *Babe: Pig in the City* (because live-action animals can't be seen to speak). But that's China. Not 'Straya.

Iran, on the other hand, will not only ban films, they'll ban antagonistic filmmakers from making the films too. Director Jafar Panahi—a prominent critic of the Islamic Republic of Iran—was kept under house arrest, leaving him no choice but to find inventive new ways to deliver his art to the world. He filmed a home 'diary', ingeniously called it *This Is Not a Film* to throw his government off the scent, and found someone to smuggle it out of the country on a flash drive hidden inside a cake. In Australia, filmmakers can rest assured they won't eventually have to bake their films into a dessert to earn a release.

Russia, Malaysia, Indonesia and North Korea (the latter famously unhappy with *Team America: World Police* and *The Interview*) ban films all the time. Yet most locals would say Australia, this bastion of larrikinism and giving everyone a fair go, could never, you galah.

Except, we totally do. In Australia, a film can be Refused Classification (RC), which means it becomes illegal to own, screen or watch, punishable by a five-figure fine and time in prison. The academic Gareth Griffith observed that the term refused classification, 'implies that nothing is banned [but] only restricted if necessary. Classification has certainly a more neutral flavour than the more pejorative term censorship.' Of course, the act of refusal is anything but neutral, so this book won't beat around the bush, and will use the terms 'banned' and 'censor' where appropriate.

Refused Classification is the most extreme rating doled out by the Australian Classification Board (ACB), a body that has an origin story more convoluted than a thicket of thornbushes, and just as fun to unpick, but stick with me here. The board belongs to the Classification Branch, which is part of the Australian government's Department of Infrastructure, Transport, Regional Development, Communications and the Arts (as of this writing). But it is ultimately independent from government. The board passes judgment on every film, TV series and even computer game prior to its release. Theoretically, if you've seen it, it's because they saw it first. In fact, if you've ever seen it, it's because they let you. It had once been known as the Censorship Board, but when VHS tapes democratised the distribution of content at great volume, it was decided the board should simply 'classify' by providing ratings and offering viewing advice, rather than 'censor' (or at least, not do so explicitly). The board comprises a director, deputy director, board members and temporary board members, with the latter called to action for as little as one day to three months should the workload require it. Today, members include academics from English literature and psychology departments, writers and actors, and, in one case, a trainer of customs officers (specifically in the areas of drug detection technology and being able to identify prohibited imports and exports.) They're armed with a handful of federal legislative documents, the *Classification (Publications, Films and Computer Games) Act 1995* and the *National Classification Code (May 2005)*. What they don't have are any enforcement powers. Those are left to the individual states and territories, which each have their own laws on classification and censorship, despite the federal legislation offering a handy, standardised template for how they should each go about it; a hangover from the earliest days of cinema in Australia, and indeed the delicate negotiations that preceded Federation. We'll get to this in a bit.

Right now, the board relies on the *Guidelines for the Classification of Films 2012* for their rulings. The guidelines outline a film's 'classifiable elements': themes, violence, sex, language, drug use and nudity. Depending on the presence or 'impact' of each of those elements, a film can be rated anywhere on a scale that includes General (G) for general audiences, Parental Guidance (PG) for content that's mild in impact, Mature (M) for content that's moderate in impact, Mature Accompanied (MA15+) for content that's strong in impact, and Restricted (R18)+ for content that's high in impact. Each classification comes with consumer advice, which is the little contextual description that accompanies a rating, and these can often read like enigmatic short stories. Consider Miranda July's *Me and You and Everyone We Know*, which was rated R18+ in 2005 for 'high level themes'. High level themes? This I gotta see!

Titles classified MA15+ are restricted to viewers aged 15 or older; anyone under the age of 15 needs to be accompanied by a parent or legal guardian (in other words, going to the cinema for an MA15+ title with an older brother or sister doesn't count—except, weirdly, in Queensland, where you can go with any random adult). Restricted titles are solely for the 18 and older crowd. Only the ACT and the NT wanted additional access to another Restricted category, X18+, named 'X' for the 'extra point-of-sale controls'. These show 'actual sexual intercourse and other sexual activity between consenting adults,' provided they don't also contain 'depictions of violence, sexual violence, sexualised violence or coercion' and the actors aren't dressed as babies—otherwise, it's a banning for them too. (Controversially, X18+ films are banned from sale in select NT communities if they are designated a prohibited material area by the Indigenous Affairs Minister, similar to how alcohol is banned in certain spots. This specific prohibition was introduced in 2007, and in 2012, an amendment was made in response to suggestions of racism, only to note that this prohibition 'does not affect the operation of the *Racial Discrimination Act 1975*'. Well, if they say so...)

If the board believes a film has gone too far in its content—taking into account context and impact—it is given the rating of Refused Classification. Even their website acknowledges that Refused Classification material is commonly referred to as being 'banned'. Strewth. If a filmmaker, distributor or other party challenges a decision by the Classification Board, it then goes to the Classification Review Board, which is made up of a convenor, deputy convenor and other members. Both boards rely on majority decisions, but the Classification Review Board starts fresh, allowing a completely new set of eyes to consider a feature, and maybe ban it all over again. Hard luck if you've already paid the initial classification fee, which is priced depending on the length: up to $2,180 for a two-hour film or $2,760 if it's three hours—but that's for a cinema release; streaming releases are much cheaper (around $900 for a three-hour flick). A streaming TV series will likely cost somewhere between $1,500 and $2,000. For each of these, it takes up to 20 working days for a decision—though you can always pay the $420 priority fee. The appeals fee is much more straightforward: a flat $10,000.

Excluding a few cultural exemptions for film festivals and the like, a distributor who decides to exhibit an unrated title—or worse, one that was banned—will face a potential fine of up to $15,000 or imprisonment for 18 months. Maybe. Enforcement of the law depends ultimately on the flagging enthusiasm (or in some cases overzealousness) of Australia's individual states and territories' police and law enforcement bodies. An Intergovernmental Agreement on Censorship was executed in 1995 (better known as the National Classification Scheme) in an attempt to bring the nation's array of hard-headed governments under one classification roof. This meant that any changes to the National Classification Code or the classification guidelines would have to be agreed upon by ministers in charge of classification matters from all jurisdictions. But the agreement was only passed once the Northern Territory and Tasmania were offered what I'll call the 'Fleetwood Mac exception': they can go their own way and reclassify content as they so choose. It's worth pointing out that the ABC, SBS and other free-to-air and subscription television providers don't have to adhere to the National Classification Code, and are regulated under separate codes of practice. For the most part, I won't be dealing with them much at all. They can go their own way too.

†

Former director of the Australian Classification Board Margaret Anderson explained to me the process of classifying theatrical films, or at least as it was during her tenure, which began in 2013 and ended in 2020:

> Literally we run the film [in one of two on-site cinemas] from start to end no stopping. You and your colleagues sit. There's a table that runs along the back of the cinema. And you have got a little light. We write on blue paper because blue paper is the easiest to read in a dark cinema with a little itty-bitty light.

It's not far removed from how the job was done in the early 1960s, as journalist Desmond O'Grady reported in *The Bulletin* at the time: '[T]here is a theatre in which feature films are screened each morning and afternoon. Usually there are only two or three people there, seated at desks as if they are undergoing an examination. In fact, they are examiners; if they want to make critical comments they switch on a discreet green light which illuminates their notebooks.' Today's process differs slightly for documentaries and films not in the English language, as those require just two assessors. Anderson tells me assessors have to watch non-English language features without English subtitles about one-fifth of the time, conceding that even when they do come with subtitles, 'you're always going to be way behind the eight-ball, culturally, because you're ignorant of the cultural mores of that society'. The process differs again for streaming and home entertainment releases: a single classifier will watch it alone at their desk, though Anderson insists the computer screens are 'really high definition'. Further leeway was offered during and after the COVID-19 outbreak that followed Anderson's period on the board, offering flexibility in reviewing conditions at home thanks to the department supplying classifiers with laptops that had increased security.

When assessors are examining films, they follow a golden rule, Anderson explains: write something once every two minutes, 'partly so that you don't stop classifying and start watching.'

> You master the art of not having to look down and being able to scribble, and what you are doing is making notes about the six classifiable elements and they are themes, violence, coarse language, sex, drug use and nudity. It doesn't matter what the intensity level is; you are making a complete note about all six classifiable elements in that film. When you get to the end, if there is anything that any of the panel is concerned about, you go back and rewatch scenes. What can often happen is in very frenetic fight scenes, for example, you might be sitting there thinking, *God, how many heads exploded? How many times did that gun go off? How many bullets were sprayed or whatever the issue might be.* You go, 'Right, let's go back and have a look at that.' Or someone will say, 'Was there actually an utterance of cunt language in that fight sequence?' One or two of you may say, 'Yes it was' and the other one will go, 'Really? I didn't think it was cunt.' I can't tell you the number of times we've gone back to listen, and we've gone back to get colleagues and we've said to them, 'We're not gonna tell you what we think was said. We just want you to shut your eyes, listen to this scene.' We've literally dragged colleagues in. It can literally be the decider as to whether or not a film gets a higher classification or a lower one.

If you're wondering what has tipped a film over an R-rating to the damned netherworld of the banned, you're not alone. The line between R18+ and RC is often imperceptible. In some cases, the RC deathblow has been handed to features that used improper and illegal filming practices, putting women and children at risk. Others, however, have been banned because of cultural misunderstandings, particularly of the gay community, or an uncertainty as to whether or not directors were depicting sexual or violent acts with the intention of titillating viewers. And it's not just those films on the furthest fringes of cinema that suffer from this sliding scale of extremity; many movies in Australia have been recut by their own distributor to ensure they get a wider audience after the board slaps them with a higher-than-expected rating. When those movies arrive on DVD, Blu-ray or streaming services, they might possibly be patched back together with their deleted footage (carrying a higher rating), but the board's power is such that, as far as cinema releases go, distributors will now self-censor for bigger box office returns. That's not always a cynical move (as we'll discuss later on, the MA-rating initially awarded to *Lady Bird* could have kept away its most relevant demographic: teen girls), and overall, the Classification Board has created a theatrical environment where parents always know what they're in for when they take their kids to a PG, M or MA15+ flick. What raises eyebrows is how the board seems to tut at sexual references only to give violence a pass, insidiously mutating the mood of feature filmmaking in Australia and beyond. There is also a concerning push-and-pull between the 'community standards' they seek to meet, and the moral absolutism that goes into their evaluations (especially when the standards and morals are set by those who raise the biggest stink: conservative pressure groups and politicians). To understand their influence better, we need to look closer at the boundaries between each classification and how prescriptive they can be, even down to the tone of any utterances of 'shit'.

A movie rated G, for General, is 'suitable for everyone', according to the board. Now, what kind of content might be acceptable for 'everyone'? Let's imagine a film about a cute little rabbit. In fact, let's make it an animated film about a bunny named Bobby. Maybe he's a mischievous rabbit who plots to steal from mean Farmer Frank's carrot field. Throughout the film, we see how selfish Bobby's hare-brained (get it?) schemes end in hilarious calamity, until he realises the value of friendship and collaboration, teaming up with his fellow barnyard pals to pull off the ultimate carrot heist. According to the board's guidelines, that would probably warrant a G-rating.

If this hypothetical movie included a scene where Bobby infiltrated Farmer Frank's kitchen at night, and was gripped by the ears as a furious Frank unsheathed a chef's knife, the board might up the G-rating to PG for mild scary scenes. That is, if Bobby got away uninjured. But if Bobby lost an earlobe in the encounter, or maybe pulled out his own butterfly knife to take a few swipes at Farmer Frank as well, the board might go and give it an M, due to its moderate impact and violence. While kids under the age of 15 can access movies rated PG and M without a parent, the rating encourages parents to consider whether or not it's appropriate for their children, providing some guidance on the picture's classifiable elements, such as violence and drug use. For instance, if Bobby the Bunny smokes a cigarette, says 'shit' seven or eight times, drops the F-bomb (not in the context of having sex, but rather, in the context of having stubbed a toe) and blows up Farmer Frank's cottage while Farmer Frank is asleep inside, his cinematic adventure may earn an M-rating (with the classification guidance noting 'coarse language and action violence'). But if Bobby says the C-word once, in almost any context, or visibly slits Farmer Frank's throat, the board will have no choice but to make it MA15+.

If we want to make Bobby the Bunny's story a little more risqué, we may open the film with a scene of Bobby procreating with his partner. If those rabbits are even slightly anthropomorphised, it may too-closely resemble human sex, and if the rabbits are really going at it, or there's some graphic foreplay involved, it's pretty likely the Classification Board will now rate the flick R18+ for adults 18 and older only. The distributor may argue that the context of the scene makes it satirically funny—they are animated bunny rabbits after all—and convince the board to keep it MA15+. (The MA15+ *Sausage Party* saw different items of animated food engage in a lengthy gastronomical orgy, so there's weirdly a precedent for this.) That case couldn't be made if two humans in fake bunny ears had performed the scene for an outré live-action introduction to the cartoon instead. And if the actors turned out to be performing unsimulated sex on screen (as in, sex that wasn't faked—though that definition opens a whole other can of worms), this bizarre artistic endeavour may be refused classification completely. The board will evaluate the context, impact and merit of its individual scenes and the film as a whole, before making a call as to whether or not it should be banned. If they decide there's not enough for it to be banned, but it's not exactly worthy of artistic appreciation, they could slap it with an X-rating, though that would mean Bobby the Bunny's exploits would only be available for sale or hire in the ACT and some parts of the NT. Enjoy, Canberra!

Of course, numerous other movies with unsimulated sex have passed muster with the board and dodged the X18+ or RC-rating; plenty more haven't. A classification category of NVE for 'non-violent erotica' was proposed to supplant the X-rating in the late 1990s, to better demarcate which erotic movies should be spared from what is effectively a nationwide ban. The proposal failed when a bunch of Nationals settled in for an evening of hardcore pornography one night in 2000, which included a viewing of the titles *Max Hardcore's Going South*, *Black Shemales*, *Backdoor Black* and *Buck's Excellent Transsexual Adventures*, having been informed by others in the party that their contents would be allowed in NVE releases. This ultimately only resulted in them pushing for stricter definitions of what could fall within the X18+ category and specific outlines for what a 'fetish' actually is. To play devil's advocate, this trade-off did also wind up protecting the X-rating in Australian law from John Howard's Coalition government—not a bad result considering John Howard had wanted to ditch the X-rating entirely. That's partly because he was apparently deeply offended by 'watersports' and reportedly didn't believe in female ejaculation, as was stunningly suggested by a representative of the adult entertainment industry during a Senate inquiry on the limits of 'personal choice'. But here's the rub, pun not intended: if X-rated releases are prohibited across great swathes of the country, doesn't that mean the X18+ classification effectively serves as censorship anyway?

The deciding factor for a ban is usually the artistic value and intent of the film in question. And here's where the Classification Board has earned the most ire, by seemingly passing moral judgments on movies as if all of cinema should meet a certain standard of respectability, even if it's in conflict with a filmmaker's carefully considered vision of rabbit erotica. For this we can thank the conservative pressure groups and moral crusaders who, at the introduction of the cinematographic arts in Australia, began to shift the early safety concerns away from packed public theatres going up in flames to an everlasting fire: the flames of hell licking beneath our seats.

EFFED UP FACT:

The Man Who Fell to Earth—starring David Bowie as the fallen starman—went through some ch-ch-changes in Australia. Nicholas Roeg's 1976 space oddity was initially classified R on first go, so the distributor sliced nearly ten minutes of sound and vision to get the downgraded M-rating. That meant much of the flick's full frontal nudity went out the window. It was thankfully restored like Lazarus for the home video release. Still, spare a thought for the young Americans: *twenty* minutes were excised in the United States. Now that's low.

CHAPTER 2
MEET THE WOWSERS

Idiotic. Inconsistent. Incomprehensible. This was the assessment of the censors in the 1970 publication *Australia's Censorship Crisis*. And that's just the I's. The book collected essays by enraged artists and intellectuals—including author and historian Geoffrey Dutton AO, theatre director John Tasker, and *Overland* founder Stephen Murray-Smith—challenging the 'moral judgments and bannings made … by confused legal functionaries or anonymous public servants'. Though the essays speak of a different era, its argument rings true today: those who are asked to define what is 'aesthetically' artistic are usually too conservative to do so, or not in touch with the community standards (specifically of the 'young and yet mature majority') they're meant to uphold. '[The] community—not policemen, politicians or magistrates—have the basic and fundamental right to determine and assert what are "community standards"', the preface notes. The authors argued little had changed since the advent of cinema. How much has changed in the 50-plus years since that book was published?

Australia produced the first feature-length film in the world with 1906's *The Story of the Kelly Gang*, but we were testing the new artform of projected film even earlier. The first cinematograph opened at Melbourne Opera House in August of 1896, followed by Sydney that September. At the time, it was considered a scientific novelty, which attracted the Salvation Army, who saw this as a way to further their evangelistic aims. The Salvationists honestly felt cinema could save souls. You can imagine their surprise when cinemagoers used the darkened movie houses to make out with one another instead. The influence of conservatives was so significant, they were able to convince some theatres to project films with the lights still on, denying horny ticket-holders the cover of romantic darkness. These hand-wringers became known as 'wowsers', coined at the start of the 20th century as an acronym for their rallying cry, 'We Only Want Social Evils Remedied!' and described in 1912 by Western Australian premier John Scaddan as 'a person who is more shocked at seeing two inches of underskirt than he would be at seeing a mountain of misery'. Wowsers began to argue against the corrupting nature of cinema, especially as the content of the features evolved. So convincing was their argument and so powerful was their lobbying bloc, judges were compelled to ban truants from even visiting the cinema, just as the bushranger genre was taking root in our national identity.

Really, the wowsers were just occupying a vacuum, as in those days it wasn't immediately clear who should monitor this new artform. Even after Federation in 1901, the Commonwealth of Australia left the enforcement of censorship to the state authorities, who relied on a patchwork of legislation that had been passed before the concept of film was even popularised. Responsibility temporarily fell to health departments, who handed out health and safety permits to exhibitors. (Despite the wowsers' complaints, governments were—at least early on—mostly concerned about theatres and their flammable film stock going up in an inferno.) If a cinema was deemed to be disorderly for what it screened, and likely to house criminals (or even, gasp, scoundrels!) the department could have its permit revoked.

Soon after, censorship became the responsibility of the customs department, which was not the worst place to put film classification. What was the importation of international smut if not a matter of biosecurity? But the customs staff of the era were perhaps not equipped for this specific task—and certainly the *Customs Act 1901*, which didn't even mention films, was not necessarily ideal for offering them guidance. Imagine poring over the Act, scanning the section on horse-drawn carts, trying to figure out how you'll apply it to, say, *The Fast and the Furious* (which is basically what the Lumière brothers' 1895 short *L'arrivée d'un train en gare de La Ciotat* was at the time).

During the early part of the 20th century, wowsers called for the banning of films that featured venereal diseases, abortion, contraception and prostitution, and offered that they should only be passed if they gave audiences a moral lesson at the end. The silent 1917 Australian feature *Remorse, a Story of The Red Plague* starred Cyril Mackay as a country boy who moves to Adelaide for business, contracts syphilis and returns home, only to be spurned by his family, friends and his long-sought after love, Nellie, ultimately killing himself in disgrace. It didn't exactly leave them rolling in the aisles. Yet even with this overwrought moralising, New South Wales police—wowsers in uniform—called for it to be banned, until the state's censorship board granted it a release restricted to those 16 years and older. Films about abortion and contraception were rarely treated as leniently by contrast; that is, until it became apparent that movies on this subject matter were rarely titillating, with NSW Board undersecretary E.B. Harkness noting the 1916 American drama *Where Are My Children?* 'seemed of a distinctly moral character and was full of pregnant information. If people go to it in the look-out for filth they must be disappointed'. That same film survived the

Advisory Board of South Australia—with some cuts—but SA's censors were even more suspicious of sexualised content, banning the self-proclaimed 'instructional' films *What Every Girl Should Know* from 1917 and *Enlighten Thy Daughter* from 1918. In 1932, they granted a release to the sex-health production *False Shame* under the condition 'it be shown to the sexes at separate sessions only'. By comparison to what flew in the 1910s, this was practically the South Australian summer of love.

The Story of the Kelly Gang was passed unmolested by censors at the turn of the 20th century, though there was a concern that it would inspire copycats, with five Ballarat pre-teens arrested for a crime spree seemingly inspired by Ned Kelly himself. ('The Children's Court will consequently have before it five infant burglars,' *The Bulletin* reported.) The Victorian government took a stand to keep the film from screening in Benalla, Wangaratta and other towns adjacent to the Kelly legend. This fed future concern that films about bushrangers would send the public absolutely batty for bushranging, especially in New South Wales, where the government ruled in 1912 that films needed to be presented for police inspection at least 24 hours before exhibition. For a short time, any police officer could prohibit a film or part of a film from showing publicly; when they lost this power, they were nonetheless encouraged to investigate film screenings and report objectionable films to the minister.

Filmmaker Harry Southwell saw his film *When the Kellys Were Out* prohibited in 1923 and again upon re-application to the NSW Censor Board in 1925, even after editing out questionable scenes. A follow-up, entitled *When the Kellys Rode*, was produced in 1934 but denied release until 1943. Other movies that were seemingly more palatable—1922's *The Gentleman Bushranger* and 1926's *Key of Fate* (which the 1978 compendium *Film Censorship in Australia* describes as 'fulsome in its praise of the police')—were still banned or edited heavily. That partly had to do with the *Police Regulation Act 1899*, which forbade any depiction of the New South Wales police force on film, primarily to protect themselves as being portrayed in an unfavourable light. Over the years, there came an understanding that depictions of crime on celluloid didn't necessarily inspire violence among the public. (Though there was a brief interlude in the 1930s when American prison break drama *The Big House* was pulled from release in Adelaide, as an actual prison break had occurred in the weeks preceding, culminating with the escapees being shot by police in the city streets; the film was reviewed five times between 1930 and 1934 but no number of cuts by the distributor were ever enough for the board to give it a pass.) Before that moment of enlightenment, a slew of scenes featuring crime and violence were excised in the first few decades of the 20th century, and numerous movies were banned, even as the censors' attention drifted to depictions of sex.

The original *Scarface*—released in 1932, just before the Hays Code came into effect—briefly reset the hand-wringing towards the glorification of criminality, with the censors banning it because 'the story would be horrifying to sensitive and refined natures but would incite the baser sort to lawlessness and crime'. Once again, the censors didn't think much of the public attending these films. 1948's *Brighton Rock* was banned in Australia for concerns it would similarly inspire violence (though it was ultimately passed with cuts), while 1941's *Strange Alibi* was also banned because, according to the censors' report, it 'clearly set out that the Chiefs of the Police Force are the Super-gangsters'. Should they have been surprised? Its director, D. Ross Lederman, was initially an extra on *Keystone Cops*, a film series that became synonymous with comically incompetent police officers.

†

Calls for a public censor had reached a peak in 1916, buoyed by religious bodies. Australia agreed to a single censorship model for imported films under the remit of the Customs Department in 1918, since most films of the era were foreign anyway. This would allow each state to hold onto their individual classification and censorship powers, but at least refer to the federal model and legislation for standardised guidance. For the most part, anyway. Tasmania defected when several unhappy conservative pressure groups (aren't they all?) formed the Federation of Women's Societies for Film Censorship in 1917, though that board was suspended by parliament the following year, and a five-man board took its place until 1934. New South Wales held out on joining the national standard until 1969. South Australia exerted their independence from the federal commonwealth in the case of *Brighton Rock* in 1948. They upheld the ban that had been overturned nationally, calling it 'harmful to public morals and [tending] to glorify crime, brutality and vice'. South Australia finally applied the (updated) national template in 2019. Queensland rebelled in its own way in 1974, though we'll save that discussion for the next chapter, because *that* story is a doozy.

The first censor for the newly formed Commonwealth Film Censorship Board was Sir Harry Wollaston, who kindly supplied the first list of 'objectionable' acts. They included 'indecent, suggestive or insufficient dress; embraces overstepping the limits of affections, or which would be contrary to propriety in ordinary life; [and] nude figures, and positions of the actors which are suggestive of sexual passion or desire'. The Commonwealth Film Censorship Board judged films on their supplied synopsis alone, though the board could request screenings at the importer's expense. They were empowered to refuse the registration of any film they found 'blasphemous, indecent or obscene ... likely to be injurious to royalty, or encourage or incite to crime ... [or] likely to be offensive to any Ally of Great Britain'.

Archibald T. Strong took over from Wollaston in 1919, which was the same year distributors were granted permission to reconstruct (AKA 'cut') and resubmit banned films. R.S. Wallace succeeded him from 1922 until 1928. It was at this time that the National Council of Women, a non-denominational organisation that nonetheless skewed towards religious morality, formed the Good Film League in New South Wales, a spin-off from its film subcommittee. The difference was that men could join the Good Film League. They insisted that children be protected from the 'evil effect of certain classes of pictures, such as those depicting crude vulgarity, gangsters and drinking scenes, etc.'. The government shot back that this ought to be the responsibility of parents but agreed exhibitors should properly classify their films to indicate their most suitable audience. Ironically, this led to some instances of unintentional self-reporting, such as when a film called *The Wild Goose* earned the attention of SA censors for its ad, which screamed in all caps, 'YOU ARE ADVISED NOT TO BRING CHILDREN!' Yeah, South Australia banned it right away.

During that period, word came down that *For the Term of His Natural Life*—a big budget Australian film about our convict days featuring scenes of cannibalism— was set to be exported abroad, making the Good Film League irate, terrified that our international image would be tarnished. In September 1926, under wowser pressure, the regulations for censorship were adjusted so that local films (or 'exports') needed to meet the same requirements as those that were imported, opening them up to censorship too. Despite this new condition, *For the Term of His Natural Life* somehow avoided prohibition in New South Wales, yet was still sent overseas in cut-down form, our reputation apparently unsullied.

When the Good Film League was formed in 1922, it stated that one of its aims was to 'extend the use, under healthy conditions, of moving pictures in school education.' It was the result of a decades-long fear of how movies might mutilate the young brains of the adolescent populace, with a *Sydney Morning Herald* article from 1921 noting an increase in 'night terrors' among children who regularly attend the movies. Edith Cowan, who famously fought for the rights of women and children in Western Australia and became the first woman member of parliament in Australia, had also noted that regular attendance at the cinema inspired 'various misdemeanours and harmful excitation of the child'. The Good Film League's aims were reprinted in the 1927 Royal Commission into the Moving Picture Industry in Australia, which was prompted by local filmmakers complaining about their treatment by distributors and exhibitors, and by wowsers concerned about the detrimental effects of American products on society and children in particular. The commission made a series of recommendations to protect children, some of them simply practical ('the audience, and especially the young, should not be seated close to the screen'), and another, which was seismic in its effect: it recommended 'the establishment of a Censorship Board and grading of films sensible for children.' Starting in 1928, a Censorship Board could classify films as 'Suitable for Universal Exhibition' or 'For Adults Only', but the latter would be limited to educational, scientific and medical films. Non-educational, non-scientific and non-medical films considered unsuitable for universal exhibition were trimmed or banned. Those that were banned or only passed subject to cuts could make a case to a new and separate Censorship Board of Appeal. Once again, it was up to each state if they wanted to subscribe fully to this federal outline. (Unfortunately, the commission did not implement the recommendation from Dr Gertrude Halley, who gave evidence that argued in favour of open-air cinemas to avoid the spread of disease, an entire century before COVID-19 would make such a space ideal.)

The office of the Commonwealth Film Censorship Board was then reorganised to meet the Royal Commission's recommendations, leading to the assignment of this new Classification Board's first chief film censor, Methodist lay preacher Walter Cresswell O'Reilly, who held office from 1928 to 1942. More than 1,000 people were reported to have applied for the role of censor, many of whom were put forward by the wowser-led pressure groups. This included Eleanor Glencross, the militant president of the Housewives' Association, who was among the first board members. But the appeals board usually comprised more art-minded folk and they often clashed with the conservative censors' decisions.

O'Reilly's lingering claim to fame may be the proposal of a 'For General Exhibition' rating in 1930; as directed by the Royal Commission. That, or the anecdote that he swapped the first and second halves of a silent film so that a climactic wedding would now precede the scenes of a cohabitating couple living in sin. O'Reilly would go on to ban films that suggested Australia had a convict past, for fear of how our nation's character would be perceived abroad. (For what it's worth, he was not the first censor to edit a movie for the sake of morality, or at the expense of narrative cohesion: his predecessors straight-up deleted the crucial death of Nancy from the Lon Chaney–starring 1922 silent adaptation of *Oliver Twist*. In a testament to our times, the full feature is available to stream as an educational resource on *Wikipedia*, with Nancy's strangulation restored. Apologies for the hundred-year-old spoiler.) At the outset of World War II, O'Reilly also withdrew the anti-war flick *All Quiet on the Western Front*—which had taken the top prize at the Academy Awards—because of its preference for 'pacifism'; this was verboten for the duration of the war. He also spared space in his annual reports to complain about American melodramas—'Why should dirty American linen be washed in the presence of Australian audiences?'—on-screen sexual intercourse—'We believe that Australians are clean living and clean-thinking, and they do not appreciate the efforts made to titillate their palate with so-called spice'—the talkies—'The soul of the film was its eloquent and vital silence'—and even, bafflingly and too-specifically, the bodies of British male stars of the time: 'Prominent English actors, splashing about in their bathtubs and spitting essential dialogue between their teeth, might be London matinee idols, but they make no appeal to Australians accustomed to the bronzed and statuesque physique of the beaches.' Okay. The point being, wowsers and the censors were now truly in sync.

O'Reilly did let *The Phantom of the Opera* starring a horrifying Lon Chaney earn a release, but horror films would still have a rough go of it over the subsequent decades. During O'Reilly's tenure, the legendarily bad-in-taste *Freaks* was banned, with the ruling in 1932 calling it 'the most repulsive picture screened before this Board'. (*Freaks* would get a PG-rating upon reapplication in 1975, a full 43 years after its production.) O'Reilly's reign was followed by that of John Alexander, who made the remarkable declaration in 1948 that 'horror films are neither entertaining nor cultural'. Not only did this organisational principle deny Australians the work of James Whale (director of the now-revered contribution to the cultural canon, *Frankenstein*, and more), but also the iconic *The Night of the Hunter*, featuring Robert Mitchum as a deluded murderer with 'love' and 'hate' tattooed across his knuckles who considers himself a reverend. (It was banned on account of blasphemy, because the censors didn't understand the character wasn't *actually* a preacher.) In 2008, esteemed film criticism magazine *Cahiers du cinema* named *The Night of the Hunter* the second-best film of all time, after *Citizen Kane*, but in 1955, to the eyes of John Alexander—a teetotalling public servant who felt horror catered only to 'a small minority of the moronic type'—*The Night of the Hunter* wasn't all that artful at all.

Alexander was supplanted as Chief censor in 1956 by Colin Campbell, another veteran public servant. Campbell was charged with the additional solemn duty of ensuring these inciteful, indecent images weren't transmitted into Australian homes at the dawn of television. However, he strove to move with the times. 'There is no doubt ... that the censor of the moment is more liberal than before,' Desmond O'Grady wrote of Campbell in *The Bulletin* at the time. The comparison was probably correct. Alexander, who had insisted images of women in bikinis would remain banned until they became 'the accepted dress on our beaches', personally recut Roberto Rossellini's *L'Amore* in 1953 after calling it 'a travesty of the Nativity'. Anyone following this procession of wowser-censors might have seemed positively transgressive.

Making his case for Campbell's liberalism, O'Grady noted that his board had retained the iconic shot of a flick-knife opening in Robert Wise and Jerome Robbins' 1961 adaptation of *West Side Story,* despite flick-knives being a prohibited import. Such apparent freewheeling broadmindedness didn't last long. The following decade, a one-armed veteran of the war by the name of Richard J. Prowse took over as Chief censor. He quickly earned the punny nickname 'One-Armed Bandit', and banned 'em, he did. Writer, broadcaster and anti-censorship campaigner Phillip Adams told me that Prowse's disability 'didn't stop him from wielding the censors' scissors.' In fact, Adams had a unique interpretation of Prowse's frame of mind: 'The chief censors' toilet was full of obscene graffiti, so obviously his exposure to smut had caused significant brain damage.'

Prowse's justifications for bans in mid-20th century Australia included depictions of mixed-race relationships, scenes that sexualised the clergy and people straight up getting kicked in the nuts. That's from the banned films we know of, because the chief censor stopped publishing his annual reports in 1964, leaving citizens in the dark for a spell. A helpful interview with *The Bulletin* in 1965 saw Prowse outline his reasons for recent bans, such as *The Leather Boys* (for 'homosexuality'); *Hit the U.S. Aggressors* (for 'propaganda'); *Die, Die My Darling* (for 'blasphemy and horror'); and *The Molester* (for 'sex'—though the title probably didn't do it any favours). Within the same interview he noted how the estimation of horror films hadn't exactly evolved in the eyes of the board over the past decade: 'We don't like them at all.' It was also flagged that he had banned 1953's *Children of the Waste-Land* for criticising colonial treatment of Indigenous Australians, however, Prowse may have accidentally made a somewhat progressive decision there. Directed by Anglican bishop of North Queensland Ian Shevill, the 20-minute documentary was inspired by Shevill's perception that most missionaries (prior to his interference) were 'smoothing the pillow of a dying race,' and reportedly 'makes no apologies for stating that Australia for years has exploited the aboriginal'. (In fact, the opening dialogue states: 'These are the aborigines of Australia. These are the people whom White Australia has exploited, denied the rights of common humanity, hunted down as animals.') But if the exposure of colonial cruelty was what Prowse objected to, he nonetheless spared most Australians from Shevill's own cruel social-engineering polemic, which according to a (glowing) contemporaneous review from the *Townsville Daily Bulletin*, '[tells] the story of real Australians of the stone age, whose life in the 20th century is filled with hope and purpose instead of bewilderment and frustration.' *Children of the Waste-Land* premiered in North Queensland despite Prowse's ruling, an early sign of that state's eventual defection.

If the censors were flummoxed by the films of the 1950s (*The White Haired Girl*, 1952, was banned for reasons of 'communism'), they were strenuously at sea in the 1960s. They were also being purposefully prodded and provoked by the Australian filmmakers who were coming up during this era of cinematic control. Artist Fiona Hooton wrote about the birth of Australian experimental film for *Metro* magazine, shining a light on the lost and nearly forgotten 1963 short *It Droppeth as the Gentle Rain*, co-directed by Albie Thoms and Bruce Beresford. Before going on to helm *Driving Miss Daisy* in the United States, Beresford and his co-conspirators from the intellectual left subculture collective Sydney Push decided to metaphorically tackle the media's fearmongering during the Cuban Missile Crisis by imagining how nuclear fallout would affect our lives. Except, instead of showing the dropping of bombs, they imagined a deluge of literal shit falling from the skies, interrupting dinner parties and terrifying the middle class into embracing Catholicism. Shot in black and white, the mud used to signify the flood of excreta was so convincing the picture was reported to police by the woman charged with grading the print of the film. The censors immediately banned it for its obscene sense of humour (and it certainly didn't help that some who saw the flick interpreted the falling fecal matter as representing God shitting on the world). Beresford would have the final laugh in the more permissive 1970s, directing *The Adventures of Barry McKenzie*, which was produced by Phillip Adams and became the first Australian movie to gross more than a million dollars at the box office—despite being rated R. The culture eventually caught up to the counter-culture. But, as you'll figure out by looking at how much of the book remains, they didn't remain in lockstep for long.

Back to the sixties. *The Bulletin* counted 113 films that received cuts in the year 1962 – 1963. Experts who've evaluated reports by the Customs Department from the period deduced that at least one in three imported films were cut in some way before screening in Australia. That includes Lee Marvin's Nazi-hunting thriller *The Dirty Dozen*; Roman Polanski's claustrophobic *Repulsion*, which lost a sequence wherein Catherine Deneuve's spiralling young woman is kept up at night by the amorous sounds seeping through the walls of her sister and married lover *in flagrante delicto*; and *The Virgin Spring*, which would go on to inspire the also banned *The Last House on the Left*. In fact, the very context of the inciting rape in *The Virgin Spring* was changed so that the sexual assault was now 'stimulating' for the victim, accidentally rendering the film far more offensive than if it had maintained director Ingmar Bergman's original intention. Sixty years later, the artistic value and contributions of each of those movies is inarguable, furthering the point that those doing the cutting didn't necessarily understand what was unfolding before them. (In a perhaps too-flattering 1962 assessment of *The Virgin Spring*'s censor, a journalist noted that 'for his pains he is criticised for allowing [cuts] at all, and for making minimal cuts'.)

Australian film critic and anti-censorship campaigner David Stratton recalled this era well when we spoke in 2021:

> Coming to Australia [from the UK], I discovered immediately two things. First of all, that the first Sydney Film Festival I went to in 1964, where I revisited some films I'd seen in Britain before coming to Australia, they had clearly been cut. Quite extensively. The other thing I discovered very quickly was that films showing in commercial cinemas were also being cut to an astonishing degree. I mean, really quite amazing, the amount of cutting going on in the most innocuous films and for the most, I thought, innocuous reasons. So, I became a member of the festival board. I moved a motion that would force the festival to stand up, publicise censorship—which they had never done before—make public what was being done to festival films, but also at the same time call for a better deal for filmgoers from the censors, so we could see, in cinemas, films that were being seen overseas at the time with no serious difficulties.

This did not make Stratton popular with those doing the cutting, especially when he became director of the Sydney Film Festival in 1966. 'The censors were aware of what a bastard I was,' he says. 'So, when I met them for the first time, when I became festival director, it was an extremely *atmospheric* meeting, because I guess they saw me as trouble, which I guess I was.'

The concern among Stratton's peers was that the Customs Department would cancel the sweetheart deal that allowed the festival to import films without paying duties, because if the charges were reinstated, the festival would simply have to cease operations due to increased costs. 'I guess I was on a moral crusade and was confident in myself—although a lot of people around me were not so confident—that the Customs Department would not retaliate,' he says now. 'Although looking back, I'm quite surprised they didn't.'

Stratton could see that censorship would only get worse in Australia as international cinema became more liberated, starting—in his assessment—with Scandinavia and reaching the United States by the late 1960s, at the cessation of the Hays Code. 'The question was how long would it take and how much would it damage the Sydney Film Festival before we had censorship reform in Australia,' he recalls.

Stratton's disdain for the slicing and dicing by the board remains to this day. 'It goes without saying if you went to go see a Jean-Luc Godard film in Sydney in the late 1960s, you were not told that you were seeing a heavily abridged version of the film,' he explains. 'Some films lost as much as 20 minutes. But there was no way the cinema or distributor was going to inform the public of this. And I thought this was scandalous.' The major part of the problem centred on those who actually comprised the Board of Censors. 'I don't think that the artistic side of a film, or any work of art that they were censoring, affected them one bit,' Stratton says. 'They had fairly rigid rules, criteria, that they fulfilled to the letter. They were not—the people who constituted the film censorship board when I first encountered them in 1966—to be honest, the sort of people you could imagine would be interested in watching a Fellini film or even a serious American or British film.' As was written of the board in *The Bulletin* at the time, '[t]wo of the women censors have university degrees, only one has a long association with the trade, but none has distinguished himself by his interest in either the history or aesthetics of films.' One of the censors during Prowse's tenure on the board—and Stratton's time with the Sydney Film Festival—was a Miss McMillan, former secretary of the YWCA in Sydney, whose 'scissors [were] reputedly particularly sharp-edged'. Further to the point, it was written in *The Bulletin* that 'importers, distributors and the public service are represented, but not necessarily those who are interested in films as an art.' Stratton echoed that rebuke, saying the board wasn't 'a particularly impressive collection of people', and the concept of films as art was entirely alien to them. 'They constantly talked of entertainment,' he remembered. '"Who'd want to go see *that* for entertainment?" was a constant refrain.'

Perhaps the most controversial banning of the era came in 1969, when director Stig Björkman's Swedish film *I Love, You Love* (*Jag älskar, du älskar*) had the gall to feature a sex scene with a seven-months pregnant woman, played by Evabritt Strandberg. Or did it? The Minister for Customs, Senator Malcolm Scott, insisted the film featured some third-trimester Swedish sex, but the film's director, actress and even a gynaecologist (summoned to provide expert comment) all insisted the actors weren't simulating sex at all, pointing out that it would be logistically impossible based on the juxtaposition of the sitting couple. (Evabritt and her co-star Sven Wollter were contacted by the *Sydney Morning Herald* to confirm that, no, they hadn't boinked.) United States Supreme Court Justice Potter Stewart famously said in 1964 he knew pornography when he saw it. Those in charge of classification in Australia were struggling to even recognise how sex worked, let alone when it was pornographic. Given the fact that the picture's ban was upheld by the Liberal government (and backed by the Democratic Labor Party), no one else from the Australian public could witness the coupling to challenge the claims made against it.

'Look, you hadn't seen too many films before with a very pregnant woman, naked, and a man in an embrace,' Stratton says of the picture today. 'But you don't actually see anything, really. There's just a naked couple embracing, and she's very pregnant. You don't see her genitals or his genitals. And they don't seem to be moving either. At least not much.' Stratton thinks the censors were confusing *I Love, You Love* with another Swedish film of the period, *I Am Curious (Yellow)*, which had earned global headlines for featuring several scenes of actual sexual intercourse, but, importantly, was not being shown at the festival that year. 'At least not then,' Stratton says. 'We showed it later.' It's possible *I Love, You Love* was largely banned because the board confused its title, and then simply stuck to their guns to avoid embarrassment. 'That's the only thing I can think of,' Stratton says, 'because of course films did change their titles. You could have a film that was shown under one title in one country and then the subtitle translation on a print we might import might be quite different.' He cites Miloš Forman's *Loves of a Blonde*, which was also cut by the censors. 'For some reason I don't understand, the English subtitle for *Loves of a Blonde* was not *Loves of a Blonde* or even *Blonde in Love*, which was another title, but *Hello Blondie*. Somehow that title sort of cheapened the film, possibly made it easier for the censors to say, "Well, this is not a serious film."' (Of the six cuts made to Forman's film, four were related to 'blasphemous' expletives in the subtitles.)

When it became clear that the censors would no longer let the festival present films that hadn't passed by their desks—despite that being the norm internationally—Stratton made good on his pledge to publicise all censorship of their submissions, and eventually ban all films that had been cut for the Sydney Film Festival, to diminish the reputation of the board and put their secretive actions under a spotlight. His argument was sound: putting aside the cultural damage that was being wrought, there was actual, physical damage to the foreign film prints that were getting sliced and resplied in Australia (and then put back in circulation). Film history was being literally garbled on our shores.

Stratton says,

> We were forced to allow [the films] to be cut, and then before they left the country—in theory—they were returned to the Censorship Board who would restore the cuts, but with 35mm film, every time you make a cut you lose a frame or two on either side of the cut, and when you put the cut back in, you lose a frame or two again, so you're sending back to the people who own the film a damaged film, and that to me was a terrible, terrible thing to be doing. It's like scratching a painting.
>
> Obviously it was very bad for the festival's status and image, but it was also bad for Australia's status and image, because we had to confess, we had to admit, and we had to apologise. We had to say, 'We're really, truly sorry, but this is what's happened.' We couldn't have known before the film was sent to us that the censors would react in this way, so we'd have to grovel and say, 'Please, send us a film again next year.'

Stratton had tried to get chief censor 'Dick' Prowse to back down from his stringent standards by saying he would go above his head and lobby the Minister for Customs, but he had even less luck with Senator Scott in the case of *I Love, You Love*. '[Scott] was just absolutely useless,' Stratton remembers. 'He hadn't seen the film. He didn't want to see the film. He just wanted to believe what the censors told him. The director of the film was there telling him that's not true, and he just dismissed it. It was beyond anything you could believe, really.' Sometimes his interactions with these film philistines worked in Stratton's favour, such as when they all watched Luchino Visconti's incest-themed *Vaghe Stelle dell'Orsa* (English title: *Sandra*) together (he could often only review films for the festival in the censors' office). Though they discussed the picture's classifiable elements at the end of each reel, which happened every 20 minutes, it eventually passed without any cuts, despite climaxing with two siblings having sex on a woollen rug by the fire (the sex act takes place just off screen). How did *Sandra* get away with it? Because once again, the censors confused the sexual circumstances. As Stratton writes in his memoir, *I Peed on Fellini,* Prowse said to him afterwards: 'Didn't you find that confusing? I thought, at the beginning, they were brother and sister.'

The debate around *I Love, You Love* is when the censorship issue cut through to the mainstream. It also preceded the declaration in *Australia's Censorship Crisis* that film censorship had evolved from Australian passion to a national disease. Stratton even considered the controversy a blessing in disguise, due to it having struck a national chord. It also coincided with the emergence into adulthood of those children who were taught to appreciate film in school following the Royal Commission of 1927 – 1928. As argued by Michael Dezuanni and Ben Goldsmith in their article for *Studies in Australasian Cinema*, 'the obvious pleasure children experienced from viewing these films at school, and the effective "analysis" of the film via discussion of the narrative and characters presented in the literary versions of the stories, is a version of film appreciation.' It mattered not that the content in schools was under the watchful eye of wowsers, and only somewhat that the Royal Commission's finding had emboldened those of the religious right to demand somebody think of the children. Three decades later, these grown-up cinephiles would be arguing against censorship and in favour of challenging, provocative cinema.

'Film for education is in complete concert with film as a civilising agent, motivated by adult critique and criticism of entertainment films,' Dezuanni and Goldsmith continued. 'It was only a matter of time before film appreciation would emerge from this as an academic pursuit in schools in its own right, a process that had already taken place in the United States.' Yet that was all a cold comfort for Stig Björkman, who had flown to Sydney to speak about a film that ultimately didn't screen, per Stratton's ban on festival selections that were cut by the censors. Björkman instead spent his time here making a short film entitled *To Australia—With Love*, all about the fuss his film had inspired. Meanwhile, back in Sweden, a shot from *I Love, You Love*'s offending nude scene adorned the poster. Skål?

'The only good thing that came out of all of that,' Stratton concedes, 'was Scott lost his portfolio—he handled it so badly it became such a national scandal—and he was replaced by Don Chipp [in 1969] who was a very different sort of person and very approachable, and who literally came to me and said, "What can we do to stop this kind of bad publicity?"'

†

New customs minister Chipp (future Australian Democrats leader but then still a member of the Liberal Party) introduced a new ratings system in 1971 that would allow films to be rated R (for those 18 and older), which was followed by the un-banning of many earlier releases. This also included the addition of the simpler 'G' and 'M' ratings, as well as 'NRC', which was for titles not recommended for children under the age of 12 (it evolved into 'PG' in 1984). Chief censor Prowse would nonetheless go on to recommend an Unclassified rating as well in 1973, later to become Refused Classification, paving the way for future bans.

Chipp was in part responding to those emerging 'film appreciators' who were stunned by the censoring of groundbreaking American sensation *Easy Rider*, directed by Dennis Hopper. (Film distributors were also frustrated, given *Easy Rider*'s global financial success.) It had been released in 1970 after a one-year delay with a 'suitable only for adults' rating. However, it arrived in censored form with most of the drug-taking removed. They deleted the drug-taking from Easy Rider. That's like deleting the motorcycles.

Chipp must have known that *Easy Rider* was just the beginning of what was coming. As Ina Bertrand put it, 'the acceptance of *Easy Rider* has codified a shift in social values, and [any] new film must provide a further challenge if it is to achieve comparable success.'

Chipp benefitted from the landmark *Crowe v Graham* case in 1968 that saw the High Court of Australia shift the goalposts on 'obscenity' and 'indecency'. It was no longer the benchmark for obscenity to be defined on its 'tendency to deprave and corrupt' using precedents set in 1868, but rather, the 'community standards test': would it offend the 'modesty of the average man' *today*? Chipp had, however, grown frustrated during his tenure that stories of sexual censorship were sending more important issues to the back pages of the paper. 'I will not have some damned government or bloody-minded bureaucrat telling me what I can read, see or hear,' he'd write in his biography, adding, 'We cannot and should not legislate for moral behaviour. Firstly, it is wrong; and secondly, it doesn't work.' Sure, his interference in the way we see films can almost entirely be attributed to him finding their controversies a nuisance, but we'll take it.

Chipp began his policy of gradualism by once again publicly reporting on censorship decisions for the first time since 1964, publishing lists of titles cut or banned in the *Government Gazette*. Prior to this, distributors had been cautiously toeing the line, willing to keep quiet the cuts made by the board so as not to anger film-lovers who were upset about the hatchet jobs being done on their beloved auteurs' works. He then invited 'special people'—including MPs, journalists and 'the clergy'—to see the banned material, daring them to print the description and outwardly challenge that which was still being cut. One film he shared was *Like Night and Day*, which he informed blushing journos at a press conference contained 'a scene that depicts a young woman performing cunnilingus on her sister, while, at the same time, a man has intercourse with the young woman by entering her from behind.' None printed the description, avoiding a furore. But ever the pragmatist, he later invited those same MPs and journalists to a screening where Stratton described the whole film's contextual and cultural value. Most in attendance were apparently bored by the film, so by the time the climactic, incestuous threesome arrived, few were flustered. As Stratton recalls Chipp whispering to him: 'I think you've made your point.' That said, the film had a champion not only in Stratton but also *The Bulletin* critic Beverley Tivey, who argued in favour of preserving the deleted ménage à trois: 'The scene is extremely short, presented in a completely matter-of-fact way and is absolutely essential to the argument of the film; it occurs in its context logically and without the shock value it might have had if inserted, say, into *The Sound of Music*.' (Now that *would* have been a shock.)

Chipp, in his pursuit of an R-rating, reiterated that community standards had changed and needed to be considered when films are being classified. It wasn't as simple as all that though; no fewer than 12 public petitions were presented to Parliament in August of 1970 insisting that censorship remain committed to 'preserve sound moral standard in the community'. At least Village Cinemas, a powerful name in Australia that began as a drive-in chain and went on to distribute films internationally under the name Village Roadshow, supported the idea of an R-rating and proved it could be enforced by keeping under-18s from driving in to see Michelangelo Antonioni's counter-cultural landmark *Zabriskie Point*.

Labor MP Gilbert Duthie was adamant in 1970 that neither an R or X-rating would be enough to stem the tide of corrupting content, saying in Parliament, 'self-righteous people want fornication, horrifying violence, sexual intercourse, lesbianism and homosexuality to be screened for everybody's viewing and legalised on the screen for all over 18 years of age.' He had been especially incensed by one of Chipp's movie nights, in which the customs minister screened cuts from the erotic French drama *Therese and Isabelle*; Vittorio De Sica's *Two Women*, for which Sophia Loren won Best Actress at the Oscars in 1961; and *The Killing of Sister George*, which was rated X in America. Duthie—who was not in attendance—was curt in his review nonetheless: 'Honourable members know what is done with sewage, it goes deep underground. I put these films at the same level.'

But Chipp's gradualism continued apace, getting the R classification over the line and introducing a five-person Film Board of Review to replace the previous Board of Appeal. And though the Film Board of Review was assembled to keep in mind 'the community'—it comprised a long-time Commonwealth Film Unit's producer-in-chief, a professor of special education, a professor of psychiatry, an Olympic runner and a television personality—they still neglected to add film writers or thinkers who might be able to evaluate the artistic merit or value of a challenging feature. Instead, the board continued to weed out scenes that might rock the fragile equilibrium of an average Australian viewer. Even Prowse was, at least coyly, unimpressed by those on the Review Board, telling *Cinema Papers* in 1974, '[I]t must be remembered that they are only a part time board and only meet once a week or once every three weeks. All the members of that board are engaged in other pursuits and are possibly a different type to those sitting on [the Classification] board.'

At the point most of Chipp's recommendations were in place, he was being accused by opponents of acting in concert with 'left wing communist pornographers who infest our universities in a concentrated programmed of subversion', which likely wasn't the worst insult he'd ever heard. A total of 21 films were the first to get an R-rating in October of 1971, among them: *Klute*, *Get Carter* and *Percy*, the latter a knees-up comedy about a penis transplant recipient that had been banned just a few months earlier. The first R-rated films shown to audiences were Robert Altman's *McCabe and Mrs. Miller* and Jerzy Skolimowski's *Deep End*. They were met by heaving throngs in Victoria on 15 November 1971 to see, at least in *McCabe and Mrs. Miller*, 'all the words so popular at South Yarra parties' according to Melbourne commentator Keith Dunstan. Critic Sandra Hall warned audiences of a 'concentrated spate of brutality in the cinema for the next few months', but that didn't stop attendees from sometimes bringing children under the age of two, having gotten so used to bringing them to the drive-ins. In fairness, adults were learning how to go to the movies anew. It also marked a turning point in how Australia's government approached many of Altman's transgressive movies in particular, given that both 1968's *That Cold Day in the Park* and 1970's *M*A*S*H* (1970) were previously slashed by the censors. In 1989, *McCabe and Mrs. Miller* was downgraded to M for its VHS release—much like *Get Carter* and *Klute* in 1985 and 1986 respectively— only to get upgraded to MA15+ in 2016 for its DVD release, because, somehow, the violence grew in impact over the subsequent decades. According to the Board's most recent decision report:

> At 104 minutes, McCabe shoots a male in the wrist. A significant blood burst is viewed upon the implied impact of the bullet. A post-action visual of the male's arm is viewed as his hand dangles, semi attached to his arm. Although the hand is prosthetic in its appearance, the significant blood detail imparts a strong impact, warranting an MA15+ classification.

Deep End, about a 15-year-old boy working at a bathhouse, has never been re-evaluated in Australia. As for *Easy Rider*, it took until 1990 for all that deleted drug-taking to be reinstated, when it received *not* an R-rating but an M-rating for VHS. Ten years later, the classification of the same cut on DVD was upgraded to MA15+. Community standards, you'll find, do not move in a straight line.

Of course, not everyone wanted to take advantage of the new R-rating. After John Travolta's signature social drama *Saturday Night Fever* scored the 18+ classification in 1978, its distributors willingly recut an M-rated edition to further its box office successes. By 1990, it had been refashioned into an even-more palatable PG feature for the VHS release, before ultimately working its way up to MA15+ in 2002. In fairness, Paramount Pictures did the exact same thing by offering 'hard' and 'soft' versions of *Saturday Night Fever* in American cinemas, but it warrants a mention in this book for a specific novelty: it is the only film in Australian history to have held four different classifications.

†

Though Stratton was heartened by these changes, he's convinced Chipp partly took action to shut him up, saying,

Chipp made it clear—not to me personally but later—that he thought we were waging this campaign to get publicity for the [Sydney Film] Festival, and of course nothing could have been further from the truth. It was terrible, negative publicity, internationally speaking for the festival. Shocking, shocking publicity. It was the last thing we wanted. But he seemed to believe we were publicity hounds and to shut us up he had to do something. That seemed to be his motivation. But to give him his due, Chipp could appreciate a good film in ways the other people around there couldn't.

Stratton would later show both *I Love, You Love* and *Hello Blondie* at his final festival program in 1983.

Unfortunately, Belgian filmmaker Thierry Zéno would likely disagree with Stratton's assessment that things improved markedly in Australia by the 1970s. Zéno's notoriously zoophilic art film *Vase de Noces* was refused classification in 1975 upon application by the Perth Film Festival and it was only later granted a screening at the festival by the Film Board of Review, though that merely caused more headaches (which you can read about in Chapter 8). It was nonetheless refused classification for proper release at two further applications, in 1976 and 1977. At this very same time, the board was wrestling with another now-iconic feature about bestiality, *La Bête* (*The Beast*). That infamous cult favourite from director Walerian Borowczyk depicts the sexual relationship between a woman and a monster, and was similarly refused classification in 1976 largely due to a four-minute sex scene in which 'passionate lovemaking exhausts the beast who collapses to the ground and expires'. It passed the following year with five minutes excised, and is since available around the world with the promotional tagline 'uncut', even though here in Australia it's still missing footage from that initial board submission. It's a better fate than that of *Vase de Noces*, which remains banned in Australia to this day. In other nations, it's available on DVD, where it sometimes goes by its alternate titles: *Wedding Trough*, *One Man and His Pig* or, according to IMDB, *The Pig Fucking Movie*.

Groups championing the pre-Chipp days of movie morality would go on to argue against the releases of Bernardo Bertolucci's *Last Tango in Paris* and Stanley Kubrick's *A Clockwork Orange* in the early seventies, with varying results. One such powerhouse was the Australian Festival of Light, the conservative Christian organisation that challenged not only the loosening censorship in Australia, but also all social change of the 1970s. Often, but not always, they just earned additional attention (and increased box office admissions) for the movies they lobbied against. To that point, the promoters of *Last Tango in Paris* were probably smacking their lips when the Australian Festival of Light, which had formed concurrently with the flick's release at a public meeting in March 1973, organised against the picture, flooding the press with interviews and letters to the editor decrying the salacious and sacrilegious Bertolucci drama. Given this was a difficult arthouse picture, the complaints ultimately gave it a marketing angle that made it must-see viewing, even to this day. Decades later, similarly conservative but savvier groups such as Collective Shout would have better success in the banning of 21st-century releases, even as Australia's arms of classification theoretically grew more sophisticated. For example, in the 1980s, the Film Censorship Board was combined with the literature censorship function to form the Office of Film and Literature Classification (OFLC). By 2006, the overarching OFLC was dissolved and the remaining Australian Classification Board found itself back within the Attorney-General's remit—for a while, anyway. But by now it was at least divorced from the customs department. This (sorta) suggested a (slightly) better understanding by the government of how to approach provocative cinema—not as the equivalent to a pest or parasite, for example.

As former director of the Classification Board Margaret Anderson told me,

> While you want consistency, you also want evolution. We don't want the Australian public sitting there going 'I haven't got a fig what an MA15+ film is anymore because I went and saw one the other day and there was [only] a picture of a side bosom and the word bitch was used'. By the same token, you have got to change—that will happen, over time—by the values and standards within your community. When and where is it appropriate to go with those changes in the community? It becomes an interesting juggle.

She also noted that 'it's a bit of a furphy to talk about the old legal concept of the "reasonable man"', referring to the concept of the average Australian and their supposed standards and expectations. 'And yet, you're trying to navigate and create that fiction because you've got to classify to that fiction, and that fiction has to exist otherwise there is no point to having classifications.'

And yet, we are currently enduring a drift of our community standards towards something more prudish, more straitlaced, more *American*. This is due to the influx of global streaming services and the abdication of the Australian government's responsibility to sensibly provide classification guidance—a shocking overcorrection that has, at once, allowed completely unregulated (and illegal) content to stream through the door, while the bar for M, MA15+ and R-ratings are raised upwards, ever more conservatively. That is why much of this book will address how censorship is still being slyly enacted, to the detriment of Australian society as a whole, even if there have been significant improvements in the way film classification is now applied.

We can take a lesson from Chipp's final year as customs minister in 1972, when Ken Russell's *The Devils* created a firestorm around the world, and was described by David Stratton at the time as 'perhaps the most sensational British film ever made'. Miraculously, this tale of orgiastic nuns was never banned in Australia, earning an R-rating on first pass. (No wonder Phillip Adams recited the following in a poem to celebrate Chipp's 25 years in parliament: 'At the setting of life's sun/ You'll know why you were born/ You kept the bastards honest/ and you gave us soft-core porn.') *The Devils* was referred to the Attorney-General of the time, the only higher appeal than the review board. During a sitting of NSW parliament, Russell's disturbing, frisky film got a mention when the Country Party's Tim Bruxner asked, 'Is the Minister aware that one well-known film critic has described this film as the sickest film that he has ever seen displayed on the screen?' Bruxner followed: 'Will he agree, also, that it was not the intention of the legislation dealing with the R-certificate classification to allow the public to view a film that has also been described in the press as disgusting, revolting and horrifying?' When his Liberal colleagues failed to defend *The Devils*—presumably because Russell's nightmarish Catholic-skewering phantasmagoria wasn't their bag—Chipp offered a unique ruling to appease both sides. Instead of adjusting the R-rating, he insisted the following message be appended to any trailers, or be shown prominently anywhere exhibiting the film: '*The Devils* is not a film for everyone. It tells of hideous events which allegedly occurred in France in 1634. Because the film is explicit and highly graphic in depicting those events, some people will find it visually shocking and deeply disturbing.'

For all of Chipp's progressive ways, there's a giveaway phrase in that first sentence of his warning: many of those who still held sway over classification and censorship couldn't fathom that a movie might not be for everyone. It was so in the first days of cinema, and it continues in the 2020s, long after the Chipp era has passed and community standards (in Australia) have apparently softened. To this day, films that 'might not be for everyone' have to make their case to a board designed to protect vulnerable consumers, for better or worse. It presents artists with a conundrum: how does one challenge the status quo, or provoke through the medium of cinema, when their very gatekeepers are charged with ensuring everything remains hunky dory? Easy: They don't. Truly, the devil is in the details.

EFFED UP FACT:

Though Dick Prowse was one of the more conservative chief censors, David Stratton refers in his biography to a time in which Prowse tried to impress upon him how the board was keeping up with the swinging 1960s. The Michael Powell film *They're a Weird Mob*, set in Australia, had just been released, based on the 1957 novel of the same name. It was a local hit. Turns out Prowse was proud that the board didn't cut the flick once, even though 'they use the word "bloody" eighty times'. Stratton must have withheld his applause.

CHAPTER 3

THE BANNED DOWN UNDER

Depending on who you ask, Peter Jackson is either the straw-chewing folk hero of Hobbiton made flesh or a Sauron-sized supervillain. To fans of J.R.R. Tolkien, he's the big-screen messiah, having cinematically realised the *Lord of the Rings* trilogy to much acclaim. To Ryan Gosling, who gained nearly 30kgs to star in *The Lovely Bones* only to be fired by Jackson prior to shooting, he's probably less revered. He's used his technological wizardry to colourise and revivify WW1 photos and footage, to clean up hours of thought-to-be-unusable rehearsal footage of The Beatles, and to convince everyone that movies looked better at 48 frames per second—each a technological endeavour that has as many detractors as champions. (I take it back: no one of sound mind liked the 48fps gambit.) And then there are those who will always adore the New Zealand iconoclast for his early, grimy, extremely gory video nasties. But there is indisputably one group that continues to curse the name of Jackson: the former Queensland Film Board of Review, who in 1991 basically all lost their jobs because of him.

Prior to this particular scandal, Queensland held its own folk reputation in Australia for being the most censorious state of an already censorious nation. By the early 1970s, as Australia started to coalesce under a singular review code, Queensland's long-in-power conservative government (largely unopposed by an also-pretty-conservative opposition) rebelled, forming their own Film Board of Review and maintaining a strict regime of prohibition in the face of what they saw as 'normalised' pornography. The Queensland Film Board of Review's sister board, the Literature Board of Review, led the charge, issuing 607 banning orders (largely for hardcore sex magazines that were available in other states) between 1954 and 1981. Their ban-frenzy peaked in 1972, with 93 banning orders, including one for *The Little Red School Book*, which the State Library of Queensland describes as having sold itself as "'a subversive reference book for young people", an invitation to "anarchy" in the schools giving advice about sex and drugs.' Though *The Little Red School Book* later saw the light of day in Queensland, the novel *American Psycho* remains banned in the state. The State Library claims to have nearly a dozen banned books in its possession, still kept from public view behind lock and key.

Queensland's Film Board of Review may have burnt out quicker than the Literature Board, but it also shone brighter. After the board was established in 1974, inaugural chairperson Des Draydon explained to *Cinema Papers* that Queensland was less concerned by 'tits and bums' and more with the public harm of a boundary-pushing release. 'Scientific evidence suggests that a film can have a harmful effect on society,' he said in 1977. 'The scientific work says it's not just a case of offensiveness. See, everyone's hung up on this offensiveness thing ... "You should be allowed to see people rooting..." [or] "I don't mind watching blood and gore on the screen or watching people being tortured." People say I don't mind watching it so what harm can it do ... that's the wrong approach. To say it again, it's not a question of whether a person is offended by it, but whether it can cause harm.' The board's stingy parochial censorship earned certain films a literal badge of honour: 'Banned in Queensland', as would be emblazoned across VHS covers upon release in other Australian states. Since the Queensland Film Board of Review didn't have the power to reclassify films, banning a picture outright was their only move. Brisbane fanzine *Mondo Gore*, published by Hank Hankerson between 1984 and 1992, kept an eye on the number of censored films in Queensland, which eventually totalled in the hundreds. These included such pictures that ultimately got the okay from the national board: *Near Dark*, *Re-Animator*, *The Last Temptation of Christ*, *Necromancer* and many more. Queensland even banned the 1989 Aussie slasher *Houseboat Horror*, which has a reputation today as one of our country's most endearingly terrible productions, and which, alongside the Banned in Queensland badge on its video cover, proclaimed to offer the 'World's 1st Gratuitous Violence and Blood Gush Guarantee'. (When you've made the sale, stop selling.) Queensland's board also, tellingly, refused to classify in August of 1986 a safe sex education film produced by the AIDS council of New South Wales entitled *Do the Right Thing* (not to be confused with the Spike Lee movie), despite it having been given an R-rating at the national level. But most notorious would be Queensland's banning of *Bad Taste*, Peter Jackson's low-budget 1987 splatter-fest, in which a group called the Astro Investigation and Defence Service (AIDS) battles a group of alien invaders made of startling puppet features and sagging skin. The title of the film is not accidental.

The Office of Film and Literature Classification—soon after its formation in April 1988—initially banned *Bad Taste* across Australia upon application in May of 1989 even though, as was related by an insider at the time, 'one of the censors was laughing uproariously throughout the entire screening.' Four groups of censors within the OFLC had to view the movie to reach a decision, but none were able to reach a unanimous agreement. It was eventually banned by a single vote, once every member of the OFLC—including the cautious chief censor John Dickie and his more radical deputy David Haines—had seen the movie and passed judgment. The distributor, CBS/Fox Video, heeded the decision and cut six minutes, but the 82-minute cut was instead given an M-rating, meaning they had sliced too much 'bad taste' for its own good. Seeking a more appropriate R-rating, CBS/Fox nudged it back up to 86 minutes, and scored the coveted 18+ classification, meaning just 66 seconds had to be deleted in total (though these critical 66 seconds included many of the picture's notoriously violent money shots). It was granted a cinema release in Australia, but three weeks into its run, Queensland's board decided to ban the flick, earning the ire of the national Classification Board (not to mention the New Zealand Film Commission, who had funded it), and demonstrating comically humiliating prudishness. As a result of the board's decision, *Bad Taste* became one of the last movies to wear the 'Banned in Queensland' badge. In 1989, Labor was returned to office in Queensland for the first time since 1957, and Premier Wayne Goss abolished the Queensland Film Board of Review in 1991 due to increasing international shame and scrutiny set off by their puritanism. But no doubt Jackson took pleasure—and maybe some credit—in the claiming of this particular group's scalp, if not the entire Country–Liberal coalition that had run the state for the past 30 years.

Or maybe you can thank Martin Scorsese, whose 1988 film *The Last Temptation of Christ* was garnering global controversy for daring to depict a version of Jesus Christ, played by Willem Dafoe, who contemplated stepping down from the crucifix, renouncing his father (God) and marrying Mary Magdalene. Reverend Fred Nile—co-founder of the socially conservative Call to Australia Party (later the Christian Democratic Party) as well as the national coordinator and the New South Wales director of the Australian Federation of Festival of Light—demanded publicly that the film be banned, in stark contrast to the Catholic Church's strategy in Australia of keeping quiet and denying the film any PR oxygen. Nile, who described the film in his typically sober manner as 'a Satan production from the studios of hell', retorted that Christians would be tacitly approving the film if they didn't protest it. In 1974, he publicised the stance he would hold for the rest of his life, declaring 'pornography [to be] totally evil and anti-Christ and anti-Christian morality and anti-human sexuality, and anti-civilisation and particularly anti-man and anti-woman.' The twist was, to his eyes, almost everything secular *was* pornography.

When the national board ultimately gave *The Last Temptation of Christ* an R-rating—after inviting church groups to a private screening—Nile threatened to sue the board for their decision. The film's release continued uninterrupted, except in Brisbane, where a fundamentalist church offered to help fund the legal action against *Last Temptation*. They didn't need to: within a week of the ruling, the Queensland Board of Review banned the picture, becoming the only state in the country to defy the national ruling, despite the roiling controversy. Having played right into the hands of its critics, Queensland brought to the public square a years-long debate among anti-censorship campaigners as to whether or not the strict board was actually kicking own-goals in its zeal for censorship. But at that point, the Queensland government doubled down, warning filmmakers that 'community standards' were actually trending in a conservative direction. This would partly lead to the board's undoing, as its power to prohibit films that were 'objectionable'—which differed from the national legislation—trod on what Queensland cabinet minutes from 27 August 1990 described as 'a range of issues some of which may raise questions as to the right of free speech'.

At the time, it was reported that a Brisbane man was running bus tours across the NSW border for Queenslanders who wanted to see *The Last Temptation of Christ*—something that had become a norm throughout the 1980s for other 'Banned in Queensland' titles. And yet, even as controversy raged and politicians in Western Australia, Victoria and Tasmania alike asked the national board to follow in Queensland's footsteps, the national board zigged, downgrading the R-rating to an M within weeks. Nile warned that violence could break out in reaction to the board's heresy, and for a brief moment, it seemed as if he was right. He would know. He had previously failed in his attempt to secure a ban of Jean-Luc Godard's 1986 release *Hail Mary*—also condemned as blasphemous by Pope John Paul II!—so he called for a protest at the gala for the 33rd Sydney Film Festival, where the film would screen. Some of the protesters threw candles at attendees like Gough and Margaret Whitlam, while 500 others chanted prayers. The premiere was ultimately delayed by three hours once fights began to break out. Critic Mark Roberts is one who recalls being 'struck heavily on the back of head with a large wooden crucifix' by the self-proclaimed 'Legion of Mary'.

As *The Last Temptation of Christ* geared up for its release, film exhibitor Greater Union hired security guards to patrol a Sydney complex on its premiere night, with clashes breaking out between Christians and moviegoers outside the cinema during opening week, resulting even in some arrests. Fundamentalist groups picketed a theatre in Melbourne; a fire brigade was called to a Canberra screening when someone smelled petrol. The plague of protest was biblical in nature. However, before the frogs began raining from the skies, the controversy simply dissipated, as it became clear the national release would not be abated. *Last Temptation* went on to be banned in some nations—and remains banned in a handful—though today it is absolutely available nationwide in Australia. In 2004, it was even nominated at the Mexican MTV Movie Awards in the retrospective category of 'Best Miracle in a Movie'; sadly, the scene in which Jesus turns water into wine—and another on-screen miracle by Jesus in *The Passion of the Christ*—lost to the moment where *Bruce Almighty* magically makes his girlfriend's boobs grow overnight.

†

As was noted in the newly elected Goss Cabinet's submission for the *Classification of Films and Literature Bill*, the '[Queensland] Films Board of Review [had] exercised its banning powers liberally,' banning a total of 172 films between 1974 and 1984, and 41 films alone in 1988–89. It also acknowledged 'religious and various right wing pressure groups will vigorously oppose the abolition of the legislation establishing State censorship boards'. Of course, we cannot simply give Queensland all the credit for being Australia's proudest prudes. Even though the Queensland Film Board of Review was dismantled—partly for its own controversy-courting buffoonery—Queensland, South Australia, Western Australia, Tasmania, the ACT and the Northern Territory each still have their own state-based legislative nuances when it comes to classification, while New South Wales' and Victoria's pro-censorship groups gained significant ground in the 21st century. In the years that followed the *Bad Taste* debacle, the national body for classification continued to censor and outright ban movies, even those of local (or, in the case of the Kiwi Peter Jackson, neighbourly) origin. It wasn't until 2004 that the board even allowed Universal Pictures to release the uncut edition of *Bad Taste* on DVD.

This repellence of Minister Chipp's policy of gradualism from the 1970s was witnessed first-hand—and warned of—by chief censor Prowse's replacement, Janet

Strickland, even though she, in some instances, helped welcome it. Having served as Prowse's Deputy Censor, Strickland took over the reins in 1979. She had written, two years prior, that 'the Film Censorship Board does in a way exert a degree of both quantitative and qualitative control over films. Quantitative control in the sense that 3 per cent of films were rejected and 21 per cent were restricted [in 1975]; qualitative control in as much as the overwhelmingly majority of those rejected were totally without redeeming social purpose or merit'. She pretty quickly asked to be called out on the 'qualitative' claim with her first significant ruling as chief: the banning of *The Tin Drum* (discussed in greater detail in Chapter 11), which was ultimately overturned on appeal. Her main concern was the film's underage actors' participation in sexualised sequences. It was for the same reason in 1982 that she challenged the pre-existing pact between the censors and the film festivals, which had begun screening films without the board's interference again thanks to Don Chipp's interventions. Believing the 1975 Film Festival Agreement that allowed fests to seek censorship exemptions to be 'elitist', she teamed up with conservative politicians to bolster her position that the Melbourne International Film Festival needed to run its '82 program past the censors. She then banned director Hector Babenco's film *Pixote* to the confusion of the Melbourne Festival's director Geoffrey Gardner, who Scott Murray quoted in *Cinema Papers* saying, 'The film has been shown at more than 12 major film festivals, and has been commercially released, uncut, in the United States. To suppress it is a decision grossly out of touch with what is happening in the best of modern cinema.' In that same report, Melbourne's premier, John Cain, added this succinctly at the opening of Melbourne Festival: 'I thought we had stopped all that nonsense 15 or 20 years ago.'

Pixote ('small child' in Portuguese) revolves around the title character, a young boy who is used by corrupt police and crime organisations to commit offences on their behalf. (The teen actor who played Pixote, Fernando Ramos da Silva, was later killed in an incident with police at age 19.) The film was initially banned for its apparent exploitation of a minor, referring to scenes in which da Silva is present while adults are engaged in sexual activity. *Pixote* was ultimately allowed to play Sydney's and Melbourne's festivals following an appeal, and later scored an R-rating from a review board that felt Strickland had overreached in trying to claim the picture breached the *Victorian Police Offense Act*. In 2022, Variety named it the 80th best film ever made; another strike against her board's credentials on so-called quality control. Protections for the film festival classification exemption were passed into law in 1983 as a result of the farrago, but Strickland had given the religious right an angle for future fights. There was an irony as she exited the role following a seven-year-stint, as she warned of Australia entering a period of social conservatism and creeping censorship. By this point, she had sued Fred Nile for defamation, after he had deemed her responsible for allowing *Hail Mary* into Australia in typically fire-and-brimstone terms. She was also critical of her successor, Dickie, and the expansion of the chief censor's remit, telling the *Sydney Morning Herald* in 1996: 'Since my time, they have moved into literature, into computer games, into advertisements on clothing. They have sought to get their hands back onto something which I gave up, which is free-to-air television. They have tried to get hold of pay television and telephone information services, too.' However, a 1984 report in *The Bulletin* acknowledged that numerous public figures had disagreed publicly with how she had interpreted her role, and offered, by way of contrast, the Labor party's attitude that adults be entitled to read, hear and see what they want. It also acknowledged her 'hardline' stance towards the festivals, and how, mere months after the festival exemption was made law, her job was being advertised.

What gives the sharply increasing prurience of the 1980s a feeling of whiplash—or, perhaps explains it—is that the preceding decade had seen Australian cinema make a name for itself internationally with 'Ozploitation' flicks that centred on cheap yet visceral gore, as well as ribald sex comedies and documentaries that burst open the box office record books. They came at a time when America's 'New Hollywood' directors (Scorsese, Francis Ford Coppola, Peter Bogdanovich, et al.) tested similar waters, having been inspired by the French New Wave and Italian Neorealism movements of the 1970s. Not that the censors let everything slide without a slap on the wrist first. A local 52-minute *Texas Chain Saw Massacre* precursor titled *Night of Fear* was refused classification in 1972 for 'indecency', and its writer-director Terry Bourke probably wasn't surprised, having described it himself as 'a bizarre and frightening picture [with no dialogue, but] weird music punctuated by occasional piercing screams'. Still, that may have been simply promotional bluster, as the censors only had problems with two scenes: a tame bit of on-screen sex and an admittedly grotesque rat attack sequence where the rats' human master, played by Norman Yemm, masturbates as Carla Hoogeveen's howling victim is nibbled away. Following an appeal, the Review Board gave *Night of Fear* an R-rating, paving the way for its profitable run in drive-in cinemas, thanks to ads that reinstated the bluster: 'The film they didn't want you to see ... a terrifying journey into a deranged mind.' (For what it's worth, at 52 minutes *Night of Fear* is a highly efficient and upsetting Ozploitation flick, and the extreme close-ups of rats' bloodied, chittering teeth are indeed very, very gross. But most amusingly, it was funded by the ABC who had intended for it to be a pilot for an anthology TV series called *Fright*. Where it would have been placed on the schedule—alongside *Play School* or *Four Corners*—I have no idea.)

In 1973, an Australian farce about a homely door-to-door salesman who becomes the infatuation of every woman he visits grossed a heaving $4.7 million, becoming the country's highest-grossing local film at the time (and would still be in our top 10 if adjusted for inflation). *Alvin Purple*, an R-rated release, became such a local sensation, it was accompanied by a televised documentary—directed by Brian Trenchard-Smith—however, the doco was pulled mere hours before airtime by the Commonwealth Film Censorship Board in Sydney, who insisted on five cuts amounting to two minutes and two seconds in length before it could return to screens. That same year, a four-part anthology titled *Libido* had similarly been a popular success, featuring stories in which a priest lusts after a nun, and a husband and wife discuss their sexual fantasies.

In 1975, John D. Lamond's documentary *Australia After Dark* sold itself as 'a film full of fetishism, libido and the liveliest liberal spirit'. Despite offering an insight into 'the grotesque, the sexy and everything that is controversial for the social contract' (including 'a furtive gay marriage in a Catholic church simulated by actors, a nude woman muddling for pleasure, [and] a nudist painting studio'), it played in what Lamond described to *Cinema Papers* as 'respectable cinemas', as opposed to 'sleazy skinflic [sic] houses'. Such were the changing tides of Australia's social mores. Five years earlier—before the invention of the R-rating—director John B. Murray had faced opposition from the censors for his own sex-centric doco, *The Naked Bunyip* (co-written by Phillip Adams and named after the fictional Australian man-eating monster of the outback, only naked). With chief censor Prowse and Minister Chipp at existential loggerheads over the ratings system at the time, Murray and Adams took a leaf from Chipp's book and needled the board's request for 36 cuts by including bleeps or a dancing cartoon bunyip—illustrated by Peter Russell Clarke—at each contentious moment, alerting everyone to the volume of their censorial demands. 'The result was the audience cheered and clapped and chanted,' Adams recalls to me in 2023. 'The most popular parts of the film were the missing bits. Prowse was apoplectic but he could do nothing about it. When it went to appeal, Caroline Jones [a founding member of the Classification Review Board]—a very pious, sanctimonious woman—was even more shocked than Richard.' It probably didn't help that the picture also includes an interview with filmmaker Aggy Read who passes this assessment on the censors and specifically their ground floor office in Sydney: 'The best thing that should be done with the censors is concrete should be poured into the basement of the Imperial Arcade and it be totally blocked up.' The film ran for several years as it toured cinemas across the country.

By the late 1970s, the popularity of R-rated local films encouraged TV stations to give them a run—with a caveat—as *Alvin Purple* and Murray's 1971 classic *Stork* went to air in late 1976 with disclaimers noting they were 'reconstructed' (AKA cut). This infuriated viewers to the point that the Commonwealth censors put out a further disclaimer noting the prints had been prepared by the distributor. But the community standards had seemingly shifted, as even more gratuitous and explicit films emerged from the pipeline. That included 1976's *Fantasm*, which was banned entirely in the UK for opening credits that were superimposed over footage of a woman touching herself in extreme close-up, and a sequence of a housewife serving as a dominatrix—armed with a strap-on—to exact revenge on a peeping tom. Lamond also returned with dual 1978 releases *Felicity* and *The ABC of Love and Sex: Australia Style*, the latter being the first to include explicit penetration in an Australian film, though the scene was ultimately censored. They each took in huge grosses at the time of their cinema releases, and became cult classics as the decades passed. All three remain R-rated to this day, and Adams even remembers this period as being the 'last gasp' of film censorship. 'It went from censorial to the practice of labelling, which was a full step forward,' he tells me more than 50 years after *The Naked Bunyip*'s release. But even if community standards shifted in the 1970s, they didn't stay shifted—or at least, the government bodies' interpretation of them didn't—as Queensland's escapades in the 1980s demonstrated. However, not to be outdone, the national board would commit a series of embarrassing unforced errors in the fifty years that followed. As we'll discuss later, one such forehead-slapping classification forced them to have to clarify that 'male nipples are *not* nudity' in a report to government. Another led directly to a police force detainment of national treasure Margaret Pomeranz. For that, they really should pray for a miracle of atonement.

EFFED UP FACT:

The 2023 horror flick *M3gan* about an artificially-intelligent killer doll arrived on Blu-ray in Australia with the proclamation that it comes to us 'unrated', despite it clearly featuring an MA15+ classification on its cover. It does however offer a point of difference to the theatrical version—which was just rated M—by now including deleted scenes. According to the Classification Board, the unrated version of *M3gan* includes more blood spray, as well as uses of the words fuck, shit, balls, ass, hell, butt and damn. I know what you're thinking: Ass *and* butt? Damn, M3gan save something for the *Unrated* R18+ cut.

CHAPTER 4

ARE YOU THERE MARGARET? IT'S US, THE POLICE

How many cops does it take to turn off a DVD? If that sounds like the set-up to a joke, well, it kind of is ... just not a very funny one. In July of 2003, Sydney police raided Balmain Town Hall to do exactly that, only to end up in a standoff with an Australian titan. Still, today, this renegade's name is merely whispered in the halls of justice. I speak, obviously, of Margaret Pomeranz.

On the evening of 3 July 2003, law enforcement strode across the stage of a makeshift cinema to a chorus of boos as the opening credits rolled on Larry Clark's banned picture *Ken Park*. Here was a film that had been Refused Classification in Australia because of its graphic sexual content, yet was being screened in protest by Pomeranz, the revered television personality, film critic and fashion icon. The police superintendent shook her hand and explained that they've come to apprehend the unlawfully obtained feature. And it was going away for a long, long time.

The crowd, assembled in defiance of the Classification Board's ruling, didn't give it up without one last act of public disobedience. As police blocked the screen while the superintendent negotiated with Pomeranz, someone snatched the still-running film projector and turned it to the wall, blowing the image up even larger than it had been previously. Video from the evening shows the audience roaring in approval at their minor victory. Officers retaliated by cutting power to the building. There was just one problem: now they couldn't eject the DVD.

'It was all a bit of a farce, really,' Pomeranz tells me nearly two decades later. As she thinks back to that fateful night, she actually recalls a bit more back-and-forth between her and the police before they took their drastic power-cutting measure. 'They turned it off and I turned it on again and they turned it off, and I went, "bugger it", and I turned it on again.' Patrons who'd come for Larry Clark wound up watching an Abbott and Costello routine.

Police eventually turned the power back on, took out the incriminating disc and invited Pomeranz back to the station—57 metres down the road—where she was briefly detained. In retrospect, the protesters could have picked a town hall that wasn't a brisk jog from the cop shop, but that's Monday-morning-quarterback talk. Upon release, Pomeranz pledged to keep seeking an outlet for *Ken Park*, a film she nonetheless described at the time as 'bleak' and 'depressing' and 'not a film you're gonna get off on'. (It was not the most convincing recommendation of her career.) This despite the fact she faced up to a year in jail for her criminal rebellion. In the end, no charges were laid, but neither was Pomeranz successful in getting justice for *Ken Park*. To date, the film remains among a select few that are Refused Classification in Australia. There are major legal ramifications for anyone who wants to screen it.

Margaret Pomeranz remains one of the most revered film critics in the country thanks to her decades-long stint reviewing movies on SBS, the ABC and most recently Foxtel. For years, she worked alongside David Stratton, a fellow crusader against censorship. She was initially an unconventional choice to sit beside Stratton, having been perceived as more of the 'everywoman' filmgoer opposite Stratton's bearded cineaste. But it was soon established that Pomeranz—quick to a croaky-laugh and steadfast in her thoughtful and well-considered opinions—knew of what she spoke. So, in 2003, when she and Stratton were at the height of their powers, her defiance of Australian law meant more than a little.

Pomeranz explained the origin of her *cause célèbre* in a 2011 televised review of Jean-Luc Godard's 1960 feature *Breathless* (*À bout de souffle*). In the review, her co-host Stratton describes *Breathless* as the 'film that changed cinema', which was contrary to how the Classification Board of the time appreciated it, having banned the film for its so-called immorality. Godard's filmic-language-altering masterpiece stars Jean-Paul Belmondo as a French hood who kills a cop, goes on the run and hides out with his American girlfriend, played by Jean Seberg. It was the English captions—taken in conjunction with the images—that inspired the censor to rule that it was 'indecent'. '*Breathless* took my breath away when I saw it in London in 1961,' Pomeranz says in the review. 'When I arrived in Australia and found it was banned here I became a rebel with a cause.' It was eventually rated R18+ in 1983 and released theatrically, but the incident had taken root in Pomeranz. 'If ever there is an argument against censorship it's [*Breathless*] being banned,' she continued. *Ken Park* ain't *Breathless*. But Margaret couldn't not be Margaret.

Pomeranz first saw *Ken Park* at the Venice Film Festival in 2002, and knew immediately it would raise a few eyebrows back home. 'I said that to Larry Clark,' she tells me. 'He said, "Ah, nonsense, they love my films down in Australia."' Clark, the iconoclastic director of controversy-magnets *Kids* and *Bully*, shouldn't have assumed he knew us better than Pomeranz. In fact, he was fortunate that *Kids* wasn't banned in 1995, when Christian organisations Project Family and the Australian Christian Coalition joined forces in Queensland to boycott distributor Village Roadshow over the explicit teen drama, to no avail. (The 2021 documentary *We Were Once Kids* reflected on Clark's filming practices with young people on that project, raising the valid, complicated question as to whether the powerful final film was worth what the stars were subjected to—or indeed urged to do—on set.)

'It was a very, very strange thing [the *Ken Park* case] because the [Sydney Film] Festival had the right to show it, but a distributor—I think on the Gold Coast, a video distributor—had applied to distribute it here prior to the festival,' she explains.

> When it went to the board, it got denied classification, RC. The festival was free to show films without classification, but once they'd been refused classification, they couldn't. There was a bit of an uproar amongst a few of us, that we were stuck with a situation where you could show a film at a prestigious international festival like Venice, and we're not allowed to see that film here. It was really frustrating and anger-making, really, about the puritanical attitude of the board. I mean, there's controversial stuff in the film; there's the implication of real sex in the final scene; there's that autoerotic asphyxiation scene, which is confronting. But I actually felt it should not even have been given [as high as] an R classification, because I thought it was a film that really spoke to young people.

The picture itself—co-directed by revered cinematographer Edward Lachman—concerns a group of disaffected teenagers and their many, *many* troubles at home. Some are abused by their parents. One is abusive towards his grandparents. All are entangled in psychosexual torment. It begins with a graphic scene of suicide and ends with a teen threesome. Admittedly, this is boilerplate Larry Clark. Fred Nile, then-director of the NSW branch of Festival of Light and whose Call to Australia Party had recently changed its name to the Christian Democratic Party, lobbied hard for *Ken Park*'s banning, arguing, 'If teenage actors portray under-16-year-olds in nude explicit sex and suicide scenes ... it is legally child pornography.' Clark, in an interview with the *Sydney Morning Herald* soon after *Ken Park*'s banning, exclaimed that all of the actors were over the age of 18, and that all the sex had been simulated, with the exception of a bravura centrepiece in which James Ransome's sociopathic character Tate climaxes from autoerotic asphyxiation. Regardless, the under-siege board declared that *Ken Park* did not meet 'the standards of morality, decency and propriety generally accepted by reasonable adults'—and certainly not those accepted by Fred Nile. At the same time, Don Chipp reared his head—at Sexpo, fittingly—to decry the churches and their special interest groups attacking films like *Ken Park* as 'singularly uninterested in starvation and slaughter but [see] a simulated act of love in a movie as an international disaster.'

I ask Margaret what gave *Ken Park* the artistic merit that the Classification Board is always looking for in films they deem challenging yet worthy of release. 'I thought it was honest about troubled kids, and how they cling together in terms of horrible situations in their own life; that what they've got is one another,' she says. 'I thought it was really good, actually, I still do. I want to believe in what I'm seeing on screen, with any film, and I believed this. I really felt that it was true, it was extremely well performed, and it was heart wrenching. Really moving. It ticked a lot of boxes for me.' It's a compliment that was echoed by some—and I do mean *some*—contemporary critics, even if it came with a number of caveats. 'Clark might very well be a pornographer, a hypocrite and whatever else you want to call him, [but] he's also the only American director working today whose work reckons with the complexities of our current generation of MySpace exhibitionists, and especially the way so many young people today seem to relish their own exploitation,' critic Christopher Kelly wrote for *Slate* in 2006. Excluding the MySpace reference, that review proves Clark's prescience about the shift towards uninhibited self-platforming youth. He continued, 'These kids know no boundaries, and Clark—who often dives right into bed alongside them—doesn't, either.'

That's why Pomeranz and fellow members of her Watch on Censorship organisation—including journalist David Marr—decided to host an illegal screening of *Ken Park* at Balmain Town Hall, which had followed a much smaller, anonymously-hosted and unimpeded event a few nights earlier at the Community Arts Warehouse in Brunswick. Pomeranz says the Balmain event, by contrast, was 'heaving' with people, though unfortunately, that also included the police, who'd heard of the event in advance—from none other than Fred Nile, who'd spearheaded a campaign against the film and alerted Superintendent Arthur Katsogiannis of the NSW police. 'When we arrived, we knew there was police presence there,' she says. 'We knew what was going to happen beforehand. That we were going to have a lot of trouble showing that film. So we were aware that the cops were out. I mean, it was quite severe. You're facing up to a year in prison and a fine of twenty-five thousand dollars. The implications for going ahead with that were actually quite serious. And for some people in the group, that had implications, because you could not take on a public role if you had been arrested.' In the retelling, she laughs while clarifying she didn't ever want to seek public office, before adding: 'I certainly didn't want to go to jail for a year, either. And I thought, "Well, if we just got a hefty fine, we could most probably get support funds from somewhere, and we would [put in] money ourselves."' So, the screening went ahead, with police waiting for her to press 'play' before stepping in.

'The police were extremely polite,' Pomeranz remembers.

> I don't think their heart was really in the shutting down of a film, but I think they were obliged to do it, because it was such a public declaration of 'stuff you' to the Censorship Board. I really do feel that the Classification Board was caught between a rock and a hard place, because if it had gone to the board for classification for a film screening, I got the impression that they would have allowed it with an R certificate. But because it had been applied for video release, which meant it could be on video shelves and accessible to young people—which I thought it should be anyway—I think they really wanted to restrict that sort of access.

Stratton was a witness to the madcap evening: 'I was meeting that evening with my grandson, and I said to him, "Margaret's gonna show *Ken Park*. Let's go along and see what happens,"' he recalls to me. 'We walked in, a bit late—we probably had dinner in Balmain—and we walked into the back of the hall and it was a throng of people, just about the time the wallopers came in, and I think the film might have just started, and they came in and took her and the film away. So, we all yelled, booed, so on and so on.' Nonetheless, as often was the case, David and Margaret didn't exactly see eye to eye on *Ken Park*. 'I wouldn't ban it by any means, but I didn't particularly like it. If you can't support it, then don't champion it. Margaret loved *Ken Park* and she championed it; good on her.' This may have seemed like a contrary position for the man who once defended the incestuous throupling at the climax of *Like Night and Day* several decades earlier, but *Ken Park* is proof positive that censors will find themselves unimpeded if films never get the chance to gain a champion. Mercifully, *Ken Park* had Margaret. Stratton adds, 'I told her at the time, "Look, I'm not going to stand on the platform with you on this because I can't really personally defend the film." Not for censorship reasons, particularly; I just didn't think it was a particularly good film.'

After the charges were dropped, neither Pomeranz nor the others in Watch on Censorship attempted another screening, even though she was given a surprise assurance that any future stint behind bars was going to be unlikely. 'I don't know whether I should say this, but in a funny coda, the Attorney-General of NSW bothered to ask me and David Marr out to lunch and assured us that we would not have ended up in the clink under his watch. That was quite nice.'

Whether they were enthusiastic about the Balmain brouhaha or not, police raids on film screenings or theatrical productions in Australia were nothing new. Seven decades earlier, Sydney police stormed cinemas to seize newsreels featuring footage of Francis de Groot, leader of the fascist New Guard of Australia, as he interrupted the opening of the Sydney Harbour Bridge on horseback. And one of the most notable pre-World War II acts of censorship occurred in 1936, aimed at Clifford Odet's anti-Nazi play *Till the Day I Die*. When the German consul complained that the play was 'unjust to a friendly power'—the friendly power being *the Nazis*—the Chief Secretary of New South Wales, Jack Baddeley, made the decision to ban it, following the direction of then-Attorney-General Robert Menzies (who would later become Australia's longest-serving Prime Minister). The New Theatre in Sydney decided to go ahead regardless with an unpublicised opening night, though police got wind of the event and interrupted the performance. As the story goes, the lead actor moved to the front of the stage and declared dryly as the police scurried behind him: 'Through that door should have stepped a Nazi. As you can see, it is a New South Wales policeman.' After asking the audience if the play should go on, and responding to their standing ovation, the actors shoved the police off stage. Nonetheless, the ban on the play would not be lifted until 1941, two full years after war had been declared against Nazi Germany, and eight years after the formation of their first concentration camp. With friends like these...

In 1968, the New Theatre in Newtown, NSW looked to stage *America, Hurrah*, by Jean-Claude van Itallie, which comprises three short plays and ends with *Motel*, in which two giant 'dolls'—inhabited by actors in costume—wreck a motel room, strip to their knickers, simulate sex and graffiti obscenities on the wall, including 'fuck', 'shit' and 'a big cock up my juicy cunt'. Five weeks into the run, despite the play being promoted as for 'Suitable Adults Only', a grandmother took her 17-year-old grandson, in what I have to assume was the most awkward night of both their lives. Afterwards, nan reportedly phoned the Darlinghurst Police Station with her scathing review. The police warned the players against performing *Motel* again, and it was subsequently banned. But two months later, at the Teachers Federation Theatre in Sydney, a free performance of *America, Hurrah* was presented. More than 3,000 punters turned up, and about 2,500 were turned away; among those who secured seats were members of the New South Wales police force, who chased the dolls onto the proscenium once they started doing their freaky thing. This time, however, the playhouse was prepared. As the police made their move, the two actors smuggled the dollsuits backstage, where they were met by five other actors in their underwear. The cops were thus faced with seven indistinguishable puppeteers in their knickers, unsure which ones to arrest. They would have settled for the dolls instead, but those had been spirited away mysteriously. Meanwhile, back on stage, there was a struggle between police and the show's crew—aided by audience members—in an effort to keep the boys in blue from confiscating the parts of the set scrawled in swear words. In the melee, the panels were wrecked and shredded. To this day, the dolls remain at large.

In 1969, a similar event took place in Brisbane's Twelfth Night Theatre, where two police, dressed as civvies, sat in the audience, having heard on good authority that the final lines of the play *Norm and Ahmed* (in which an Australian archetype torments a Pakistani victim) included the word 'fuckin' …' followed by a slur. The police waited until the line was delivered, and then jumped onto the stage, asking the actor to confirm whether or not he really had just said what they thought he said. He confessed, and the police retreated to HQ with their report suggesting a swift edit to the script. The players refused, and the next night, at the same point in the play, the actor was arrested. After some arguing in the courts, a verdict found that the actor had contravened the *Vagrants, Gaming and Other Offences Act*, which condemns 'obscene language' in a public place, 'whether any person is therein or not'. Quite literally, Queensland had decided that if someone swears in the woods and no one is around to hear it, they're still committing a crime.

Also in 1969, Mart Crowley's celebrated queer drama *The Boys in the Band* moved onto Melbourne's Playbox Theatre, following a successful seven-month run in Sydney without complaint. It took just three weeks for Victoria's Vice Squad detectives to attend and—toting stopwatches and notepads—document all the ways the actors were guilty of public obscenity. Producer Harry M. Miller fought the charges in court, primarily as an act of shrewd publicity generation, forcing the detectives to recount their notes, leading, most likely, to the very first time a detective said the phrase 'supertwat' before a magistrate. John Tasker—the director of both these contentious productions of *America, Hurrah* and *The Boys in the Band*—offered his thoughts in 1970, writing:

Theatre has been a substitute for an indigestion powder—or after-dinner mint—only in the last few decades. The entire previous history of theatre is that of a public forum where the concerns and the problems of the day may be discussed and perhaps resolved; where the foibles of mankind and society are held up for ridicule. Theatre has been a place of ritual and ceremony and mystery and terror. If we insist that every play which is presented in the theatre must be acceptable to a twelve-year-old, to a policeman who has not been to the theatre for fifteen years, to a granny out for the night with her box of Winning Post, then we debase the art of theatre to that of a sideshow.

He continued, 'For centuries theatre has led the thought and ideals of society. The question should never be asked "Are we ready for such and such a play?" If a play arrives and the country is ready for it, then it is out of date. The theatre should be the leader in thoughts and values. It should be one of the most responsible components of community life. When theatre is recognised as the art in which we speak most directly to each other, there will be as little need for censorship as there is in the bedroom.'

In the subsequent decades, it would not have been unreasonable to apply Tasker's description of theatre as a component of community life to the art form of cinema as well. Certainly the wallopers and the wowsers felt cinema could infect the populace in the same manner as provocative theatre. Cinema raids began in Australia at the earliest emergence of the art form, with police in 1902 hauling in an exhibitor for showing 'allegedly suggestive pictures'. Australia's reputation was such that none other than H.G. Wells remarked, 'a barrier of illiterate policemen and officials stands between the tender Australian mind and what they imagine to be subversive literature.' Encounters like these saw their modern return in the dramatic, slapstick saga of *Ken Park*, and more battles since. 'We had quite a few fights,' Pomeranz says of her relationship with the board. 'It feels like a century ago that we had to fight for, oh God, trying to get *9 Songs* [which contained unsimulated sex] off the X classification [in 2004]. What an insult that was.' That feature, from director Michael Winterbottom, was initially classified X18+ by the OFLC for its scenes of unsimulated sex, including a shot of ejaculation. The X-rating aligned it with regular non-violent and thus not-banned 'erotica', nonetheless assigning it closer to the category of 'pornography' rather than 'legitimate' cinema—though, being X-rated was a kind of 'banned', as so few states were allowed to even show X18+ movies. It was later reduced to R18+ by the Classification Review Board in a 3 – 2 majority decision. The main argument was that the media's exaggerated assessment of its frequent sex scenes was overstated, and that 'the Classification Review Board only determines that 'actual sex' is depicted when it sees actual penetration (of some kind), actual manipulation of genitalia or actual climax.' As such, *9 Songs* could be downgraded. Still, it was a tumultuous time, as Pomeranz recalls. 'I think distributors have become more cautious,' she adds, when asked about the fallout to *Ken Park*, and even *9 Songs*. 'It's expensive to get the rights to a film, and then when you're not allowed to show it, it's almost not worth your while.'

So, what does Clark have to say about all this? 'If there are countries that have a problem with it, then fuck it, they can't show it, I don't care.' Clark—now in his eighties—declined to be interviewed for this book through the Luhring Augustine Gallery in New York that showcases his decades of photographic work; however, the gallery provided me with a trove of press clippings from the days of the *Ken Park* controversy and beyond. That quote comes from the English translation of a chat with a French journalist in 2007, who asked about his stoushes with censorship boards over the years. 'I'm always fighting censorship, or I'm not fighting it, they are fighting me, you know?' he argued. 'I just make the work.' He also justified the morality of his projects, despite the inflammatory accusations about his intentions: 'I've been called many, many names, "pornographer," "child pornographer," "garbage," 'trash,' "he's romanticising drugs," and on and on and on … But there is a moral centre to all the work and the moral centre is consequences. Consequences for everything that we do, and that's just a fact.' In that same conversation with the outlet *Art Press*, I learnt why an amended version of his still-banned feature never made its way to our Classification Board, and why the Classification Board will have to blink before Clark if they ever want to evaluate the film again for Australian release: '*Ken Park* could never be cut one frame, the contracts all say it could never be altered or changed or cut or censored in any way.' Hence: 'Fuck it, they can't show it.' How's that for consequences?

Pomeranz knows there's another way to see *Ken Park* in Australia. 'It's almost like the Classification Board has become redundant with the web,' she says. 'You can access just about anything that you want to, even disgusting stuff. I sort of felt then, and I do now, that the Classification Board's role is to advise people of material that may be upsetting, so they are warned about the content of films, so people have the right to make up their own decision; whether they want to embrace this material or not. I felt that then. I feel it now.' And when it comes to *Ken Park*, she continues to feel the same way. 'It gave me great pleasure—and I don't suppose I should say this—to pick up a copy overseas and bring it back illegally.'

EFFED UP FACT:

The National Film and Sound Archive houses the first known porno made in Australia, shot—according to reporter Peter Luck—most likely by a newsreel crew going off script. Presumably filmed in the early 1920s, it appears to have been made west of Sydney, in the Blue Mountains area. There's no sound, or even credits, rendering the participants, a hundred years later, completely anonymous. James Cockington, author of *Banned*, was among the 'serious researchers' granted permission to view it in the archives, and he describes it as 'graphic as any X-rated movie made today, performed with enthusiasm by participants who were relaxed enough to show pleasure in their performances.' Folks, if you love what you do, you'll never work a day in your life.

CHAPTER 5
YOU CAN'T SAY THAT

If I called you a dickhead, would you hold it against me? I certainly know how the Australian Classification Board would react: they'd rate me PG. According to the ACB's official internal coarse language guide, you can get away with using 'dickhead' in a PG movie, along with 'arsehole', 'bastard', 'bullshit', 'douchebag', 'knob', 'slut' and 'wanker'. Those words won't fly in a G-rated film, but the guide says general audiences can withstand the usage of 'bum', 'effing', 'jerk' and 'nuts' (though, maybe not all in the same sentence, and definitely not in that order). A single 'fuck' will get you slapped with an M, as will 'screw' (in a sexual context) and 'motherfucker' (in a non-sexual context). But there's only one word, no matter the context, that'll earn a film an instant MA-rating. And it's basically Australia's favourite word: cunt.

It's believed the word 'cunt' either derives from the Indian goddess Kunti, the Norse phrase 'kunta', or the Latin words 'cuniculus' (meaning 'rabbithole') or 'cuneus' (meaning 'wedge'). The jury may be out on the etymology, but most experts agree it's derived from the word sound 'cu', which can be found in the early versions of the feminine words 'cow' and 'queen'. Today, in most English-speaking nations, it's regarded as the ultimate conversation-halting curse, despite simply being a slang stand-in for vagina. But in modern Australia and the UK, it's so much more than that. It's both a cutting insult and a term of endearment; it partners well with 'funny', 'mad', 'right' and 'silly'; it's versatile enough to be used as a noun, an adjective and, with a little imagination, a verb; you can even peg it at a Prime Minister and not be convicted of offensive behaviour. No, seriously.

That's what happened to activist Danny Lim in 2017, when he stood on the side of busy New South Head Road in Edgecliff, NSW, wearing a sandwich board that called then-PM Tony Abbott a cunt. (Well, technically he wrote 'can't' with an upside down 'a', but the meaning in the sentence 'TRICKY LYING TONY YOU CAN'T [line break] SCREW EDUCATION HEALTH, JOBS & THE ENVIRONMENT' was not lost on anyone.) A judge initially ruled that Lim's not-so-subtle wordplay counted as offensive behaviour to a 'reasonable person', which includes any behaviour considered likely to invoke anger, outrage, resentment or disgust. But, in a twist, the decision was overruled on appeal, precisely because, in

Australia, compared to other more sensitive nations, 'cunt' just doesn't have the same ring to it.

And yet, as recently as 2021, movies that would otherwise appeal to and be relevant to a wider audience have earned MA-ratings for their usage of cunt alone. How else to explain Aussie teen comedy *Ellie & Abbie (& Ellie's Dead Aunt)* getting downgraded from MA15+ to M after a single instance of 'cunt' was excised by distributor Arcadia Films, and replaced with the sound of a squawking crow? This cunt-to-crow switcheroo is the only difference between the wide-release feature and the version that played festivals.

Take also, for example, 2019 features *Rocketman* and *The Australian Dream*. The former is a fantastical musical biopic based on the ribald life of Elton John, in which Elton, played by Taron Egerton, at one point cheekily calls himself a cunt. The latter is a contemplative documentary about the racial vilification experienced by Indigenous Aussie Rules footballer Adam Goodes. In the Classification Board's decision report for *The Australian Dream*, they cite 'three audible uses of very strong coarse language in the form of the word "cunt" in addition to written use of the word "cunt"'. They're referring to the instances where Goodes remembers being called 'a black monkey-looking cunt' by footy fans as a twenty-something player and when fellow Indigenous footy great Nicky Winmar recalls hearing someone refer to him as 'a black cunt' during a game. Later, the film shows a scrolling page of social media posts also including 'cunt' and vile variations. Per the board's hard and fast rules, usage of 'cunt' guaranteed that *The Australian Dream* would get an instant MA-rating. Perhaps most ironic in this situation is the synopsis for the film written in their decision report: '*The Australian Dream* is an Australian documentary, focussing on Adam Goodes, the Indigenous AFL legend and his story of race, identity and belonging in a society still immature and mostly ignorant with regards to its historical identity.' The key words here are 'mostly ignorant'. If only there was some way to help people of all ages learn more about it.

But that's the way the cookie crumbles. Or is it? Because Paramount Pictures, the distributor of *Rocketman*, was able to successfully challenge its MA-rating, appealing on the basis of context. The board concurred: 'It is the view of the Classification Review Board that the dramatic biographical context does mitigate the impact of the language, and specifically, the one instance of the use of strong coarse language.' Madman, the distributor of *The Australian Dream*, never appealed their MA-rating, having told me they didn't even think a downgraded rating was possible.

As far as they knew, usage of 'cunt' warranted an immediate MA15+, so why cry about it? In this one and only instance where *Rocketman* and *The Australian Dream* can be considered in contrast, you start to see the shortcomings of the Classification Board's supposedly reliable rulebook. In theory, it empowers censors to classify accurately without having to make captain's calls on each and every title, but the wriggle room is almost non-existent, and when a film does wriggle free, it's never clear how that one managed to do it over others.

It took a conversation with the director of the board at the time, Margaret Anderson, to get to the bottom of the issue. In the matter of *Rocketman*, she believes the fault lay with the distributor and the review board, emphasising that the Classification Board and Classification Review Board are two distinct bodies. 'Paramount, who was the film distributor, they are notorious,' she began. 'If you want to know who appealed [more than any other studio], Paramount did. It was amazing.' After Paramount submitted a version of the film without final effects and end credits, the picture received an MA15+ for the single utterance of 'cunt', but all involved knew it would need to be resubmitted once the last elements had been integrated. 'That is not uncommon where a film distributor—especially one of the major film distributors—has a film and they want to get an idea of where the classification is going to sit,' Anderson explained. At Paramount's request, she embargoed the board's decision, and also embargoed the MA-rating given to the next iteration of the movie with all effects and credits included. But five days later, the film was brought to the Classification Review Board, who awarded it an M. 'There was not a great deal of love or respect between the Classification Board [and] the Classification Review Board,' she says.

> And the reason for that was, the Classification Review Board basically went on a frolic of its own. It is meant to still apply the Act, the Code and the guidelines. They would regularly come up with these bizarre decisions that you would read and go, 'How in God's name is that in accordance with the film guidelines?' The problem with them making *Rocketman* M is that M is not a legally restricted classification. MA15+ and R18+ are the only two restricted classifications. G, PG and M are simply advisory classifications. So in relation to M, it's suggested that it's really for a mature audience, hint hint, so maybe children won't want it. The moment that *Rocketman* was made M meant that you and I could take our

eight-year-old to see it. And no one was going to be stopping us. It may be that you and I are quite fine about our eight-year-old going to see a film with cunt language in it; a film that otherwise is dealing with adult issues and adult considerations. But the issue was that the Classification Board itself, in its own reports, had already drawn attention to the fact that, yeah there was a single use at 112 minutes; the film guidelines are really clear that strong coarse language—and cunt is considered strong—gets you an MA15+ classification. We had already said in *Rocketman* that we noted there was other coarse language justified by context, in the form of the words fuck and its derivatives, and bitch and shit and bastard, which could easily be accommodated in a lower classification category. By the review board doing what they did, they basically said this film is okay for everybody—*everybody*—in Australia to watch. And that was just something that the [Classification] board itself thought, 'that's wrong'.

On the matter of *The Australian Dream*, Anderson was resolute in her team's rating (which never went before the review board because, as a Madman spokesperson stated, they didn't like their odds). In her opinion, if a parent wants to show it to their child, they can, and if a teacher wants to show it to their student, they can follow the Department of Education's policies to gain approval from parents. 'All [we're] doing is giving an advisory. You don't have to watch the film. You can look at the DVD box or look at the streaming service, it will say, 'MA15+, scenes of racism and strong coarse language.' And that's what this is all about.'

The 2017 feature *Lady Bird* also found itself at the centre of controversy when Universal Pictures Australia amended the US edit and replaced both usages of the word cunt before even submitting it to the board for approval, fearing an MA-rating. In one instance, they even got star Saoirse Ronan to overdub one 'cunt' and replace it with 'cooze'. That same year, *John Wick: Chapter 2* was released to cinemas rated MA15+, featuring close-up footage of Keanu Reeves' assassin killing exactly 128 people. Without seeing the board's conversion chart, we can still deduce that individual deployments of the word 'cunt' equate to about 64 on-screen murders.

Anderson remembered the *Lady Bird* incident well, even if it hardly set a precedent. 'There have always been different versions of films released in the different markets around the world. Always existed. Always will exist.' She pointed to the sliding global scale of community standards: 'Scandinavia, very relaxed over sex and nudity. Like, really relaxed. Americans, stunning prudes over sex and nudity. Chop the baby's head, eat its intestines, that's all fine. Violence is hunky dory. But stunning prudes over the sex and nudity.' Yet she was particularly irked by Universal's decision to remove the cunt language in the theatrical release of Australia, of all places, and record Saoirse Ronan saying 'cooze'. 'We played that like five times, going, "Cooze"? What the frick? Honest to God.'

'Every film distributor is interested in the box office taking,' Anderson continued. 'So it was not a surprise at all that for the sake of the holy dollar Universal butchered *Lady Bird* for the theatrical release in Australia.'

Anderson mostly felt bad for *Lady Bird*'s director. 'Greta Gerwig made a film [and] she was telling a story and she was happy with the way that she had filmed it and had it edited.' But Anderson ultimately understands why Universal had attempted to get an M-rating on first pass. 'They had obviously done their number-crunching and there were a truckload of 12, 13 and 14-year-olds who they were expecting to see *Lady Bird* that were more important to them than those who were able to see it as a MA15+ film.' Little did Universal know that *Lady Bird* would still get an MA15+ for featuring a shot of Ronan reading a *Playgirl* with male nudity, but more on how they tackled that particular issue later.

†

The historical usage of 'cunt' in the movies is interesting in and of itself. It's widely believed that Jack Nicholson was the first person to say 'cunt' on screen, but that's not true. Perhaps it's become apocryphal because it's just so easy to imagine it rolling it off his tongue, like so many other swears he'd deliver over the years. The honour actually goes to Jack Smith in the Ken Jacobs short art film *Blonde Cobra* from 1963, in which he describes 'young ladies [who have] thrown themselves upon a plaster statue of, well, Jesus—I mean they've been shoving the thing up their cunts.' The infamous, blasphemous stand-up Lenny Bruce would go on to also drop the bomb in his video-recorded 1965 comedy set. The first mainstream movie to feature 'cunt' was William Friedkin's adaptation of the aforementioned play *The Boys in the Band* in 1969. And *then* Nicholson steps into the lineage, with Mike Nichols' 1971 drama *Carnal Knowledge*, where he shouts at Ann-Margret, 'Answer me you ball-busting, castrating, son-of-a-cunt bitch!' Later in the same picture, reflecting on his exes, he refers to one he 'banged in Berlin' as 'a real cunt'. If there's a trend in the trailblazing of the c-word, it's that it was never seen to exit the mouth of a woman in those early days, and often used in a derogatory, even misogynistic fashion, as with *Carnal Knowledge*. It's harder to identify the first usage by a woman, but most signs point towards 1979 British ITV drama *No Mama No*. The HBO series *Sex and the City* would go on to normalise its on-screen usage by women (even though its first utterance is from a male character) several decades later. Nine Network in Australia actually let an episode of *SATC* play on free-to-air television with the word uncensored, though viewers in regional areas had their purity preserved: for them, 'cunt' was bleeped. Not that this cured the entertainment industry and classification boards or censors of their fear of language around female genitalia for all time. In 2006, Shonda Rhimes coined the term 'vajayjay' for her medical soap opera *Grey's Anatomy*, because she was instructed to stop using the clinical term 'vagina' so much.

It didn't have to be this way though. In fact, in an alternate and more matriarchal universe, this chapter might have been about the words 'lad' or 'prince' or 'fellow', which are just some of the neutral/positive masculine terms that aren't considered offensive. So says Amanda Montell, a US-based linguist and author of the book *Wordslut: A Feminist Guide to Taking Back the English Language*. As she explained to me over an early morning video call during coronavirus isolation mid-2020, 'These are just a handful of the masculine terms that have not undergone this process of pejoration, which is a form of semantic change where a word that starts out with a neutral or positive meaning devolves over time to mean something negative.'

She says,

> With masculine terms, you more often than not see the opposite process occur, which is called amelioration, where a word starts out with a negative or neutral meaning and evolves to mean something positive. We can look at some minimal pairs, like the words 'buddy' and 'sissy', which back in the day were synonyms for brother and sister, but the term 'buddy' ameliorated over time to mean a friend and pal, while 'sissy' pejorated over time to mean a wimpy man who, God forbid, reminds you of a woman.
>
> For a long time, for hundreds of years, cunt was used to reference female genitalia without any negative nuances. It was just an objective word to describe female genitalia, but like so many of these other terms referencing

female sexuality, it gained those negative connotations over time. That's directly related to the history of female sexuality in our culture.

Though Montell appreciates Americans are even more sensitive and skittish about 'cunt' compared to Australians ('It might have to do with the two cultures' distinct senses of humour; vaginas just aren't funny here, vaginas are scary'), she's not surprised it can still be used and understood as offensive down under. 'It all just really says something about female sexuality's place in our culture, women's place in our culture, that over and over again we see terms designating femininity at some point over their lifespan be reduced to a sexual slur,' Montell says. 'We often use the pronoun "she" to refer to things that are beautiful but also dangerous, like cars and storms and oceans and planes and countries and indeed dangerous epidemics.' (Just ask the Académie Française, the official guardian of the French language, who officially declared the phrase COVID-19 'feminine'.) 'We have a history of equating femininity and womanliness with being in danger; things that tempt us but need to be conquered and tamed and reeled in, because they can be our undoing,' she adds. 'That's how we've been taught to perceive female genitalia.' It's been that way for a long time too. In 1856, live performer Lola Montez gained notoriety in Australia for touring her seductive 'Spider Dance', earning ire in *The Ballarat Star*. Montez proposed meeting with the editor Henry Seekamp at a hotel in front of invited guests to debate the merits of her act. It was a trap. When he arrived, she attacked him with a horsewhip, and then continued on with her tour, performing to packed houses. Okay, the danger in that instance was real, but so too are the pre-emptive attempts to control female bodies.

Montell believes it also helps that 'cunt' is effective in its pronunciation too. 'I think the phonetics of the word cunt also contribute to its strong expletive sound,' she explains. 'Plosive consonants, stop consonants are all over our vocabulary of vulgarities. Cunt has the 'thwack' of 'ck' and 'tuh'. It sounds like a powerful, almost violent word, phonetically.'

Australian journalist Donald Horne once called on the censorious government of the '70s to admit to their skewed stance around genitals: 'If the State decides that certain parts of the human body are obscene, it should name them. If it doesn't want people to use certain words it should write them down ... It would be fascinating to find out what words, what sexual acts and what parts of the body the state found obscene.' Today, the list exists. You read it at the top of this chapter. And you saw which word the modern-day state considers most obscene: the one related to female anatomy. And yet, over the decades, censorship has been presented as a way to maintain the purity of the female viewer, from the wowsers within the Good Film League who fought 'to encourage the presentation of moving pictures of high ethical and artistic standards,' to Senator Brian Harradine, a right-wing independent from Tasmania who campaigned against X-rated exports from the early 1990s through to the 2000s because it 'sullies the image of Australian women [and] depicts them in a manner that indicates they are generally highly promiscuous and available.' (He also spurred that infamous Nationals' party room porn marathon in collaboration with Nationals MP De-Anne Kelly.)

In my conversation with Montell, we agreed that the pejoration of the word 'cunt' is largely ridiculous. Nonetheless, Montell argues we shouldn't be so dismissive to compare the violence of one film (such as *John Wick*) as necessarily more impactful than the usage of a word. 'I think the word "cunt" earning a film the same rating as 100 bloody war sequences really speaks to the inherent power of words to destroy people, to take away their power, or to elevate them and make them feel empowered. I don't think people give language the credit that it's due all the time, because we have idioms like "sticks and stones will break your bones", or "they're just words", but people really can be harmed in a material way with language.' Take 1996's Red Riding Hood riff *Freeway*, which was refused classification and ultimately rated R18+ only after the shortening of a scene in which wolfish Kiefer Sutherland threatens Reese Witherspoon's hitchhiker with sexual assault, calling her a 'fucking cunt'. Much of the exchange was initially erased in both Australia and the US, though that piece of dialogue was restored locally for Australia's 2007 DVD release.

'I think also our relationship to certain slurs—which are individual—are directly related to the oppression that we or our communities have experienced as a result of that word,' she continued. 'So, the word "cunt" has been used for a long time to disempower women, to put them in their place, to silence them.' Depending on the context, Montell believes we need to pay language like this some reverence, considering all those who have been disempowered, damaged or emotionally abused by the weaponisation of the word.

Even though what's done is done, that doesn't mean it can't be undone. Montell says we should be open to 'ameliorating' or 'reclaiming' the word. 'I like the idea that slurs deserve to be reclaimed, and one of the ways that that happens is by only using it in positive contexts moving forward,' she says. 'So, if people are attached to the positive or fun and friendly version of the word cunt, then maybe they can commit, just within themselves, to only using it in that context.' This, perhaps, will shift the tide on how the word cunt is perceived, though, Montell concedes, 'there are plenty of folks who would disagree with that.' Either way, we have our homework cut out for us.

EFFED UP FACT:

So, which film uses 'cunt' the most? *Nil by Mouth* may hold the unofficial record with its 82 deployments. This 1997 film, helmed by Gary Oldman in his directorial debut, concerns a family wrestling with heroin abuse and domestic violence, and was rated R18+ on first go by the Classification Board on account of 'adult themes, drug use, high level coarse language', though based on the hierarchy of its consumer advice, all those 'cunts' were the least of the board's problems.

CHAPTER 6

THE 10,000 DAYS OF SODOM

I own two copies of *Salò, or the 120 Days of Sodom*. One more copy, and I'd have a full year of Sodom in my DVD collection. Of course, two copies is plenty; some may argue it's two too many. I initially ordered it over eBay for the purpose of writing this book. I had rented it previously in 2010, but didn't buy a copy at the time, because, admittedly, the film's rewatch value is pretty low. A decade later, and within a week of receiving the DVD, I somehow lost it. I promptly ordered a second copy from the same dealer on eBay, who must have raised an eyebrow as he packaged up this new delivery. I couldn't help but imagine their perplexed fulfilment of my order—*Who is this Salò obsessive?*—wondering if I'm ending up on a list somewhere as a result of this double-dip. Do I sound paranoid? Given the censorship history of this notorious film and the mysterious fate that befell its filmmaker, I had reason to be. It was banned for more than 10,000 days over 35 years in Australia, having been banned, unbanned, banned again and then unbanned once more. Who knows how long until it's banned a third time? Maybe having two copies in the house isn't such a bad idea.

Salò, or the 120 Days of Sodom is the work of director Pier Paolo Pasolini, but we mustn't give him all the credit. His 1975 feature was inspired by the Marquis de Sade's book *The 120 Days of Sodom* from 1785, which was also once banned in Australia for obscenity. Pasolini, who co-wrote the script to *Salò* with Sergio Citti, neatly adapted the Marquis' tale of libertines indulging in four months of teen-torturing gratification into a satire on Italy's history of fascism. He transplanted the story to the Italian Social Republic (AKA the Republic of Salò) during the dying days of World War II. There, four powerful fascists—the Duke, the Bishop, the Magistrate and the President—arrange for the arrest and imprisonment of 18 teenage boys and girls in a palace, and spend, you guessed it, 120 days degrading, raping and murdering them for their personal pleasure. *Salò* definitely falls into the one-and-done category: watch it once and never again. Unless you're me, that is, buying copy after copy by the armful—at least according to my eBay dealer.

'All things are good when taken to excess,' is one of the first things said in *Salò*, and boy howdy, Pasolini really puts that maxim to the test. Of the picture's 808 shots, 131 feature naked characters. A later line of dialogue, delivered in the direction of the trapped teens, turned out to be not so prophetic: 'You are beyond the reach of any legality.' The Australian government proved otherwise. In March 1976, a 'narrow majority' of the Classification Board refused to classify *Salò* because of its 'indecency', a decision that was upheld by the review board. That was the word for 16 years. But in December 1992, the divide on *Salò*'s suitability for audiences somehow got larger upon its resubmission by a new hopeful distributor, with even more board members than before voting to ban it. In their 1993 Annual Report, the board explained the majority's opinion: 'It thought that the reasonable adult person would find the film's intellectual thesis neither clear nor compelling and would therefore, be more inclined to perceive the general character of this version of the film in pornographic, voyeuristic and exploitative terms.' Nonetheless, an appeal in January of 1993 put forward by Premium Films saw the review board relent, awarding *Salò* an R-rating for 'disturbing adult concepts and high level violence and sex'. 'The film is generally considered to be a metaphor for fascism and oppression and a critique of capitalist exploitation,' the review board wrote in their decision. They continued:

> According to Mr John Cerrone, representing the appellants, Premium Films, it has been approved for showing in 16 countries, including France (where it was first shown), Britain and the United States. The Board of Review considered a detailed response by Mr Cerrone to the report of the Film Censorship Board on its most recent decision. In a brief presentation to the Board, Mr Cerrone contended that *Salò*, if approved for restricted exhibition, would be seen, in the main, only by serious and generally older film goers and film enthusiasts in arthouse cinemas, and would be exhibited with any appropriate warning or advisory message which the board might require.
>
> Notwithstanding the extreme character of much of its imagery, and intense feeling of horror and revulsion it might arouse in some audiences, it seemed to the Board appropriate that decisions taken as long as seventeen years ago on a film of undisputed importance should be looked at afresh, in an atmosphere unclouded by indignation and

controversy attending the film's initial screenings abroad. *Salò* presents us with the most stringent test to date of the basic principle that adults in a free society should be at liberty to see what they wish. That principle, endorsed as part of the comprehensive revised guidelines by Commonwealth, State and Territory Censorship Ministers in 1979, we have taken to be fundamental. Approaching *Salò* from this standpoint, we agreed that its depictions, while frequently shocking, were integral to the filmmaker's purposes, and therefore not gratuitous; nor were they in any way erotic or titillating.

Under the proviso that Premium Films only show Salò in small, selected cinemas with appropriate discretion in its advertising—and not subsequently release it on video—Pasolini's film opened in Sydney and Melbourne theatres in July 1993. By August, the chorus to ban it again had begun to swell.

The first petition to re-ban *Salò* was put to the Queensland Legislative Assembly on 24 August 1993 by Labor's John Szczerbanik, with 143 signatories 'praying for urgent action'. Then-Nationals senator Julian McGauran joined the fray seven days later, presenting three petitions to the federal Senate over the next fortnight in favour of banning *Salò*. Two of those petitions had 16 and 20 signatures respectively. On 6 September 1993, Senator McGauran informed the Senate that the Victorian police—including the head of the rape squad, the head of the gaming and vice squad and the department's chief serial crime expert—had been told to see *Salò* and report back their findings. 'In my casual conversation with some of those who attended the movie,' Senator McGauran said, 'They told me that, following the movie, these men of the police force who had experienced many hardened situations had to take a walk down by the Yarra just to get their breath.' It is not known if Senator McGauran provided any of the unmoored officers with smelling salts to wake them from their stunned stupor. After learning that the chair of the review board, Evan Williams, had argued *Salò*'s artistic merit trumped its more scandalous elements (key quote: 'we thought it was a good film'), Senator McGauran called for Williams' dismissal as chairman: 'Not only do I believe that Mr Williams' position is no longer tenable because of the flagrant breaches of the [classification guidelines] but also I question his competence to be a judge of community standards. This belief was confirmed by the incredible assertion by Mr Williams that he could see no evidence to link a level of sexually violent crime to sexually violent movies. His opinion clearly shows poor judgment and it could be supported only by a very small minority of people in society.'

McGauran closed with what is, undeniably, a startling image: 'The unacceptable alternative is simply to wish our children luck as they ride the pendulum of censorship towards the outer limits.' The next day, the senator presented a fourth petition, this one with 13 signatures now requesting the Attorney-General sack Williams 'on the grounds that he has lost touch with community standards'. At the same time, Fred Nile joined the campaign, specifically concerned with Pasolini's depiction of 'teenage girls' and for the film's promotion ('by implication') of 'child pornography'. Nile did take solace, however, that 'the producer of *Salò*—apparently a sexually perverse person—finally killed himself.' It seems he was referring to Pasolini, who was found dead in suspicious circumstances on 2 November 1975, a few weeks before *Salò* debuted in Paris. It's not clear why Nile used the word 'finally'.

Senator McGauran kept on presenting petitions and in February 1994 he turned a Senate Estimates hearing over a new computer for the OFLC (to store its financial and classification records) into another referendum on Pasolini's film. South Australia's Attorney-General, Trevor Griffin, ultimately decided to ban the film in his state, which was then followed by similar requests for bans in Queensland, Western Australia and New South Wales. Senator Brian Harradine—who once reportedly delivered a box of porn to Prime Minister John Howard's office to shock him into banning X-rated features—revived the *Salò* debate in February of 1995 as a means of having the entire review code (particularly the R18+ and X-ratings) re-evaluated. And on and on. The campaign to ban *Salò* raged for much longer than the duration of the 120 Days of Sodom themselves.

In June of 1997, years after *Salò*'s theatrical run had ended (and with no video release allowed or proposed), Queensland's Attorney-General Denver Beanland continued to lobby to get the film back up in front of the review board (which now comprised new faces) and banned. Though the R-rating was upheld, this time, the advice was changed to say it contained 'Adult themes of high intensity, strong depictions of violence [and] strong sexual references'. That wasn't enough for the new prudes of the 1990s.

A refreshed argument that arrived only a few months later would prove to be fateful, as Liberal MP Trish Draper and Senator McGauran both raised the spectre of 'paedophilia and sexual abuse of children', suggesting *Salò* was either guilty of the crime or at least capable of inciting it. In February 1998, the review board was urged by Queensland AG Beanland to give the picture yet another look, and finally, they refused it classification once more. Their decision indicated a new interpretation of *Salò* that apparently warranted its banning. It was not simply that it contained 'indecency' and 'offensiveness'. That was already well appreciated. Instead, it was now 'the age of the young people' within the movie that deserved scrutiny, in combination with indecency and offensiveness.

Their report stated

> A majority of the Review Board believed that the apparent youth of some of the abducted teenagers was also matter for concern. Some of the young people who were sexually abused throughout the film could have been under the age of 16 years. Further, there were many scenes in the film in which they were dressed as school children, and gave this emphasis to their youth. However, in the view of a majority of the Review Board, the age factor by itself was not considered to be of [sufficient] certainty to cause the film to be refused classification, as would have been required if any of the abused young people had 'looked like they were under the age of 16 years' (National Classification Code). The youthfulness of the abused was nevertheless seen by the majority to be an important factor, and one that should be taken into account when considering the issue of 'offensiveness'.

Several years later, even after the movie had been successfully re-banned, Senator McGauran couldn't let it go, noting in March of 2000 during a Senate discussion on the costs of classification that *Salò* had been guilty of 'exploitation of minors'. What had initially begun as mere suggestion had now, in his opinion, become fact.

This controversy swirling around *Salò* is no matter to take lightly, and it's complicated by the fact that Pasolini met Ninetto Davoli, whom he described as the love of his life, when Ninetto was just 15 years old. Even fan of the film John Waters (a director who's had plenty of his own brushes with obscenity) exclaimed at a Toronto screening in 2010, without evidence, that the teens in the film were underage and that the production had, basically, been illegal. But when a modified version of *Salò* (now with accompanying making-of material) went back to the Classification Board in 2010, distributor Shock Films refuted the argument by Senator McGauran and Nile's FamilyVoice Australia (previously Festival of Light, who had of course taken the case to the courts) by saying the victims in the film were sexually mature—visibly so, in fact. With that in mind, the board rated it R18+. That latest and, as of this writing, still-held decision followed two further failed attempts at a re-rating in 2003 and 2008, and several confiscations of imported *Salò* copies by customs officials.

The Classification Board accepted that a modified version of the film could receive an R-rating on DVD in April of 2010, for 'scenes of torture and degradation, sexual violence and nudity'. The kicker, this time around, was the assurance by Shock Films to the director of the Classification Board, Donald McDonald, that the picture would be accompanied by '176 minutes of additional material which provided a context to the feature film, mitigating its impact.' The board added in a media release, 'this film is classified R18+ based on the fact that it contains additional material. Screening this film in a cinema without the additional material would constitute a breach of classification laws.' Senator McGauran, expectedly, called for the resignation of McDonald for releasing what he called 'a paedophile's treat ... a hand book for deviants [that] could trigger crazed minds'.

Conservative Christian groups renewed their attack, and the Labor government's minister for home affairs, Brendan O'Connor, requested a review in May of 2010. The review board upheld the latest classification, further explaining that the actors appeared sexually mature, despite conceding that was a fairly subjective interpretation. 'It is the view of the Review Board that the film does not contain descriptions (in stories related during the film) or depictions of child sexual abuse which are exploitative or offensive.' McDonald reiterated in a Senate Estimates hearing, while being grilled by Senator McGauran, 'This film does not contain actual paedophilia.' On this point, the senator surprisingly agreed: 'Of course it is not.' Still, he called McDonald both a 'coward' and a 'smart alec'. The senator then took the matter to the Federal Court—in collaboration with FamilyVoice and the Australian Christian Lobby—seeking a reversal on the board's decision. They failed. The film hit DVD and Blu-ray, and went on to have its TV premiere in Australia on Foxtel's World Movies channel on 5 September 2016. Four years later, I purchased two DVDs for $10 apiece. No one—as far as I know—batted an eye.

And now we arrive at the question that was rarely raised, and seemingly only answered by the board's former chair, Evan Williams: Is *Salò* any *good*? Williams seemed to think so. At the very least, he and his board felt the film had enough artistic merit to warrant its disturbing content. Unfortunately, we do not have a robust sample of critical analyses to pull from, to argue whether or not *Salò* is more than problematic misery porn—at least not in Australia. The movie is more than 40 years old. Australia has only been trusted with it for little more than a decade. On Rotten Tomatoes, there are just 40-odd critic reviews for *Salò* (in comparison, *Avengers: Endgame* has 555), and only ten of those come from those designated 'Top Critics'; none of the latter are Australian.

Viewing it in the 21st century, you have to conclude that some of the cited moments that caused Senator McGauran and his conservative friends palpitations are, by today's standards, positively quaint, such as a scene in which masturbation is implied with such broad strokes (seen only from behind) that you'd more likely mistake it for a cow-milking or the restringing of a cello than a hand job. Other moments are, to this date, horrifyingly graphic and upsetting by any standard of morality. There is no period in any of the past six decades in which the watching of *Salò* wouldn't raise alarm. It contains obscene gropings of helpless young bodies against their will, conducted by nauseating fascist figures (in particular the hideous President with his plastered, serene smile); there are bared genitals as the prisoners are exposed and evaluated, as if in a meat market; and there's the mass eating of human excrement. In fact, that sequence of coprophilia alone makes it stand out among all the films ever given a rating in Australia. This act was once described explicitly as an 'offensive fetish' in the Classification Guidelines and instantly triggered a Refused Classification rating, until it was removed entirely from the guidelines in the early 2000s as the X-rating was being re-evaluated. However, it was nonetheless expected a title would still be refused whenever coprophagy reared its head (or headed into its rear). The few other exceptions include *Pink Flamingos*, which was initially banned multiple times, and, technically, the South Korean feature *Lies* from director Jang Sun-Woo, which was censored in its home country but played internationally and arrived on VHS in Australia with its coprophilic centrepiece involving a sadomasochistic couple intact. The point being, no one would accuse *Salò* of being subtle, in its dialogue or in, say, its sequence where the enslaved teens have to eat a meal comprised of their collective diarrhea. As the Duke says while a young boy is whipped, 'I rejoice when I see others degraded and can say to myself: I am happier than the scum they call the people.' But there is, remarkably, restraint here too. In the final sequence of ritualistic mutilation and murder in the estate's garden, we are held at arm's length, watching from the central fascistic foursome's binoculars back in the building; the violence is seen in only elliptical cutaways, with the bars of the window they're peering from obscuring our view.

It can also be comical in its absurd, detached way. How else to explain the part in which the incoming prisoners are informed the 'Hall of Orgies' will be 'adequately heated'?

And yet, you can still get sucked in by *Salò*, even all these decades later, recoiling from its horrors and forgetting that it's just a movie. That was the apparent masterstroke by Shock in their 2010 re-release: adding nearly three hours of contextual material to remind you that, actually, we're watching special effects and make-'em-ups, not actual torment. In one doco, Pasolini explicitly describes his desire to depict 'what the power does to the human body'. Some critics have noted that the detached, panoptic gaze of Pasolini's camera reflects the regime of control he's criticising. Paolo Russo, writing in *Senses of Cinema* in 2015, countered that take, saying if Pasolini had employed a detached perspective, it 'would make *Salò* visually anti-erotic and anti-pornographic' when, Russo argues, he is in fact using the staging, coverage and repetitive filmic structure of pornography yet replacing 'pleasure with shock' to make his point. Both arguments, albeit contrary, confirm the same thing: a director has framed content that is obscene by definition, yet used the cinematographic arts to contort them to convey a particular message. In one moment, a girl begs for death and the Duke says he's never been so excited. It's not that the movie *couldn't* theoretically spark arousal in viewers, but as the movie itself indicates, to be aroused by its nightmarish visions would equate you to fascist murderers. Pasolini's entry in the cinema of cruelty can be dissected many ways—and his approach can be validly questioned—but Senator McGauran and the like had to have wilfully misread Pasolini's extremely obvious meaning to think it would corrupt the apparently chaste and unblemished hypothetical viewers in Australia.

Pasolini's choices are displayed and described in the DVD's additional features. For better or worse, *Salò* was now following the trend established with the advent of DVD technology at the turn of the century, when each movie—no matter its contribution to the cultural canon—arrived with making of documentaries and audio commentaries for the intention of convincing film-lovers to invest in a new viewing medium. In recent years, with streaming platforms threatening to upend the cinema business, auteurs like Christopher Nolan have gone to bat for the big-screen experience. Specifically, Nolan wants audiences to get lost inside of movies, reiterating that's how the medium is meant to be. But Australian audiences have never been trusted to get lost inside of *Salò*, even after they were finally granted permission to see the damn thing. Though Shock was successful in 2010, they tempered the viewer's experience of *Salò* by quieting concerns with the insistence it's *just* a movie, clearly outlining the director's intention. Doing so removes the real visceral reaction, which is precisely the point. It reduces the possibility of debate. It makes *Salò* a little academic, and if movies were simply meant to be explained and justified, directors would just publish a script and an accompanying message of intent rather than try to bring them to life through vision, sound and story. To understand and appreciate *Salò*, you have to acknowledge the blood, shit and mania. That doesn't mean you have to like it. And many don't. That's fine. I only hope those people don't confuse *Salò* for fact. It's a fiction, and one shot artfully and with great intention. You can sense the global influence: on Wales' Peter Greenaway, Italy's Luca Guadagnino (particularly his *Suspiria* remake), Austria's Michael Haneke, America's David Lynch, Spain's Albert Serra, France's Catherine Breillat and Claire Denis, South Korea's Park Chan-wook, Greece's Yorgos Lanthimos (make that most of the modern Greek weird-wave) and even England's Monty Python crew (on *The Meaning of Life* especially). Whether they were all fans of *Salò* or hadn't seen it matters not. And whether or not *Salò* is good or actively bad isn't important either when evaluating its artistic merit for classification purposes. What counts is it uses a cinematic language we can appreciate as having meaning and mattering. It demands confrontation, and any film that does deserves to be met halfway. Porn has never required so much of us.

When I ordered (and reordered) my copy of *Salò* in 2020, it arrived in different packaging than I had remembered from 2010. Gone was the subtle, simple lettering of S-A-L-O on a white background, and in its place was an image of a torturous orgy featuring men in climactic agony and ecstasy. A threshold of decency had seemingly been crossed, and on the *cover* no less! Also gone: the second disc with the all-important context-setting features. Now, the movie was simply accompanied by a music video. I asked Shock if something had changed in recent years allowing them to distribute the movie without the makings-of. The Classification Board's decision listing online certainly didn't seem to suggest so. I was instead told by a Shock spokesperson that the stock came from a distribution deal via a now-defunct company called VEG Group, and that, once those discs are exhausted there will be no more. After all these years in limbo (or censorship Sodom), the complaints against *Salò* simply fell away, and so too did the policing. *Salò*, finally fulfilling its prophecy, was now beyond legality. But maybe the wowsers and the censors won after all: they blunted *Salò*'s power and reach in Australia, and subsequently diminished interest and demand. If I wanted to give this chapter's conclusion a sunny spin, I'd say at least the uncut film remains. Though, that won't be true here for long; only until we run out of discs. And I lost one of them. Sorry about that.

EFFED UP FACT:

In 1980, free-to-air station Channel 7 briefly interrupted their telecast of the Australian Open for an important announcement, or rather, the accidental broadcast of pornography. James Cockington shares a brief anecdote in the book *Banned* about the network apologising for the rude interlude, in which tennis players were suddenly supplanted by a very different kind of ball boy. Accident or prank? Either way, it's just not tennis.

CHAPTER 7

ONE OF THE MOST REVOLTING, DISGUSTING PIECES OF SHIT DAVID STRATTON HAS EVER SEEN

The review screener for *A Serbian Film* arrived unceremoniously at my desk in July 2011, without any accompanying artwork, and simply a title scrawled in permanent marker on its plain disc face. It likely arrived in a package with dozens of other upcoming DVD releases from Australian distributor Accent Films. In the early 2010s, this is how independent production companies got the word out about their upcoming releases: en masse, frantically scribbled upon, stacked on spindles. At the time, I was accumulating literal bundles of movies at a time, and only able to pick a select few out to review each month for the movie website at which I worked. *A Serbian Film*, with its unremarkable title and little accompanying information, was not a priority. In fact, I only got around to watching it when it was suddenly illegal to do so.

Turns out I had been unaware of a burbling scandal that had been building up for many months, culminating with the last big watershed fight against film censorship in Australia; a fight that was lost, and cost all involved dearly.

A Serbian Film opens with a young boy watching his dad having rough alleyway sex in an old hardcore video, and yet, it's us who will likely wind up more traumatised by the time we get to the final credits. Srđan Todorović stars as Miloš, an aging, down-on-his-luck and now domesticated ex-porn star saddled with a wife and son. Like so many cinematic characters before him, he is offered one last job to pay off his debts forever. He's hired by the repugnant film producer and former child psychologist Vukmir, (played by Sergej Trifunović) to participate in 'artistic pornography of the highest level' for wealthy private viewers. Miloš can't see the script in advance, and instead must turn up to a kindergarten, where filming will commence, wear an earpiece to follow Vukmir's direction, pay no attention to the roaming cinematographers and respond to the circumstances, ideally, by having sex with those he's presented. Vukmir, still in salesman mode, explains what he's making by reeling off keywords: 'Art. Naked art. Truth. Real people, real situations, real sex, minimal editing.' Ironically, *A Serbian Film* would be victim to more than minimal editing, urged by Classification Boards around the world, as a result of whom Miloš comes face to face with, and what, exactly, Vukmir wants him to desecrate, including drugged women, corpses and children. (Sound extreme? 'That's film,' Vukmir exhales in ecstasy shortly after a character is eye-fucked to death by a raging Miloš. I suppose that's one word for it.) The feature builds to a truly dark climax—yes, even beyond what I've described—which is followed by a wretchedly grim dénouement, and a deranged final comic beat. The thing is, *A Serbian Film* doesn't only get more horrifying as it reaches its end. It also gets more illegal.

A Serbian Film was refused classification twice by the Australian Classification Board—the second time for a modified version—before an even-more-modified cut got an R-rating. That was until wowsers reignited the spat and got that third version successfully banned in SA one day before its home entertainment release, and then nationally several months later. The DVDs had all been printed and distributed to vendors. Now, Accent had to ask for them back.

'The sad debacle of *A Serbian Film* is a long-distant memory now,' Peter Campbell, Director of Accent Films, tells me a decade later. 'As I recall, I edited, tweaked and shaved it minimalistically both in tandem and to comply with the [board] at the time. There was a back-and-forth but finally an approval. They knew we weren't being exploitational since the film was supposed to be a Serbian allegory.' Well, kinda. Director Srdjan Spasojevic (who, as of this writing, hasn't produced another feature), made no secret that he intended it as a gob of spit in the face of Serbia's state-funded, self-serious cinema. It followed decades of extreme government control over artistic output and overarching ideological supervision. (For instance: no sci-fi, thrillers or horrors were allowed after WW2 until the 1980s—and as the academic Alexandra Kapka notes, there are only a couple dozen Serbian movies you'd describe as belonging to the horror genre even to this day.) *A Serbian Film* was in fact the first independently funded feature within the nation, and anyone who's seen it won't need an explanation as to why. 'This is a diary of our own molestation by the Serbian government,' Spasojevic explains on the introduction to the UK DVD. 'It's about the monolithic power of leaders who hypnotise you to do things you don't want to do. You have to feel the violence to know what it's about.' It's true that there are allegorical elements to the flick. At the horrifying climax, the picture's villain describes the sight of unspeakable familial carnage as representing 'a real, happy Serbian family'. But it's also a provocation by design. The artistic goal here was to make a film that's virulently distasteful, politically incorrect and, indeed, on the fringe of what's lawful; a conflagration to rile up and revolt against Serbia's strict society, generally, and the state's narrow film-funding focus, specifically. You could call it masturbatory, and not just because the main character re-watches pornography, starring himself, for his own sexual gratification. But as a would-be porn producer opines to the film's lead, 'You weren't just a porn star, you were an artist,' almost in justification for *A Serbian Film*'s hoity-toity aspirations. It wants to be reckoned with, and not simply discarded like a used tissue. So, if a film like that causes a firestorm so incendiary it winds up banned and unseen in nations across the world, is it a triumph or a failure? As Kapka writes, the picture is so outrageously gory, and its metaphors so opaque, it doesn't so much shine a light on Serbian atrocities as it reinforces 'the very reductive understandings of Serbian national identity the film set out to subvert'. But that's only for those who are allowed to see it.

Australia was not the first or only nation to approach *A Serbian Film* with alarm. It was also banned in Germany, Malaysia, New Zealand, Norway, Singapore, Spain and, briefly, Brazil. It was slashed and cut in the UK before going out to its public, and Sitges Film Festival director Ángel Sala was charged with the exhibition of 'child pornography' after screening the film in Spain. (The charges were later dropped. In a 2020 interview with the website *Monsters, Madness and Magic*, Spasojevic alludes to providing 'tons and tons of statements, pictures from the set, videos proving we didn't kill or rape anyone on the set' in defence of 'ordinary people' who were 'prosecuted for possessing the film'.) But just like with *Salò*, Australia had to make the classification process as messy, drawn-out and drama-filled as possible.

It began when the Classification Board gave *A Serbian Film* its first RC-rating in November of 2010. In their decision report, the board conceded that there was 'a degree of artistic merit and dramatic intent ... evident in this fictional film'. I personally like to think they came to this conclusion after witnessing the training montage in which the camera takes a penis-eye view as Miloš, trying to regain his lithe form, attempts to summon an erection without looking at or touching his penis.

Truly, *A Serbian Film* is not a cheap-looking video nasty, nor does it bear any similarity to cinema verité snuff, or even poorly lit porn. It's polished and in some sequences recalls the nightmare voids of David Lynch's filmic worlds, even predating the cavernous horror of Jonathan Glazer's *Under the Skin*, which is now a trope unto itself. Its score is similarly world class; a genuinely catchy, throbbing, Trent Reznor-esque pulsation that is obscured, as the movie reaches fever pitch, with atonal screeching. This is, in the audio and visual language we understand, a real movie. Alas, the board's decision continued: '[We are] of the opinion that the film ... is very high in viewing impact and includes an explicit depiction of sexual violence. The film therefore exceeds what can be accommodated within the R18+ classification and should be Refused Classification.' This decision—shared via a Freedom of Information request that nonetheless blanked out all the offending examples from within the film—appeared to be a new, even more conservative approach than that which the board took with their torturous review of *Salò*. Here, they could acknowledge from the get-go that it was a movie with dramatic and allegorical intent. And yet, for them it still went too far. Perhaps more than ever before, a line was drawn for what artists should and could attempt. There was no argument from the board that *A Serbian Film* was veering too close to pornography; merely that it was too impactful in its content.

Of course, they subsequently relented after Accent made further modifications, but they had put a target on *A Serbian Film*'s back with its initial Refused Classification rating and eventual reversal. By April of 2011 (after a 97-minute cut was once again rated RC in February), *A Serbian Film* had been trimmed down to a 96-minute edit for Australian audiences and rated R18+ for 'high impact sexual violence, sex scenes and violence'. 'In the Board's opinion, while the impact of depictions of violence and sexual violence contained in this film are at the upper limit of the R18+ category, this modified film no longer contains classifiable elements that exceed a high impact level,' their new decision found. Gone was footage that had survived the UK's 99-minute cut, as well as the most troubling shots from the original 103-minute edit, such as the moment in which a newborn baby is raped. (Accent Films never even attempted to get the 103-minute version across the line, starting with the edited 99-minute cut.) Most of what was deleted included sequences in which sexual activity took place in proximity to children or as video footage of children played in the background, especially those sequences where the children themselves, albeit doing nothing controversial in isolation, were intended to arouse the film's characters. Spasojevic stressed to Indiewire that the child actors' parents were present on set, and that their scenes had been filmed separately from the staged violence and sexual content, which was edited in during post-production. It relieved no one.

Being a small local distributor, Accent not unreasonably tried to capitalise on the controversy in a press release that, perhaps, overcooked it: 'With hellacious extremities of realistic simulation *A Serbian Film* explores new zones of discomfort. Various members of audiences at festivals around the world have found themselves being carried out of the screening such is the notorious pedigree of the film's already fugitive reputation.' One of those patrons may have been former Melbourne International Film Festival director Richard Moore, who witnessed the picture at Cannes in 2010 and declared to *The Age*, 'There are enough perverts and weird sadists out there who'll just get off on this sort of material.' He wasn't a fan.

Thankfully, this was not Accent's first rodeo. They had previously triumphed in battles against 'Fred Nile and his crony army', as Campbell puts it, in the cases of *Irreversible* and *9 Songs*, which narrowly landed R-ratings. The board only received nine complaints against *A Serbian Film*'s release, but by 18 August 2011 the Attorney-General of South Australia had interceded and banned the film in the state. 'I was first made aware of this film after a DVD store manager decided to refuse to stock the film in his store,' Attorney-General John Rau said in a statement at the time. 'Some of the scenes in the DVD are so depraved that I am not prepared to even describe them in any detail.' (With the exception of what I've already outlined above, Rau was perhaps also referring to the moment in which Miloš holds his own penis at knifepoint, which survived all of Accent's, ahem, cuts.) Having been referred to the South Australian Classification Council (SACC), which was the stubborn state's separate classification arm, they considered whether *A Serbian Film* had 'literary, artistic or educational merit that would justify classification'. Their conclusion was simple: 'it did not.' Intriguingly, Accent did not have the support of anti-censorship campaigner David Stratton, who tells me today, 'As a lifelong opponent of censorship, I can understand why that film was censored and I am sorry I saw it.' In fact, he really didn't hold back, calling it 'one of the most revolting, disgusting pieces of shit that I have ever seen'.

'I guess what I feel is that whoever wanted to show that in Australia should have thought twice,' he adds. 'I know it may seem to be going against my own principles, but [*A Serbian Film*] involves child pornography, and child pornography is something I personally find reprehensible. Here you are, I'll say it: I think child pornography of that type [including fictional recreations] should be banned. I find the mindset behind *A Serbian Film* to be repugnant. I guess we all have our lines beyond which we're not willing to cross, and that's mine.'

Nonetheless, at the time of the SACC's review, an R-rated cut was being scheduled for the Melbourne Underground Film Festival, where it was badged 'the sickest film we have ever played'. The screening went ahead unimpeded on 19 August 2011, but by 14 September, the national Classification Review Board had received an application to consider banning *A Serbian Film* again. This one came from newly formed advocacy group Collective Shout, founded by Melinda Tankard Reist, who spent 12 years working as media and bioethics advisor for the anti-abortion Senator Brian Harradine. Collective Shout claimed they could not comprehend why the classifiers were ignoring the film's depictions of sexual violence against children and women, suggesting the board was desensitised and in need of replacing. By 19 September, the review board had decided to rescind the R classification and change it to a Refused Classification rating. Tankard Reist celebrated the announcement on her personal blog. In January 2012, she was profiled in the *Sydney Morning Herald*, her reputation as a crusading rabble-rouser and self-proclaimed 'pro-life feminist' cemented. The profile was so combustible online it inspired numerous follow-up think pieces, including one by journalist Julia Baird in the same outlet that distilled the backlash thusly: 'Tankard Reist's opponents believe she has for years tried to capture attention by painting herself as a renegade feminist, so that she will not be dismissed as a conservative Christian when talking about porn.' To this day, the RC-rating for *A Serbian Film* stands, though the scrutiny into Tankard Reist's intentions has faded away, with the ABC as recently as 2021 simply calling her 'director of the women's empowerment organisation Collective Shout' and even commissioning her for an article titled 'Why "consent" doesn't stand a chance against porn culture'. Without dismissing outright the advocacy Collective Shout does on behalf of women and children today, especially in the realm of sex trafficking and consent education, there's a fair argument that it used a simmering culture war to establish its bona fides in a way similar to far-right religious and conservative groups in the years that followed (and years preceding). If anything, its 'win' against *A Serbian Film* helped develop a social media–driven template that would breathe new life into film censorship in Australia, and later, other conservative-leaning campaigns. We'll get to that in the second half of this book.

†

When the national ban on *A Serbian Film* was announced, Accent Films took the accusatory route, focused instead on the initial complainant in South Australia, tweeting, 'Funny how the DVD store owner who complained about the film to SA AG has never returned the DVD screener. They know our address. Waiting ...'. Privately, they were scrambling for a solution to what would be a costly exercise: recalling and destroying all copies of the DVD distributed to video stores. 'As a possible option, I got hold of the [legally released] UK version from the director and lined it up in the edit timeline with our version and ironically the scenes we had to remove remained in their version, whereas others they had edited out remained in ours,' Campbell recalls. 'So that was a dead end.' In their initial statement, Accent reiterated that 'we have a great relationship with [the] Classification Board. This is really not their doing. It's political.' It's a stance Campbell holds to this day: 'The targeted criticism submitted to the board was so cunningly manipulated and peppered throughout that it was pointless to move forward, and the [board] had no further options but to ban it. The [board] personnel working with me were naturally very embarrassed and upset at the ruling and outcome as it also made a certain mockery of the entire system.'

It was a bellwether loss for those concerned with censorship in Australia; a unique and uncommon instance of a classified film being pulled from release and banned. However, it also took a larger, lesser seen toll on filmmakers and distributors who traffic in boundary-pushing and provocative films from across the globe. 'Not only was it an enormous cost to us, but it signalled the end of our trust and belief in the discriminatory Australian censorship regulations,' Campbell says. 'It also showed that any disgruntled group had a capacity to lodge submissions to overturn classifications after a film release. So classification certainty was basically obliterated.' Accent was no longer willing to acquire controversial films, and retail outlets started pushing back on R-rated features as well. 'Sadly, the entire industry has gone pear-shaped now.' In Accent Films' initial statement about the banning, they shared a concerned warning: 'To those who have already purchased the DVD, we THINK you are safe but, nowadays, we cannot rule [out] a house search and arrest by [the Australian Federal Police]!'

In Serbia, which has seen only approximately 100 or so local features produced in the decade since, provocations are acknowledged to be bad for business as a result of *A Serbian Film*. The government certainly won't fund films critical of itself, but neither will private investors entertain a dalliance with provocative cinema after

A Serbian Film, which struggled to find purchase in the international marketplace. As Spasojevic told *Monsters, Madness and Magic*, 'For some it will be forever taboo, for others something meaningful. Maybe in the future, in a few decades, when *A Serbian Film* would be considered a film about some other time, some other society, some other bad people but not us, things could change... But at the same time some other artwork will be declared unfit and banned. Those things will always repeat. We move in circles not forward.'

But this is not the end of the story. Because while that was the most recent, most significant censorship snafu in Australia, it occurred at a time in which the internet affords digital citizens access to international goods. And in this unique circumstance, physical media had already been distributed publicly, on an easily replicable format. (I'll remind you that my review screener was burnt to disc and shared by the distributor themselves.) A cursory search online revealed that you can easily access a torrent of both the 99-minute and 103-minute versions, though you'd need a virtual private network (VPN) to get around Australian internet service providers' government-mandated block on pirating sites. *A Serbian Film* can also be ordered on DVD from overseas online retailers, provided you get an intermediary to receive and send it on to Australia, though this comes at risk to both you and the sender. (NSW Police once confiscated a contraband copy of the 99-minute cut on a USB stick in February of 2019.) Or, you can simply take your laptop with you on your next trip to the United States, where the film is rated NC-17, and stream the full, graphic 103-minute iteration on Amazon Prime Video, where it currently holds a 3.5-star average from 466 reviews. In fact, it's actually harder these days to get your hands on the 96-minute edit that was once considered acceptable at R18+ by our board. Banned doesn't necessarily mean what it used to mean.

As for Accent Films, their social media presence has slowed to a crawl, and their online eBay and VOD stores mostly promote a few challenging gems (*Irreversible, 9 Songs, Heaven Knows What, Pusher, White Reindeer*) from the early 2010s. We know full well these movies are still being made, though not necessarily in Australia. There was a time when a local distributor was needed to carefully midwife them. Not anymore. Not here.

Postscript: When the government disbanded the South Australian Classification Council in 2019, SA's first female Attorney-General, Vickie Chapman, noted, 'The last decision made by the South Australian Classification Council was in 2011, when it banned *A Serbian Film* from release in this state at the request of the then-Attorney-General.' She continued: 'Given this, the fact that the Council's most recent meeting was held in 2014 and that all functions undertaken by the Council in South Australia are already dealt with by the national body, I see no need to continue operating a separate classification body in South Australia.' The SACC was formally abolished on 5 December 2019. Though the damage has been done, Accent Films can at least lay claim to outlasting the Board that sought to deliver its fatal blow. But then, Collective Shout outlasted them both, so what does that say about the beneficiaries of these contests of ideas?

EFFED UP FACT:

In 2005, Greg McLean's dizzyingly nasty *Wolf Creek* became the country's highest grossing locally produced R-rated feature of all time. When its sequel got slapped with an R18+ in 2013, McLean (who, he reiterated, had final cut of the movie) went back to the cutting room and sliced a few minutes off until the board awarded it a coveted MA15+ classification. No doubt distributor Roadshow Pictures was pleased. The gore would be returned for the Blu-ray release. Regardless, I stand by my assessment of the R-rated version that was initially screened for critics, calling it in my review 'loathsome, detestable and disgusting in all the right ways'.

CHAPTER 8
FESTIVAL OF FILTH

Over the years, certain states within Australia have earned a reputation for being bigger pearl-clutching conservatives than their fellows in the federation, at least as far as film censorship goes. Queensland, obviously, takes the cake; its state flag may as well be a bleeding fist popping pearls off a tightly-clenched necklace. South Australia, not going down without a fight, continues to make its reputation for puritanism known, with *A Serbian Film* just a semi-recent example of how it has responded to jarringly provocative cinema—and even to not-at-all jarring or provocative cinema, having a decade earlier forced Warner Home Video to add a state-specific M-rating to otherwise PG-classified DVDs covers of *Wild Wild West*, resulting in a visual pile-up of crescendoing classifications. But then again, director Rolf de Heer shot his incendiary and notorious features *Bad Boy Bubby* and *Alexandra's Project* in Adelaide, which may give the SA capital a lifetime exoneration.

However, Western Australia—that parochial colony always threatening to secede—should never be forgotten. It was Western Australia's transport ministers (!) who called for the banning of David Cronenberg's *Crash*. It is Western Australia that makes a point of specifically clarifying in its classification code—unlike the other states—that it's unlawful for a publication to feature the use of urine or excrement in sexual conduct (the state doth protest too much, methinks). And it was in Western Australia that a provocative film festival—piggybacking on but then exceeding the brazenness of the Sydney and Melbourne fests—was ultimately threatened by the WA government and strong-armed into financial ruin. But then, maybe WA should get some credit for being the home of such a troublemaking festival in the first place. After all, in the 21st century, it remains the site of one of the country's best and most singularly bizarre screening series: the annual Revelation Perth International Film Festival, which began in a pub basement in 1997 before moving above ground to Perth's pre-eminent arthouses, and has since hosted titles as diverse and squirm inducing as 2001's *Semi-Private Sub-Hegelian Panty Fantasy (With Sound)* and 2017's *Assholes*. Most of the pictures they play aren't even available to see or rent elsewhere ... except on their dedicated streaming platform RevStream.

But before Revelation, there was the Festival of Perth, which continues today and was founded in 1953 by University of Western Australia's Professor Fred Alexander. Known these days largely as a performance arts festival—under the updated and succinct title Perth Festival—the original iteration introduced the concept of showcasing films in UWA's pine tree–ensconced Somerville Auditorium. The idea for the film program reportedly came from John Birman, a European émigré who brought with him a desire to showcase foreign films in WA. Alexander, being the Director of Adult Education and seeking a program for the mature-aged public attending its summer school in January, gave Birman the thumbs up to screen international movies accordingly. Cut to the 2020s and Perth Festival's film program continues to screen local premieres of Australian productions and acclaimed international features (including many that have already been co-signed in other parts of the world: *Memoria*, *The Father*, *Benedetta*, *The Salesman*, and so on). Some are still certainly provocative, especially for the attendees who are simply seeking a night of wine and cheese under the stars (the nun-sploitation of *Benedetta* may have caused a few to drop their quince and camembert cracker into their cab sav). Mostly, though, there are few if any who might run screaming into the pines at a Perth Festival film session. However, with its inception, the festival indirectly inspired a startling movement within WA. Their early screenings in the 1950s only caused controversy among audiences unaccustomed to seeing subtitled pictures, but a shift occurred in the 1960s, when the Festival of Perth—and UWA's Adult Education Board—became a distributor unto itself, rather than claiming films already playing interstate. It imported and provided the Australian debut for the filmed opera *Der Rosen Kavalier*, which certainly appealed to its particular market, yet also earned the festival and its board the reputation as a buyer of 'art' films. Its early successes in this 'arthouse' arena—combined with the burgeoning film society scene—led to the formation of the Perth Film Society in 1964 by Ian Channell, considered Birman's offsider at the festival. At the end of the year, Channell passed the responsibility over to John McKracken, who was well established in the film society movement. McKracken would end up playing the provocative Luis Buñuel and Salvador Dali collaboration *Un Chien Andalou*; it was the festival's most well attended screening. The match had been struck.

David Roe was one such audience member at these increasingly artsy film society screenings, and he became central to the newly enlightened film appreciation movement. In 1972 he founded the Perth International Film Festival (also known as PIFF, not to be mistaken for Revelation), which would become the country's most notorious fest. Aged just 22 and a member of the UWA Student Guild, Roe had a particular predilection for testing the boundaries of censorship—and good taste. He started seeking out international films that weren't earning local releases, and importing them for his fest. Using PIFF precisely *for* distribution was the whole point. As its 1975 program proclaimed, the festival's line-up reflected the growth of independent cinema, and specifically, cinema unencumbered by the odious ideology of mass produced-media. This included another Buñuel picture: 1961's merciless satire *Viridiana*, which was, in 2022, placed 53rd on *Sight and Sound*'s decennial poll of directors on the greatest films ever made. The film wasn't released in Australia until 1972 for the reason of blasphemy; a delay that saw Australia aligned with the Nationalist government of Francisco Franco in Buñuel's native Spain. They too banned it until Franco's death in 1977, despite having submitted it to the Cannes Film Festival (where it won the Palme d'Or) presumably without watching it first. The 'blasphemous' film concerns a would-be nun who visits her uncle before taking her vows; she is almost assaulted, and winds up with the deed to his estate alongside her male cousin, where they offer shelter to rowdy local vagrants and climactically consider incest. *Viridiana* was wild enough to send the Aussie wowser brigade barmy when it was locally rated M in 1972. (The picture's themes are legitimately transgressive, even today, given that Buñuel's appears to make the case that acts of charity—Christian or otherwise—are for rubes, yet that's what makes *Viridiana* feel so alive with ideas all these decades later.) Those who had become upset with the Chipp policy of gradualism and the introduction of the R-rating in 1971 started picketing PIFF for screening *Viridiana*. Roe may have actually enjoyed this. That is, if he could remember even programming it. Such was the ordinariness of the festival causing a stir. That was their bread and butter.

'Firstly, how come you know about it?' David Roe asks me as a prelude to our interview about his festival, 50 years after its debut. He clarifies that he's more 'curious' than surprised, given that the fest had run its course within just a few years. And it's a fair assessment to say it has been somewhat lost to the annals of history. But its influence—and the consequences of the festival poking the governmental bear—certainly lingered. 'When we started in '72, [the WA government] weren't all that keen,' he says. 'I remember dealing with officers from the [customs department] who were frankly not very well informed. They were quite ignorant when it came to the art. They certainly saw me as, I think, a pest, because I was, at times, campaigning against censorship and had done that at the university through the student newspaper there and when I finished university and started up this festival, they were suspicious.' He adds: 'There were some kerfuffles that followed.'

Though his memory of even programming *Viridiana*, let alone the protests that followed, are faint, he specifically recalls—and regrets—selecting *Vase de Noces* for the 1975 schedule, especially at a time when the permissive federal Labor government of Gough Whitlam had been replaced by the Liberal party under Malcolm Fraser, and Sir Charles Court—of the WA Liberal Party—had taken over the state's reins. 'I haven't seen it since 1975,' Roe notes. 'I don't remember even particularly liking it. It was allegorical with nothing explicit in it all,' he adds, countering the suggestion made by its incendiary nickname *The Pig Fucking Movie*. Scott Murray concisely summarised the plot in *Cinema Papers*: 'Dominique Gary plays a man who has an affair with a pig—though a rather one-sided one judging by the pig's frantic fleeing around the yard.' Murray added that it was 'an insufferably tedious film', but Roe programmed it for both its international bona fides and combustible subject matter. 'I thought, "Here's a film selected by serious critics [at Cannes] that might possibly infuriate the authorities as well." I don't doubt that was in the back of my mind. But it qualifies as a film of artistic significance because of some considered reviews and because it was selected by the Semaine de la Critique [International Critics Week section] of the Cannes Film Festival. If I was doing it all over again, I possibly wouldn't select it, because it caused a huge amount of difficulty in that the state government tried to ban it, even though the festival had been given a dispensation; they didn't stick to the agreed ground rules and objected to the film's screening, even though they hadn't seen it. So we immediately appealed to the censorship appeals board. I was in Perth, I flew over to Sydney with the director, Thierry Zéno, and we went into the screening of the film with the appeals board.' Here, Roe's memory is crystalline: Zéno explained his intentions and how there was really nothing explicit in the film. It worked. Immediately, the board overturned the ban, and Roe flew back home, but not to a hero's welcome.

> We came back over to Perth and of course all hell broke loose. There was a demonstration outside the cinema; some right-wing, prohibitionist, Pentecostal group holding up placards saying 'Perth Filth Festival'. The government was furious that they had been outmanoeuvred by a pissant little film festival and their attempt to suppress the film was blocked.

We showed the film and [Premier] Court was outraged, so they then amended the legislation such that it prevented future appeals from being made, I believe. So why I probably regret it is we inadvertently caused the cause of censorship [legislation] to go backwards [in WA] over one small film.

And yet, that wasn't the death knell for the Perth International Film Festival, which just kept on doing its thing. By this point, PIFF had been invited to affiliate with the International Federation of Independent Festivals, which also included the likes of the Directors' Fortnight at Cannes, the International Forum of New Cinema in Berlin, the Edinburgh Film Festival and the Rotterdam International Film Festival. This, for a pissant little film festival in Perth, was *legitimacy*. And it was against this backdrop that Roe—eventually serving as chairman—and Sylvie Le Clézio—who took over the running of the festival—later programmed the Australian 'junkie' film *Pure Shit*, which had been raided by the vice squad at its Melbourne Playbox premiere in May 1976 (a precursor to the storming of *Ken Park*—though this time, the police were looking to arrest drug dealers, not DVDs). Initially banned by the censor, the 16mm production—shot over four weekends by director Bert Deling—was renamed *Pure S*, rated R, and ultimately found purchase at PIFF. At the same time, a *Herald Sun* writer called it the 'most evil film I have ever seen'. For Roe, it must have felt right at home.

The Australian film publication *Lumiere* declared PIFF's 1973 program 'as extensive as has ever been shown together in one festival in this country and as up to date with current trends in the cinema as was possible'. However, as the academic Tom O'Regan recalls in his article *Film Societies and Festivals in WA*, the top-tier nature of the programming was not necessarily equalled by the presentation, given how often the projection equipment (not to mention the projectionists) would damage reels or show them in the wrong order (or aspect ratio). Much of this cheap and cheerful DIY attitude was due to the fact Roe paid for most of the festival from his pocket, and as the years pressed on, the organisers argued that the government was actively obstructing their funding ability, while the government responded that organisers had neglected to get their grant applications in on time.

The Perth International Film Festival would last just five years, with its proposed 1977 program canned after a request for $40,000 in funds was supposedly met with derision by the WA government. This was seemingly the direct result of the firestorm incited by their prior fest. In 1976, Roe and Le Clézio sought to program

Nagisa Ōshima's masterpiece *In the Realm of the Senses* (sometimes translated to *Empire of the Senses*), which was based on a true story and contained unsimulated sex acts between its lead actors, and thus became an early example of high art intermingling with pornographic activity on film. Eiko Matsuda plays the insatiable young geisha Sada opposite Tatsuya Fuji as her older innkeeping employer Ishida; they engage in a film-long consummation of their affair across the entirety of his inn, even as chambermaids try to tidy up around them. You have to wonder if the censors found this all so egregious because Sada's female pleasure is platformed so prominently, given how that remains such a regressive taboo. Of course, it's not only unsimulated sex that made this such a controversial feature. After all, Japan's genre of 'pink films' had long before established an acceptable presence of real sexual activity in softcore domestic releases (albeit with pubic blurring or 'fogging' to obscure genitals with a white mark). But *In the Realm of the Senses* set off a global storm in no small part because of its climax, which includes a (mercifully simulated) severing of a penis and death by erotic asphyxiation. Censored heavily in Japan, the picture was nonetheless selected to play at Cannes, where 13 screenings were required to sate audience demand. It was a highly political work that thumbed its nose—among other appendages—at Ōshima's immediate ancestors in Japan's tapestry of cinema (including Yasujirō Ozu and Akira Kurosawa, who were quaint by comparison). He sought a return to the nation's Meiji era, where uninhibited sex was often explored artistically. Instead, Ōshima found himself facing obscenity charges for publishing the script complete with pictures from the film. (He was only acquitted in 1982.) During his trial, he argued that the very concept of obscenity should be struck from the dictionaries of democratic nations, especially when concerning consenting adults. *In the Realm of the Senses* pushes that concept to its logical conclusion with Sada and Ishida's fatal, coital agreement.

Other than Cannes, *In the Realm of the Senses* was a natural fit for the Perth International Film Festival, which desired to premiere the picture in Australia. But even more than its previously flammable selections, *Senses* was just high-profile enough to catch the attention of the federal censor—in this case, Richard Prowse, who had not so long ago been made an example of by David Stratton at the Sydney Film Festival over *I Love, You Love*. When the WA authorities saw that the Perth International Film Festival was seeking to debut the feature down under, they called for a ban and left it in the hands of Prowse, expecting him to step over the unofficial festival exemption and ban the film outright—which he did. (The festival exemption would not be drafted into law until the 1980s, once Prowse had left the profession and during Janet Strickland's tenure, much to her annoyance.) The Western Australian authorities reportedly then insisted to Roe and Le Clézio that every future film would need to be submitted to the censors going forward, a cost-prohibitive and pre-emptive exercise that effectively rendered the festival dead (and censored). PIFF withdrew *In the Realm of the Senses* in 1976, but it would screen uncut a year later at Stratton's Sydney Film Festival. Ironically, as he recalls in his autobiography, Stratton received a call from Prowse prior to the screening, insisting on seeing the film first; Stratton denied and invited the board to view it with an audience instead, writing in his memoir that it screened without issue, and that Prowse told him his imagination had prepared him for something more explicit than the reality. A heavily edited version of the film was released with an R-rating in 1977. As Jan Dawson wrote in *Cinema Papers*, 'It is not Sada, but the censors who ultimately wields the knife.' *In the Realm of the Senses* wouldn't receive an uncut theatrical release in Australia until the year 2000, and on DVD until 2001.

'The branding [of PIFF] was it sought out films that were outliers, that were interesting, by and large,' Roe says. 'And we showed some really interesting films. Not all of them. But there were some that were absolutely fantastic. But they were all ever so slightly alternative.' He continues: 'We saw the festival as having a function above and beyond existing for its own sake. I always thought that the big festivals in Sydney and Melbourne just existed for their own sake; just existed to entertain that audience. What was the point beyond that? What purpose did that serve? We saw our role as a much smaller festival, it gave us advantages. We did our best to get those films that we selected into distribution. So there was a purpose in sending a film to Perth; it was the prospect of finding a distributor and we did our best to do that.'

As for *In the Realm of the Senses*, Roe feels vindicated by his initial choice to program it. 'It was an Ōshima film, and it was provocative, it was pushing the envelope. It was pushing its luck. But it was a very serious film; a much more significant film than *Vase de Noces*. It was an important artistic achievement; I don't think there's any question about it now. I'd seen it. There was nothing prurient or pornographic about it, even though it was explicit; fleetingly explicit. But it was not remotely pornographic. It was clearly an important film, and why would we not want to show it?'

PIFF's ignominious end meant Perth wouldn't see another provocative film fest until the formation of Revelation two decades later. The film festival exemption faced another challenge when the Office of Film and Literature Classification was established in April 1988 to incorporate both the Film Classification Board and the Literature Classification Board, with John Dickie the new chief censor, and David Haines his deputy. Dickie started whittling away at the film festival exemption when Queer Cinema—the film festival arm of the Sydney Gay and Lesbian Mardi-Gras—attempted to screen the Spanish feature *Tras el cristal* (*In a Glass Cage*) in 1995, nearly ten years after the picture's original release in Spain. The film concerned a sadomasochistic relationship between a Nazi paedophile and his underage victim. Dickie hedged his bets by insisting it be classified first, before granting the exemption; to suss out 'community standards' and see whether or not the film was in breach. *Tras el cristal* was refused classification, a move that instituted a loophole to the 1983 exemption ruling: once struck with an RC-rating, a film festival release could no longer be exempted. Queer Cinema's appeal went to the Federal Court, to no avail, and the picture—released without incident in most other international markets—was deemed by the judge a 'child abuse film'. For this and other reasons, Haines was no fan of Dickie, considering him a bureaucratic public servant whose priority was simply pleasing the varied Attorneys-General and sparing them from difficult questioning in Parliament. No wonder Haines would eventually turn to producing porn himself—but more on that later.

Revelation had its own drama with the exemption soon after in 1999, and for another film about sadomasochism, coincidentally. The documentary *Sick: The Life and Death of Bob Flanagan, Supermasochist* saw its film festival exemption for Revelation overruled by WA's censorship minister Cheryl Edwardes, only for Edwardes to walk her decision back just six days later, after receiving advice from the Western Australian Censorship Advisory Committee. As Revelation founder Sowada recalled to me, 'I set up a private screening for them at Luna [Palace Cinemas in Leederville] and in walked their assessment panel: a nun, a priest and a military guy in full uniform. I pretty well thought I was sunk until at the end of the movie the nun walked out in tears proclaiming it was the best documentary she'd ever seen.' It nonetheless helped that the OFLC merely gave *Sick*—about the titular BDSM celebrity's battle against cystic fibrosis—an extremely palatable R-rating even after Edwardes made her concerns known that 'the standards of morality and decency generally accepted by reasonable adults had not been met' and that 'the film contained a scene about self genital mutilation.'

Sick aside, that pesky film festival exemption would continue to wreak havoc across the decades, and even occasionally backfire on distributors and programmers of challenging, provocative international cinema. The Australian Security Intelligence Organisation (ASIO) even had dossiers for most film festivals on account of their organisers' apparent subversiveness. Conservatives like Senator Brian Harradine from Tasmania—*especially* Brian Harradine—were galled that these pervy film folks were getting any leeway from government. (Welcome, Tasmania, to the 'most conservative state' royal rumble!) Harradine had been elected to the Australian Senate in 1975, where he remained until 2005, finding himself—in the late 1990s—powerfully positioned to influence Prime Minister John Howard's Coalition government. Since he was pivotal to parliament's balance of power, Harradine was being courted by the government for an all-important vote to fulfil Howard's dream of privatising Telstra, and to pass a tax reform package. Harradine leveraged this by joining Senator Julian McGauran, Senator Richard Alston and others in their 'Lyons Forum', a coalition of extremely conservative members of parliament thought to be instrumental in the election of John Howard. Together they argued for even stricter classification, the outlawing of pornography (which they sought to redefine as anything we understood as 'R' and above), the introduction of filters and protective apparatus on computers and televisions, and for the bulk blocking of offensive websites on the internet. This was all for the sake of children, at least they claimed, when a cultural shift closer to Christian conservatism is more likely the source of their agenda. Harradine even argued for more 'ordinary' Australians to join the ranks of censors, seemingly influencing a list of suggested board members submitted by the Howard government. (None made it to the interview stage.) ABC's *4 Corners* reported that McGauran had spent time trying to convince Howard that unwanted members of the board should be pressured to resign. As Howard's prime ministership went on, the Lyons Forum saw many of their passion projects humoured. This would include a campaign to ban all X-rated films, and upgrade all films to higher ratings, promoting all R-rated features to the X18+ tier and deeming them pornographic. Extreme? Not to Harradine, who believed films were pornographic if they even attempted to arouse its audience. It was apparently never raised—or too scandalous to suggest—that the growth and normalisation of internet pornography could actually be a reflection of community standards. Nor did anyone appear to point out that the interference of politicians speaking on behalf of a community they hadn't consulted was counter-intuitive. But this wasn't exactly a fertile time for good-faith arguments.

Shortly after the *Classification Act* was amended in 1995—already bent to the whims of Senator Harradine—Jim Jarmusch faced the first banning of his career with

Dead Man, due to a blink-and-you'll-miss-it sequence of 'sexualised violence', per the Refused Classification guidelines. Upon appeal, the Classification Review Board granted it an R-rating. Here's how they described the contentious shot:

> The scene, some 12 minutes into the film, takes place as Blake [Johnny Depp's character] walks through the town of Machine on his arrival. Different facets of the town's degradation are revealed as he walks. Down an alley he sees a man leaning against a wall with a woman kneeling in front of him, implicitly fellating him. A gun held loosely in the man's hand is raised towards the horrified Blake as a warning to move on. The scene lasts approximately four seconds.

Jarmusch himself offered a defence on appeal: 'Without the gun there to represent force, the woman would merely be viewed as [a] common, vulgar whore, and the scene would reflect on her character rather than, as is intended, on the character of the town itself. With the gun however, she is clearly the victim of the town's obvious acceptance of coercion, violence and corruption on every level.' The Classification Review Board concluded the shot was important to the narrative, and hardly exploitative, adding that 'the reaction of the viewer, as of Blake, is one of revulsion.' This simple line points to the complexity of banning that which is offensive to a reasonable adult: What if a reasonable adult is *meant* to be offended by the art? The review board—understanding the contemporaneous culture of conservatism—reinforced the view in its ruling by saying they are 'mindful of community concern, reflected in the film and video classification guidelines, about portrayals of sexual violence, and in making its decision in relation to this particular film does not wish to convey the impression that its commitment to upholding the relevant guidelines have been diminished.'

The other unspoken but clearly defined phrase here is 'reasonable adult', which history—and certainly this period—solidifies as someone who holds Christian values. It was reinforced by John Dickie, then-chief censor, who believed *Salò* and even Sam Peckinpah's rape-revenge drama *Straw Dogs* would have been banned if put before him; the latter specifically because of the 'ambiguity' of the rape sequence, suggesting, ironically and oxymoronically, that a reasonable adult needed everything spelled out for them. Dickie missed out on getting his *Back to the Future* moment and retroactively disappearing a distasteful film, but just two months after his term as director ended in January 1998, the board decided to change the R-rating for 1978 rape-revenge shocker *I Spit on Your Grave* to RC, suddenly banning an admittedly infamous ten-year-old movie. It stayed that way until 2004, when distributor Force Entertainment resubmitted a DVD with an explanatory director's commentary, which allowed the reinstatement of its R-rating.

The Lyons Forum continued to influence government policy on matters close to Christian groups such as marriage, sexuality and, of course, censorship. (Membership ultimately numbered in the 50s, including 15 front-benchers and Howard's parliamentary secretary, Chris Miles, who led the charge on the 'say no to sodomy' campaign.) This is the group that fought to ban X-rated videos, and decided the freedoms won in the seventies needed to be tightened back up. Secretary of the Lyons Forum (and eventual minister of multiple portfolios) Kevin Andrews clarified what that meant in a public statement, calling for all films rated MA15+ and above to be pushed to a higher rating—i.e. MA15+ to R18+ and R18+ to X18+—which ultimately meant the redefinition of 'pornography' as anything that had previously been restricted to adults 18 and older.

During the public debate over Catherine Breillat's sexually explicit *Romance* in 2000 (discussed in Chapter 12), it was leaked by an ex-censor that more conservative members of the board were holding greater sway and finding themselves promoted, while the more liberal-minded classifiers felt that their career progression had been hindered. Brian Harradine was also specifically mentioned by one source as a particular politician the board should seek to placate. The keywords used to define the board's priorities and strategy were 'conservative' and 'damage control'. Keep in mind this was happening at the same time as the Classification Code was being used to govern the web. The laws instituted at the turn of the century allowed the federal government to remove any content from the internet that could conceivably be rated R18+ or worse in Australia. The government didn't even need to publish the details of the decision nor the URLs that were taken down. This made Australia a first-world trailblazer as far as internet censorship was concerned, though not the good kind. American Civil Liberties Union (ACLU) spokesperson Barry Steinhardt called it the 'most censorious measure in effect in any democratic nation ... The law will harm Australia's reputation in the democratic world and make it more difficult for Australian content providers to compete in the global marketplace [of ideas].'

Romance ended up being the tipping point; the board agreed that the film was a serious work that approached the themes and depictions of sex in an artistic—rather than arousing—manner, yet was still denied classification. Based on editorials at the time—perhaps with people's patience having boiled over in the preceding decade—many Australians were tired of being treated as idiots, or 'unreasonable' adults. The government's tightening of the guidelines had meant to diminish the prevalence of violence, but had largely and primarily restricted sex and sex themes, transparently to soothe the ill-tempers (and gain the political favour) of those on the religious right.

The idea of 'persons aggrieved' who might be able to complain against a classification decision was even amended to include religious groups following the Howard-era shake-up of the classification rules and regulations—though this shift can be largely attributed to Adrian Lyne's remake/readaptation of *Lolita* in 1999. When the board gave it an R-rating, Western Australian groups Helping All Little Ones (HALO), Adult Survivors of Sexual Child Abuse (ASSCA) and an individual representing Child Protection Connection (CPC) applied for the review board to take a second look—but based on the existing definition, none met the criteria of 'persons aggrieved'. No doubt thanks to the coordinated letter-writing campaign that saw 945 complaints about *Lolita* directed to the Attorney-General, the wording for 'persons aggrieved' was legally changed in 2001 to 'a) a person who has engaged in a series of activities relating to, or research into, the contentious aspects of the theme or subject matter of the publication, film or computer game concerned; (b) an organisation or association, whether incorporated or not, whose objects or purposes include, and whose activities relate to, the contentious aspects of that theme or subject matter.' Senator Harradine specifically cited the failed *Lolita* review as an impetus while speaking in favour of the bill. But letter-writing campaigns from these soon-to-be-christened 'persons aggrieved' weren't always indulged, despite the long-held belief that MPs consider one letter equal to 1,500 constituents. Kevin Smith's *Dogma*, starring Alanis Morissette as God and Matt Damon and Ben Affleck as murderous fallen angels bringing forth the apocalypse on Earth, inspired 17,904 letters of complaint in 1999. It turned out that 17,500 of those letters were pro-forma postcards charging blasphemy. The movie was released unmaimed, unless you count the reviews.

Campaigners also argued against *Salò* and Gaspar Noe's *Irreversible* (which featured fleeting glimpses of actual sex and a brutal yet simulated rape) yet not Todd Solondz's *Happiness*, in which Dylan Baker plays an exposed paedophile, primarily because it did not come with a pre-fabbed target on its back like *Salò* or *Lolita*, which were both controversial as books before. (A few years later, once Howard's ten-year pledge to ban the X-rating had failed, the long-refused *Cannibal Holocaust* was released on DVD with nary a complaint from the wowsers, who were now solely concerned with filmed depictions of sex.) Community panels across Wagga Wagga, Sydney and Melbourne—60 people total—were put together in 1997 and 1998 to evaluate a series of releases and understand where the line for 'reasonable' persons was drawn. None of the participants called for any bans, and in fact, all groups suggested more lenient ratings for the evaluated films than was awarded by the board. Some years later, Senator Richard Alston—serving as Howard's communications minister—proposed a novel new interpretation of what 'community standards' should really mean in classification law. He suggested it be understood as 'what you think community standards ought reasonably to be'. This kind of doublespeak would give the religious right all the scope for appeals they'd ever need. Alston would also eventually order the investigation of ABC reporters to monitor them for balance and bias, which was both the terrifying extension and ramification of the Classification and Online Safety upheavals.

Can all of this really be blamed on the Perth International Film Festival attempting to screen *In the Realm of the Senses* with its uncut severed penis, or *The Pig Fucking Movie* that didn't actually feature any pig fucking? Was it the unexpected extension of a bruised Richard J. Prowse looking to enact revenge on David Stratton? Or could it be that the moral understanding in Australia of pornography—of 'filth'—within the modes that other countries have accepted as 'art', can be attributed to John Howard's attempts to privatise Telstra—per the redefinition of community standards by Richard Alston? Maybe all three can be true at once.

Of course, we can't just solely blame folks like Richard Prowse or Richard Alston, but as this chapter and the next argues, when it comes to censorship, there's usually a dick or two involved.

EFFED UP FACT:

Censorship creep was already being identified by the authors of *Australia's Censorship Crisis* in 1970, when noting that Melbourne International Film Festival director Erwin Rado had decided against selecting Jean-Luc Godard's *Week-end* because 'a) it was not a good film and b) it could have caused trouble with the censorship authorities'. Still, I don't buy the first excuse. The merits of *Week-end* are indeed debatable, but geez, if major directors could get excluded from film festivals for simply having produced minor works, we all could have saved a lot of valuable hours over the years.

CHAPTER 9

'PEOPLE ARE SCARED OF A HARD PENIS'

In 2017 Australian critic Luke Buckmaster openly accused the Classification Board of being 'homophobic' for classifying the Dome Karukoski-directed *Tom of Finland* R18+. The picture tells the life story of the famed homoerotic artist, who finds his creative voice upon returning from service in WW2. Margaret Anderson, then-acting director, penned a response to Buckmaster in a media release, clarifying that the 'Classification Board is of the opinion that the sexualised imagery and nudity in the film is high in viewing impact.' She continued:

> In response to Mr. Buckmaster's charges in the article that the Classification Board has a 'hostile attitude towards homosexual-themed content' and is 'homophobic, erotophobic, genophobic and archaic', it should be noted that, on 9 June 2017, I granted Palace Cinemas' application seeking a cultural exemption to screen unclassified films, including *Tom of Finland*, as part of the 2017 Scandinavian Film Festival. Their application included the following screenings of *Tom of Finland*: 13 screenings in Victoria; 10 screenings in NSW; and 4 screenings in Queensland. Furthermore, at the time of lodging its application for this Festival, Palace Cinemas sought to have me impose R18+ conditions on the screening of *Tom of Finland*, which I did.

Buckmaster later tweeted that someone gave him a framed print-out of the media release, alongside a picture of it hanging above his toilet. It was a fittingly inelegant coda to an undeniable history of homophobia in film classification, which was often spurred by protestations from special interest groups (and I use the term 'special interest' as an unflattering euphemism) eager to badge queer content as pornography. The 'porn' tag has been slapped on films like *Baise-Moi*, *Romance* and *9 Songs*; almost anything with unsimulated sex, really. Of course, all of those were eventually released in some form. It can't be a coincidence that risqué movies with LGBTIQA+ subject matter (male-on-male, especially) are protested most enthusiastically, and are the ones often banned outright by the board. That's what happened to independent art films *L.A. Zombie* and *I Want Your Love* in the last decade alone, with the former even leading to a raid on the home of Melbourne Underground Film Festival's organiser. The tragedy is that queer erasure in cinema has been successfully lobbied under the guise of pornographic moderation, meaning that champions of so-called 'moral' censorship such as Fred Nile have in a way already 'won' this conversation: we can't talk about the censorship of queer cinema without discussing pornography too.

L.A. Zombie comes from underground filmmaker Bruce LaBruce, who has long entwined the ethos of indie cinema with hardcore porn. And indeed, it features unsimulated sex scenes between male actors. A horror-comedy with a $US100,000 budget, it advertised itself with a tagline that left little to the imagination, and even less to the realm of logic: 'He came to fuck the dead back to life.' Though a softcore version of the film was scheduled to play the Melbourne International Film Festival in 2010, it was refused an exemption by the Classification Board. Festivals aren't normally required to submit the actual films when seeking an exemption, but according to *The Age*, the board requested a DVD of *L.A. Zombie* after reading a plot synopsis, their ears pricking up at the apparent suggestion of implied sex with corpses and wound penetration. LaBruce, commenting to *The Age*, at first welcomed the controversy: 'I'll never understand how censors don't see that the more they try to suppress a film, the more people will want to see it. It gives me a profile I didn't have yesterday.' However, he also confessed he was surprised that the film was refused an exemption, seeing as the board gave his previous film *Otto* a pass, reminding readers, 'that also had a zombie penetrating another zombie.' His 1996 feature *Hustler White*—co-directed by Rick Castro—was initially refused classification in 1997, and resubmitted in edited form by Potential Films, who admitted on Facebook

> at the time of submission there was a very strict policy against an R-rated film showing 'actual sexual activity' and although fleeting instances of this had been passed previously, it seemed unlikely some scenes in *Hustler White* would be passed ... [though] the board claimed there was still some actual sex (masturbation) visible in one sequence. Sitting with an editor it took several viewings to spot what they were alluding to. A token cut was made and the film was passed.

There were no plans to make token cuts to *L.A. Zombie*.

In August 2010, the Melbourne Underground Film Festival jumped at the opportunity to illegally screen the film and publicly protest the ban. Festival organiser Richard Wolstencroft attempted to keep its location a secret for as long as possible, anticipating a police raid not unlike that which befell *Ken Park* supporters Margaret Pomeranz and company in 2003. However, the screening went off without a hitch at Melbourne bar 1000 Pound Bend, with Buckmaster reporting for Crikey that Wolstencroft kicked off proceedings by declaring 'fuck the censors'. Another screening followed in Sydney, following a debate moderated by Revelation Perth International Film Festival director Jack Sergeant, featuring LaBruce via video chat from Toronto. Again, no police revealed themselves to the organisers. Turns out, they were biding their time. On 11 November 2010, Wolstencroft was met on his doorstop by three detectives seeking *L.A. Zombie*; he insisted his only copy had been destroyed post-MUFF. Though he faced a maximum penalty of two years in jail or a $28,688 fine for the screening, the court accepted a diversion order, with no conviction recorded against his name. Wolstencroft instead made a $750 donation to the Royal Children's Hospital. MUFF continues on, as does LaBruce, whose films in the last decade include 2020's *Saint Narcisse* and 2017's *Sodomise Me*. But the chilling effect on even the most audacious of festivals had commenced.

As for Wolstencroft, he suggested he would resign from MUFF in 2017 after receiving backlash to his vocal displeasure at the achievement of marriage equality in Australia, calling the announcement of the public plebiscite's result 'a horrible black day of infamy'. Despite an initial apology for his comments, he had a change of heart a year later and then decided to stay on as director of MUFF; that is, until Melbourne Underground Film Festival was deregistered as an incorporated association in July 2022 and the name was taken over by another nascent fest in 2023.

†

Compared to LaBruce's work, *I Want Your Love*, from director Travis Mathews, is a more traditional romantic drama, albeit with unsimulated sex, not so different from *Romance* and *9 Songs*, et cetera, even though it employed a pornographic studio (NakedSword) for its production. The movie tells the story of a 30-something gay man moving back home to San Francisco and navigating complicated relationships with friends, old and new. This puts it closer on the spectrum to Zach Braff's

Garden State than, say, Max Hardcore's *Going South*. Yet, the Classification Board refused to offer it an exemption to screen the Sydney Mardi Gras Film Festival or the Melbourne Queer Film Festival in 2013. (*I Want Your Love* is nonetheless available to stream online today via Vimeo provided you have a VPN, courtesy of UK distributor Peccadillo Pictures, as it received an 18+ classification under Her Majesty's watch.)

According to a statement by the Melbourne Queer Film Festival, the board had claimed that the film warranted an X-rating, apparently because, in their eyes, 'it contains explicit sex scenes without the narrative context to support the sex scenes', and was therefore 'not available for the sorts of exemption processes the MQFF follow each year'. The festival could have submitted it for classification (at a larger cost), though a potential X-rating would have only allowed it to be legally screened in the ACT and parts of the NT, so the festival applied for a second ruling on the exemption, with the following argument: 'The MQFF disputes that reading of the narrative of *I Want Your Love* and insists that the sex is in context with the narrative. We're shocked that Classification Australia have taken this path. *I Want Your Love* has screened to critical acclaim at dozens of festivals around the world. Australia is the first film festival to have it banned. We're sorry our audience won't be able to make up its own minds about adult content.' Alas, no exemption was ever forthcoming, despite Mathews indeed being a legitimate filmmaker (not to diminish Bruce LaBruce, whose intentions are just as status-quo challenging as Mathews, if intentionally more outré).

One may ask: 'Well, why do these filmmakers need to be so transgressive in the first place?' Reflecting on the situation in 2021, Mathews explained his reasoning to me: 'I knew I was being provocative, but I felt like—in queer cinema at least, but across the board—there was not the time given to the narrative possibilities of things that happen, communications verbal [and] non-verbal, when two people have sex. At the time, I was wanting to tell stories where the intimacies that were not sexual were as raw and naked and honest as what you were seeing with the sex.' It's true that, had his or these other films not featured unsimulated sex, they might have gotten through the Classification Board's clutches unscathed. But those transgressions can sometimes be the point, and they come after decades—centuries, even—of censorship and literal policing of gay activities that, not so long ago, were unlawful in the eyes of the courts. In these examples at least, queer cinema takes the form of protest, challenging the censors to reveal themselves as reactionary, in the face of exaggeration or honest depictions of previously hidden sexuality.

The reality, of course, is that this is mostly a problem for queer cinema featuring men (while acknowledging that the entire LGBTIQA+ community has been historically suppressed). I initially spoke to Mathews on that point in 2013, as he was promoting another picture entitled *Interior. Leather Bar*, which he co-directed with James Franco. In that documentary, the co-directors captured their attempts to re-stage the fabled 'lost' 40 minutes cut from William Friedkin's much-maligned *Cruising* from 1980, which became widely regarded as a retrograde thriller that demonised New York's underground gay hook-up scene. The deleted scenes were comprised, apparently, of hardcore sex between male extras; Franco, keen to explore what this might have looked like by re-enacting it with game participants, recruited Mathews for the collaboration based on his handling of *I Want Your Love*. (Franco later recorded a video in support of Mathews when the board banned *I Want Your Love*, expressing his disappointment at the decision and confusion towards the revulsion over on-screen sex compared to stylised violence. In 2018, Franco would find himself facing allegations of inappropriate and exploitative behaviour for his handling of sex scenes in some projects unrelated to those made in collaboration with Mathews.)

When I asked Mathews at the time about the board's decision to refuse an exemption for *I Want Your Love*, he was even-handed in his criticism, even though they had also refused an exemption for his earlier film, *In Their Room: Berlin* for Sydney's Mardi Gras Film Festival in 2011 as well. 'I think it is being misunderstood by your classification system, but when I think of Australia, I don't think of all of Australia being to blame for that. I think of the handful of people who are responsible for that. My feeling is that it's a very antiquated and backward classification system that needs to be revisited.' As for that handful, you'd have to attribute a few specific fingers to Fred Nile, who, as leader of the Christian Democratic Party, had long railed against the Mardi Gras Festival for blasphemous and, by his definition, 'illegal' activity. 'Is it a fact that three of the so-called festival feature films contained violent and explicit real sexual acts, which are illegal to be screened publicly in New South Wales?' he asked, a year prior to the *I Want Your Love* incident, during Questions Without Notice in NSW parliament. 'Can the Government explain why it funded an illegal activity?'

†

I wondered if *Interior. Leather Bar*—which was given an exemption to screen at festivals, but has never been otherwise released down under—was an attempt to demonstrate how sex scenes are actually made, even when unsimulated; that they're clinical and unsexy, and that with the right director, the participants can be thoughtful participants and collaborators. (This was of course complicated by the specific accusations faced by Franco some years after the film's production, but it was never suggested anything untoward occurred during the making of *Interior. Leather Bar.*) Mathews' understanding of why censors—and the systems that enable them—rejected his sex scenes was much more specific: 'I think it's that people are scared of a hard penis. If it's two women, that's much more permissible in most cultures. If it's a man and a woman, that's more permissible but a little bit less if a hard penis is involved. And then if it's two men and there are hard penises involved, it's threatening in all of these ways that a lot of cultures still are grappling with.'

So how long is the perfect penis? About three seconds. That's what producer Judd Apatow found when screening his ultimately MA-rated music biopic spoof *Walk Hard: The Dewey Cox Story* for test audiences. In one sequence, after a particularly orgiastic night in the hotel room of John C. Reilly's Johnny Cash stand-in, a nude man keeps stepping into frame behind Cox's head, dangling dick on full display. According to interviews with Apatow, the penis was visible for much longer in the original edit, and the audience revolted (and was revolted), presumably because, um, they had forgotten what the film was called. Twenty-two people reportedly walked *out*. Eventually, after some trimming, the scene was considered palatable to crowds. Size may not matter, but when blown up on a big screen, length can at least counteract the intimidating girth. Nonetheless, former director of the Classification Board Margaret Anderson suggests, contrary to Apatow's efforts, the Australian public is not accustomed to seeing penises on screen precisely because of American media's avoidance of the unsheathed member. 'That really is going to be a jolly great surprise to the Australian public because they're not used to seeing full frontal male nudity, albeit non-sexualised,' she explained. 'That's one of the things you are going to be talking about over gin and tonic post-film.'

Nonetheless, in a 2020 submission by the board for a review into the classification system, a table was suggested outlining how much nudity might be allowed within each rating: G could accommodate 'brief full frontal nudity in documentary/archival contexts (colour or black and white footage and still photographs) [or] Naked animated characters, where the animation is basic and simple (e.g.: *The Simpsons*).' In a PG film, you could theoretically see 'brief visuals of breasts and buttocks which are not the focus of the scene; full length nudity shot from behind or side view, to obscure genital detail; [and] full frontal nudity, with genitals, in a documentary context or archival footage.' Films rated M could contain 'breast nudity with nipples and areolae', though there is a specification: 'male nipples are *not* nudity' (emphasis theirs, and for good reason, as will be discussed in humiliating detail in Chapter 15). MA15+ features, like *Walk Hard*, may showcase 'full-length frontal, including genitalia; genitalia may be in close-up (no sexual arousal)'; and R-rated movies can include 'genital focus [with] sexual arousal.' An example of the latter is a rare sighting indeed. It also explains why *Jackass Forever* got away with an MA15+ classification in 2022: 'Chris [Pontius] stands nude, his penis depicted in close-up, squashed completely flat between two pieces of perspex.' Visible arousal at that point would just be downright impressive.

As Mathews suggests, male nudity in cinema has always been taboo, albeit in its own special way—compared to the lascivious usage of the female body—usually earning a film an instantly 'adult' classification. However, it came to be normalised—somewhat—by Apatow in the early 2000s; in fact, once he became a household name, it was his pet project, which at least differed from most charitable celebrity endeavours. (George Clooney uses his Nespresso money to pay for a satellite that surveils atrocities in Sudan. Apatow's big fight was to allow Jason Segel's limp phallus to hang sadly in *Forgetting Sarah Marshall*. We are each called to service in our own way.) But Apatow wasn't exactly a trailblazer, even if the male penis became something of a mascot for his movies. His nude men were never presented as figures of lust, but of comical impotence. Adjacent American comedies like *The Hangover*, *Borat* and *Hall Pass* would also use these dangling appendages similarly, or to instigate gay panic in its characters (referring to the ugly yet common comic beat of a straight man becoming apoplectic at the thought of being in proximity of a gay man, or confused for one). Notably, these penises were not seen in romantic sequences. Regardless, the Classification Board doesn't see dicks—hard or soft—as a laughing matter, and in the case of *The Hangover*, a penis played for laughs earned an R-rating, with distributor Roadshow eventually deleting the incriminating dong and resubmitting for a new MA15+ classification. *The Hangover* specifically avoided its R-rating by deleting a shot from the closing credits of a polaroid in which Zach Galifianakis' prosthetic penis is employed in a simulated sex act. (It was later released in full, rated R18+, when it came to DVD.) Universal Pictures Australia had to find a similar solution in 2017 for Greta Gerwig's *Lady Bird*, when Saoirse Ronan's character flips through a copy of *Playgirl* on her 18th birthday and gifts us a scant glimpse of static penis. Margaret Anderson outlined the thought process in classifying *Lady Bird* for me:

> The problem is [the male model] has a semi-erect penis draped over his left leg. If he'd been completely flaccid it may have been a slightly different story. By the time we get to a semi-erect penis, whoo, okay we're all taking notice at this point. The next image, in the bottom right, is the same man seated holding the base of his vertically slanted erect penis, so that's like, 'okay, we've got sexual arousal here', I can't ignore this kind of sexualised nudity. So, congratulations Universal, you've got an MA15+ for brief strong nudity.

(To be fair, they may have been cutting *Lady Bird* some slack, at least based on the suggested classification of R18+ for the sight of aroused genitalia.) Universal, wanting the more inclusive M-rating, pulled out the scissors and gave the naked gentlemen in the magazine the cruellest cut of all. Viewers would have to wait for the MA15+ DVD and Blu-ray release to see the penises restored, since they didn't make it to Australian cinemas. I've checked and you can see them on streaming services too. They appear for one literal second.

Though the word 'cunt', as discussed at length previously, is enough to set censors hyperventilating, on screen female nudity doesn't rankle quite the same way male nudity does. If you want to be academic about it, you could say it's a tradition that has carried on from the earliest days of sculpture and painting; our elevated and enlightened minds are not shocked or surprised by female breasts or a vagina, so ingrained are they in our understanding of beauty and art. More realistically, we have to acknowledge that cinema has been used as a tool to commodify the female form, and its usage has become so widespread it's not so scandalous when an actress goes nude (except in extreme circumstances). But male nudity? And not played for comedy? In an industry that has long been dominated by the heteronormative male gaze? This is unprecedented stuff, folks, with only a handful of male actors famous (actually, infamous) for dropping their dacks, Harvey Keitel being the patron saint.

Another common argument for the restrictive ratings handed down on instances of male nudity is that the erect, tumescent penis is visibly 'aggressive', or considered 'proactive' when compared to the 'neutral' vagina and breast (as far as non-pornographic cinema is concerned); this reading of course requires one to subscribe to an outdated understanding of sex—and consent—that suggests sexual intercourse can only be initiated by aroused changes to the male biology. The 2020 submission prepared by the board says the MA-rating can accommodate genitalia in close up with 'no sexual arousal'. However, the R-rating allows for both 'genital focus' and 'sexual arousal' and I don't think it's unreasonable to assume that both of these conditions around 'arousal' are code for erections, and not a change in the state of a vagina, which, in close-up, would likely exceed the R-rating. Just ask John Howard.

Consider the aforementioned argument of the former Classification Review Board's convenor Maureen Shelley who wrote the following when arguing why the rating for *9 Songs* should be downgraded from X18+ to R18+: 'Generally, the Classification Review Board only determines that 'actual sex' is depicted when it sees actual penetration (of some kind), actual manipulation of genitalia or actual climax. This is generally simpler to determine in scenes involving men rather than those that centre on women.' To that point, *Mulholland Drive* director David Lynch blurred the pubic region of actor Laura Harring in one sequence for the picture's initial global DVD and VHS release, seemingly to protect her modesty and prevent screencaps from hitting the internet; it ultimately gives the dreamlike sex scene with Naomi Watts that follows a 'sexless' quality—while also suggesting a complete misunderstanding of how sex between women even works. The nudity was restored for the Criterion Collection re-release several decades later. But still, it's *especially* rare to see an erect penis in legitimate cinema, so all these claims of flaccid penises appearing aggressive or proactive are, quite literally, a fallacy. In the closing lines of his negative 1969 review of the notoriously graphic *I Am Curious (Yellow)*, Roger Ebert reflected on the fact the male lead 'makes love detumescently', which is to say, un-erect. 'I say the hell with the movie; let's have his secret,' Ebert concluded. To this day, the secret remains unspoiled, with erect penises appearing less frequently on screen than Daniel Day-Lewis. Take *Fight Club*, David Fincher's provocative excavation of toxic masculinity and needling of modern society and mores, which closes with a not-so-subliminal spliced-in frame of a semi. If Fincher couldn't get it up for the final 'fuck you' in his R-rated feature, who could?

Australia is far from the only nation to discourage penile appendages in its movies. For decades, most filmmakers have just gone ahead and edited penises out accordingly, in subtle and obvious fashion alike. American Stanley Kubrick digitally altered his *Eyes Wide Shut* orgy to block instances of nudity with objects; a method popularised a couple years earlier, but purely for yuks, in *Austin Powers*. Kubrick's countryman Todd Solondz used a giant red box in *Storytelling* to cover up anal sex between a black college professor (Robert Wisdom) and his white student (Selma Blair), but only for the American market (on the DVD, you can watch both versions). And the climactic reveal of a trans woman's member in the Irish thriller *The Crying Game* was blurred upon release in Japan (a process known as *bokashi*), despite having been partly funded by Japanese organisation Nippon Film Development and Finance.

†

When I reached out again to Travis Mathews in 2021 to see how he now felt about the experience of being banned in Australia, I asked if he believed his thesis—that people were afraid of a hard penis—had held up. Intriguingly, eight years after *I Want Your Love* was banned, Mathews identified a slight culture shift—a tremble, maybe—in the direction towards, well, erections. 'I just saw this movie *Violation*,' he tells me over Zoom. 'It's like a female revenge film. There is a long scene that's warranted and also narratively driven, where there is a man with a hard penis, and I just saw this like a month ago and I actually had this thought [that attitudes are maybe evolving]. One thing that I feel has been changing is that you are seeing flaccid penises a lot more. But a hard penis, which I'm starting to see—that's an example, *Violation*—is still something I immediately register as, "Wow, that's different." Anyway, I recommend the film.'

On the banning of *I Want Your Love*, he recalls it being 'kind of a crazy moment'. And, intriguingly, not an entirely unpleasant one. 'From my self-interested perspective, having a movie banned in a country—especially when it's a small movie that's kind of edgy, that could almost use controversy in terms of getting people interested—was actually kind of exciting,' he explained. 'I didn't have a huge film where [controversy] was gonna suppress the box office. If anything, it would make people more interested. *'What* got banned?' But also, it was an education for me, for sure, just about the [Australian Censorship Board]. I didn't really have any thought or understanding of whether that was a conservative institution or not, so it was interesting to learn what had passed through before in somewhat recent history, and then try to understand how this film was banned.'

It is undeniable that films with graphic lesbian sex scenes that *appear* to have been unsimulated (but indeed *were* simulated) such as *The Handmaiden* or *Room in Rome* encounter little trouble getting past classification boards unscathed and uncut. (Chantal Akerman's *Je Tu Il Elle*, with its raw climax—a 10-minute full frontal sex act between Akerman and Claire Wauthion—earned an R-rating in 1982, though it was submitted nearly eight years after its initial French release and with three minutes missing. It's unclear what was actually cut. Exchanges with both the Australian Film Institute (AFI)—who submitted the film—and the Classification Board were friendly but fruitless, with neither having any detailed records of the classified content.) It merely speaks to the mainstream perceptions of gay sex, as Mathews mentions. You need only look at movie posters to understand how one type is sold, and the other type is shielded. When director Sebastián Lelio's *Disobedience* arrived in Australian cinemas in 2018, it was promoted with a poster of Rachel Weisz and Rachel McAdams in a provocative pose, almost kissing. In the film, the Rachels play childhood friends (and onetime lovers) who reconnect as adults, still constrained by their strict Orthodox Jewish community. If the title didn't give it away, the poster paints a clear portrait of what audiences can expect: forbidden tongue-touching. It's a striking one-sheet, and it brings to mind another McAdams movie with a similarly lusty title and poster: Brian De Palma's *Passion*, co-starring Noomi Rapace as her almost-kissee (though this movie is more salacious than *Disobedience*). The posters for *Disobedience* and *Passion* aren't so far removed from those for queer dramas *Blue Is the Warmest Colour*, *First Girl I Loved*, *Below Her Mouth*, *Allure*, *Women Who Kill*, *Entre Nous* and *A Perfect Ending*, which were all released within the last decade. Clearly, the near-kiss is a trend in queer movie posters. In fact, we probably have enough examples here for an entire Near-Pash Film Fest.

'I think it's definitely empowering,' says Dr Stuart Richards, senior lecturer at University of South Australia and author of *The Queer Film Festival: Popcorn & Politics*, whom I interviewed in 2018 for *Disobedience*'s release. 'If you look at a lot of queer films that have been nominated for Academy Awards—*Monster*, *Brokeback Mountain*, *A Single Man*, *The Hours*—where there are explicitly queer characters in those films, in all of the marketing materials, you do not see intimacy. So, definitely seeing something like *Disobedience*, where we have two A-level actresses being intimate on the poster, I think that's incredibly liberating and should be celebrated.' However, Dr Natalie Krikowa of University of Technology Sydney—and director of the satirical theatre production *All Our Lesbians Are Dead!*—disagrees, telling me she 'wasn't a huge fan' of the *Disobedience* poster or its stars' positioning. 'The way that it's framed is not for a queer gaze at all,' she says. 'If it's for mainstream audiences, what they're presenting is this one type of intimacy and that type of intimacy is a sexualised one. There's a complexity to love, and we're only being presented with one vision of that love, and that is, two women looking lustily at each other.'

So why aren't movies about queer male leads (think *Call Me by Your Name*; *Love, Simon*; *God's Own Country*; *Moonlight* and *BPM: Beats Per Minute*) commonly advertised with the same level of erotic intimacy as their queer female counterparts? (Although we should shout out 2022's *Bros*, the first mainstream queer rom-com from a major studio, whose poster featured a close-up of two men gripping one another by the butt through their jeans. The movie was an infamous bomb.) 'Audiences are generally more comfortable seeing women kiss than men kiss,' Dr Richards says. 'There are several reasons for that: One is because intimacy between women is more culturally accepted. It also is titillating for heterosexual male viewers, whereas that's probably not the case for male kissing.'

'There's a longer history of men having to hide their intimacy,' he adds. 'Even straight men have to hide their intimacy, for fear of appearing too gay.' Dr Krikowa echoes this, saying, 'It's still not socially acceptable. But "two women" has always been that straight male fantasy. That gets a lot of people going, "Ooh, that should be good. That should be interesting." When the straight male producer is making the film, he's okay with that level of sexuality in females but not in males. And that's still unfortunately the case with most distributors of mainstream Hollywood cinema.'

'My hope is that things are improving; I feel like they are improving,' Mathews said to me back in 2013. 'It's a process.' Nearly a decade later, he conceded, 'I don't feel like that's changed very much. But I also feel like the power of those voices [who challenge queer cinema] continues to shrink or they become louder to the point that they become caricatures of themselves.' Of course, not so long ago, aforementioned flicks like *Moonlight*, *Call Me by Your Name* and *Disobedience* might have been relegated to the fringes, rather than well-regarded hits with major stars. And yet, representation remains a massive issue.

There was also the curious incident in 2020 when Netflix's self-classifying tool (which we'll discuss more in Chapter 15) rated *Moonlight* MA15+ upon its debut on the service in Australia, despite it having already been given an M-rating by the board several years earlier. After I raised it with the Classification Board, they removed the additional MA-rating from their site, and upon alerting Netflix, the streamer changed the rating back to M. Still, what were the nuances that led to *Moonlight* getting a harsher classification on this latest go around? Would the Netflix Classification Tool have given this film an MA-rating if it wasn't about a queer black man? It's hard to imagine what *Moonlight* would even look like (or be about!) if you removed its LGBTIQA+ themes, so it's not as simple as suggesting that the tool would have awarded the picture an M if lead character Chiron was straight. However, this re-rating follows a trend of queer stories not being considered acceptable for younger audiences, as if anything other than heteronormative content goes beyond acceptable norms. And it ties back to the movie poster problem, in that the issue isn't simply that queer female leads are more sexualised on these one-sheets, or that those featuring queer males sometimes hide their queerness; it's that there are simply so few types of mainstream queer movies being made, and even fewer being made by queer voices. 'In queer cinema, you've got two stories that get foregrounded, and that's either a coming-out story or "I've fallen for the straight person and I get my heartbroken"', Dr Krikowa says. 'We're not really getting any counter narratives or anything beyond that from alternative perspectives.'

One could argue that the counter narratives—and the ones intending to normalise gay sexuality—are the kinds of pictures made by LaBruce and Mathews, even if they occupy very different spaces. But these more graphic efforts are the ones being cast into the wilderness, and reducing in frequency as a result. Take, for example, Comstock Films, which was founded in the late 1990s by 'Tony Comstock', who produced movies featuring 'real people, real life, real sex' until 2011. (The name was an alias inspired by the notorious 19th-century American censor Anthony Comstock.) 'Tony' started Comstock Films in New York with his future wife Peggy as a means of showcasing experimental shorts that depicted real love, sex and relationships, among other topics (their website notes common recurring themes including '9/11', 'indigenous fisheries' and 'the visualisation of God', so they really cast their net pretty wide). In 2006, he triumphantly blogged about an impending illegal screening of his X-rated documentary *Damon and Hunter: Doing it Together* at MUFF (a reminder that X-rated pictures aren't allowed in Melbourne, or almost anywhere in Australia). In the picture, long-time lovers Damon DeMarco and Hunter James have unsimulated sex on screen. Comstock said he could not afford to challenge the board (or OFLC, at the time) on their X-rating 'as *9 Songs* did', because of the approximate $8,000 cost, 'with no certainty of success'. Regardless, it screened in defiance of the ruling, and went on to even take the Best Documentary prize. Success was its ultimate curse, unfortunately. After receiving an invite to play the higher profile QueerDoc festival, held by Queer Screen in Sydney, the OFLC informed them that they'd be violating the law.

Comstock's tone in his blog posts shifted significantly after learning the festival organisers could be on the hook for major fines, and even jail time. 'Of all the films the OFLC might target for censorship,' he wrote, '*Damon and Hunter* seems like a particularly inappropriate choice.' He continued,

> Aside from the recognition the film has so far received as an outstanding work of cinema, it's also been recognised for its value as a life-affirming and educational document. *Damon and Hunter* is held in the Kinsey Library at the world renowned Kinsey Institute at the University of Indiana. It's already being used by the Gay Men's Health Crisis in New York, and by the San Francisco Sex Information Hotline. Just this week it's been passed around by delegates at the 16th Annual World AIDS Conference in Toronto, Canada. Why? Because *Damon and Hunter* is singular in its compassionate, humane, frank, and erotic depiction of gay love and gay sex. And apparently that's something that the government of Australia needs to keep the people of Sydney, especially the gay men of Sydney, from seeing.

He went on to produce an edited version—'no erect penises, no touching of each other's flaccid penises, and no butt cracks'—for OFLC review, but after telling the *Star Observer* of his frustration that he was considered 'fucking criminal' simply for showing 'two people who love each other making love, which is an incredible part of being a human being,' he pressed his luck, titling the new edit, '*Damon and Hunter: Doing it for the OFLC*'. Comstock then claimed the OFLC complained that this softer cut was 'defamatory', as the explicit content had been replaced with a tile that read, 'Footage Removed by Order of the Australian Office of Film and Literature Classification'. Not only did the flick never end up playing QueerDoc, but Comstock alleged that because of 'the stink' he raised for *Damon and Hunter*, he was advised by the board to 'tread lightly' in how he discussed recuts of the film—and others— in future. True to their threat, the board prevented his next film, *Ashley and Kisha: Finding the Right Fit*, from getting an exemption to screen at MUFF.

In a surprise twist, the OFLC did owe Comstock for one thing, per his blog on 28 August 2006: 'We received, by post, a request from the OFLC to retain our film for use in their Classification Training Workshops. No, I'm not kidding. The OFLC would like permission to lift 3–4-minute segments to be used on training members of the film, television and videogame industry about the classification process. As you try to wrap your brain around this, please keep in mind that only two days before the OFLC informed us that if an Australian counterpart to The Institute for Gay Men's Health or The San Francisco Sex Information Hotline were to use *Damon and Hunter* with their clients, or merely kept the DVD on their library shelves, they would be subject to fine and jail time.' Unfortunately, irony does not pay the bills. Comstock Films has been out of commission since 2011.

†

'Whether somebody deems something pornography or art is also something that is such a subjective argument to have, especially with my films I think,' Mathews told me in 2013. 'My definition of pornography is very much around, "if it's conceived of, produced for and then it's mostly consumed for the sole purpose of getting somebody off, then it's probably pornography". But it's very rarely that I shoot anything with sex that the intention is to get someone to the point of orgasm. It's much more around character, around story and around different types of male intimacy that I feel are so rarely seen in films that have a narrative involved.' He conceded, at the end of our chat, that the systems themselves, and those sitting at the top of them, would need to change before we saw a demonstrable shift for filmmakers within the queer scene. 'Aging, white, straight men in the world, they feel threatened by so many different things that are happening,' he explained at the time. 'An erect penis is definitely still at the top of their list.'

In 1971, David Stratton wrote hopefully in *The Bulletin* for the cause of movies about queerness, thanks to the advent of the R-rating at the time. However, he remained sceptical that they'd all be rapidly welcomed by the board. 'Still, I suppose we'll have to be grateful for all the other movies we *will* be getting,' he offered in conclusion. That would go on to include director Doris Wishman's *Let Me Die a Woman* from 1977, an empathetic, quasi-educational documentary about the lived experience of transgender men and women that nonetheless sees the sensationalist Wishman present gender confirmation surgery in all its graphic glory.

(The Australian DVD cover leant into the queasy expectations established by Wishman's prior sexploitation cinema: 'All true! All real! See a man become a woman before your eyes!') The censors slapped *Let Me Die a Woman* with an R-rating in Australia upon application in 1981 (for 'transsexualism'), but not before toning down the surgery sequence on account of 'gross surgical detail'. The picture's reputation today is mixed at best though it was considered valuable enough for Criterion to enshrine it in their collection, noting it's 'a rare historical record of the transgender experience in the 1970s—and features cinematography by trans photographer Andrea Susan Malick.' But the Criterion Channel streaming service isn't available in Australia, and *Let Me Die a Woman* has never been reclassified (or reconstituted) for Australians since 1981. Clips from its centrepiece surgery would instead find its way into the *South Park* episode 'Mr Garrison's Fancy New Vagina' in 2005—rated MA15+.

In 2021, I asked Mathews what he felt had nonetheless been lost in the near-decade since *I Want Your Love*, and films like it, were banned across Australia. 'I think the queer youth of your country miss out,' he says. 'Imagine you are a heterosexual couple with a queer child who is 15 years old, and you hear of these banned queer films. It makes it, like, a scary world that they're entering in. Just knowing that there are these queer films that are being banned, it's like, "What kind of world is my young son entering into"? It might make them more conservative or protective. I have no idea. It's like one message among many messages, but for sure it's not a positive effect on people.' However, Mathews was heartened after asking 'people manage to see these films in Australia, yeah?' *I Want Your Love* can indeed be accessed locally via VPN, for now at least. In June of 2021, Australian parliament passed the controversial *Online Safety Bill*, which, among other reforms, accommodates the sending of removal notices to Australians hosting content that could meet the currently described standards of the R18+, X18+ or RC film classifications, with a possible fine exceeding $110,000 for each offence. Though that won't affect international sites, it could indeed promote the chilling effect that we see on local distributors of international content. Should that happen, it won't be just filmmakers like Bruce LaBruce or Travis Mathews who feel the chill. In the meantime, Mathews ultimately feels his film's ban was 'advantageous', having earned him attention and a reputation, adding 'there was a little work I needed to do to quietly convince [producers] that I wasn't just "the porn guy"'. But as he noted, 'The conversation is more important than any of these films, in a way.

Because a lot of people are going to hear about these films and talk about these films, but not a lot of people will actually watch them.' All these years later he could only think about the queer youth of Australia absorbing the unspoken message of the bans, and how their parents should feel. 'I would be furious,' he said.

After a pause, he could only repeat himself: 'I would be *furious*.'

Robert Mitchum as Harry Powell in *The Night of the Hunter*. Australian censors banned the picture in 1955 for 'blasphemy'. (Stanley Cortez / Metro-Goldwyn-Mayer, Inc. / United Artists)

Jean-Paul Belmondo and Jean Seberg in *Breathless*. Jean-Luc Godard's film was banned in 1960, having been deemed 'indecent'. Like *The Night of the Hunter*, it is now widely considered among the best films ever made. (StudioCanal)

Carla Hoogeveen as 'The Woman' in *Night of Fear*, from Australian director Terry Bourke. It was also refused classification for indecency in 1972. *Night of Fear* was rated R18+ on appeal and advertised as 'a terrifying journey into a deranged mind'. (Peter Hendry / Umbrella Entertainment / Terryrod Productions)

I Love, You Love (*Jag älskar, du älskar*) set off a storm of controversy in 1969, and was banned for a perceived sex scene featuring a pregnant woman. A shot from that same scene adorned the Swedish poster.
(Stig Björkman)

Margaret Pomeranz and David Stratton on the set of ABC's *At the Movies*. The beloved film reviewers had infamous stoushes with the censors over the decades. (Australian Broadcasting Corporation)

David Roe, founder of the Perth International Film Festival
(PIFF), pictured in a 1975 issue of *Cinema Papers*.
(Scott Murray)

Eiko Matsuda as Sada Abe in Nagisa Ōshima's *In the Realm of the Senses*.
David Roe had to withdraw the banned film from PIFF's 1976 program.
Senses didn't screen uncut in Australia until the year 2000.
(Hideo Ito / Cité Films)

A mock wedding from Pier Paolo Pasolini's *Salò, or the 120 Days of Sodom*, one of the most notorious films ever made. It was only released in Australia under strict conditions. (Tonino Delli Colli / Metro-Goldwyn-Mayer, Inc. / United Artists)

Caroline Williams as 'Stretch' in *The Texas Chainsaw Massacre 2*.
This scene was the main reason the film was banned in Australia for twenty years.
(Richard Kooris / Metro-Goldwyn-Mayer, Inc. / Cannon Films)

Peter Jackson (and a friend) behind the scenes of 1987's *Bad Taste*. This cheap and cheerful gorefest was one of the last films to wear the 'Banned in Queensland' badge of honour. (WingNut Films)

James Ransone as Tate in *Ken Park*. Margaret Pomeranz was detained in 2003 for attempting a public screening of Larry Clark's banned picture. (Edward Lachman / Busy Bee Productions / Cinea / Marathon International / Lou Yi Inc. / The Kasander Film Company)

Srđan Todorović as Miloš in *A Serbian Film*. The Classification Board first rated it R18+, and then later banned it on appeal. David Stratton called it 'one of the most revolting, disgusting pieces of shit that I have ever seen'.
(Nemanja Jovanov / Contra Film)

Top: Monster Pictures co-founder Neil Foley (left) and Simon Miraudo at a 2011 Q&A screening of *The Human Centipede 2: Full Sequence* in Perth, WA. Mere days after the screening was held at Luna Leederville cinemas, Australian censors banned the film.
(Monster Pictures)

Bottom: *The Human Centipede 2: Full Sequence* star Laurence R. Harvey (left) and Simon Miraudo.
(Monster Pictures)

'Lena Watson' as Elli in Sandra Wollner's *The Trouble With Being Born*, which was disinvited from the Melbourne International Film Festival in 2020 after a news outlet asked experts if it was 'masturbatory' material for paedophiles. (Timm Kröger / Panama Film)

Katia Pascariu as Emilia in *Bad Luck Banging or Loony Porn*, a 2021 Romanian comedy that satirises the concept of public obscenity and pornography. (Silviu Ghetie / microFilm)

Prano Bailey-Bond's 2021 horror film *Censor* stars Niamh Algar as Enid, a censor who turns murderous during the UK's 'video nasty' era. (Annika Summerson / Silver Salt Films)

Violation's co-director Madeleine Sims-Fewer, in character as Miriam, moments before a sexually explicit scene that ends in shocking violence. The picture was initially released unrated on Shudder in Australia. (Adam Crosby / Dusty Mancinelli / Madeleine Sims-Fewer)

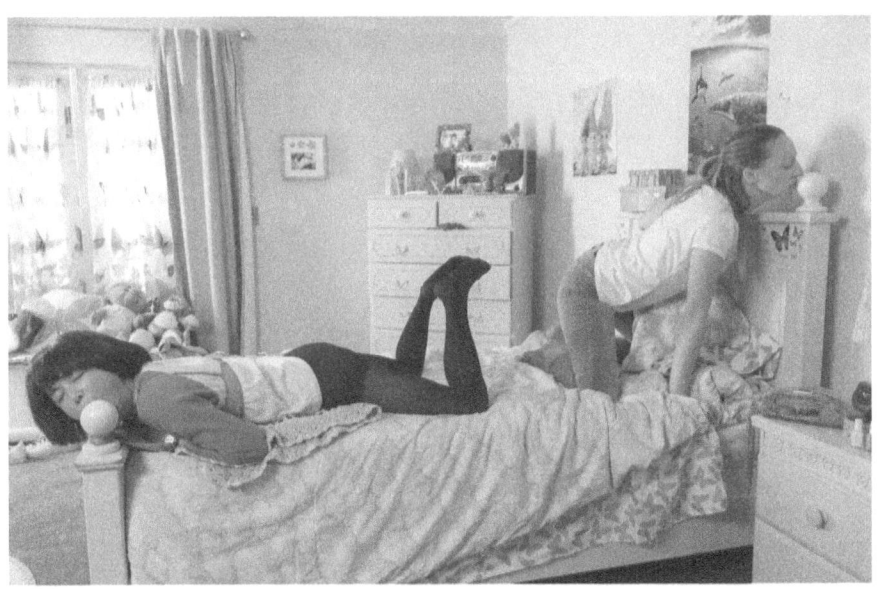

Maya Erskine as Maya and Anna Konkle as Anna in the coming-of-age comedy series *Pen15*. The show was never submitted for classification in Australia by the streaming service Stan. (Andrew Rydzewski / Lonely Island Classics / Odenkirk Provissiero / AwesomenessTV)

CHAPTER 10
RAIDING THE STATE-SANCTIONED SPANK BANK

If a stopped clock is correct twice a day, how often did the censors get it right? A couple times a century? That rate of success makes a smashed timepiece seem positively infallible. But it's through gritted teeth that even the sternest anti-censorship advocate might have to concede the censors occasionally made an agreeable edit, even if they usually only did so by accident. Turns out, in their efforts to reduce the amount of nudity and violence unleashed upon sensitive audiences, early censors were actually limiting the on-screen misogyny of the era's predominantly male filmmakers.

To see this in practice, one would have to sort through the deleted footage and the censors' written reports by delving into the labyrinthine, end-of-*Raiders-of-the-Lost-Ark*-style warehouse in Canberra, wherein these decisions and deletions have been stored for nearly a century. Filmmaker Sari Braithwaite stumbled upon them in Canberra's National Archives by accident while researching a short film about David Stratton in the early 2010s. A few years later, she had a pallet of these VHS tapes shipped to the National Archives office in Melbourne so she could compile *[CENSORED]*, an essay film comprising found footage, though calling the footage 'found' is probably too passive a description of what she actually curated. Spending years poring through the scenes deleted by the Australian Classification Board, she sought to liberate these lost cinematic moments from between the years 1958 and 1971 (there were 1,191 cut scenes in total).

At her movie's start, the deletions Braithwaite shares are ordinary and expected: cowboys in a punch-up; an exposed breast; two men holding hands while dancing down a church aisle. The kisses that were deemed unsuitable by the censors are not so different from what would soon after be considered passable. One uncovered smooch even includes Dame Maggie Smith, meaning the eventual Dowager Countess of gran's favourite TV show, *Downton Abbey*, had once been deemed too saucy for Aussie cinemagoers. To further the point of the absurdity of these edits, we learn that three essential minutes were removed from Ingmar Bergman's *Persona*, in which a youthful sexual encounter is vividly described, despite the fact that no sex is depicted on screen. *Persona*, non grata?

Braithwaite, in her narration, notes how celluloid could be 'quietly altered' by censors in a way that songs and books of the time couldn't, making their censoring particularly insidious. However, after viewing these scraps of story, isolated from their context, she grew to hate that which she had intended to liberate. 'I didn't see the obvious,' she says via voiceover. 'That all these films were directed by men. That this was a distilled collection of male fantasies, imaginings and desire. I was liberating a state-sanctioned spank bank.' And she's right. So many of the images clearly objectify women or are violent towards them. Braithwaite wonders who it benefits to uncensor these visuals: 'Tear down one power and another power reveals itself.' In fact, she sees only one scene directed by a woman in the entire collection: a post-coital exchange from Agnes Varda's *La Bonheur*, with fleeting nudity shot by a fluid, floating camera. As Braithwaite puts it: 'This archive is only the artifacts of what had the privilege to be made. The artifacts that expose how men have always told their stories.' As happened to Bergman's *The Virgin Spring*, many of the rape sequences of this era were, if not deleted, toned down to now appear consensual. Same goes for Roger Corman's *The Wild Angels* in 1966, which had a 'violent sexual attack ... cut that it looks no more than an undignified scuffle', *The Bulletin* reported at the time, just as these edits were gaining further scrutiny. 'Greatly reduce struggle between girl and man in which he undresses her, and makes love to her and hits her', one instruction by the board reads for an unnamed film, as pasted on screen during *[CENSORED]*. 'There are hundreds of clips in this collection,' Braithwaite concludes. 'Most were dull and unmemorable, instantly forgotten unless I played them over and over again.' And yet, others had her sympathising with the censors. 'Some clips felt so intolerably vile to watch, so dark and ugly, that I don't dare grant them exhibition. If I had the opportunity, I think I would have destroyed those clips. Are these the actions of a filmmaker or a censor? But maybe they aren't so different; these forces that we imagine in opposition. Both filmmaking and censoring are expressions of power. Both dictate what is seen.'

This temptation to censor was not Sari's alone. My passion for defending artists' unfiltered visions had run aground in the face of footage that seemed to serve only ugly impulses. Watching *[CENSORED]* brought to mind the sequence from Bret Easton Ellis' novel *American Psycho*, in which the sociopathic serial killer Patrick

Bateman admits to obsessively rewatching Deborah Shelton's infamous death-by-drill in Brian De Palma's *Body Double*. Fox, the Australian distributor, had already self-censored that scene from *Body Double* before putting it to the Classification Board in 1983, though it was restored for the VHS the following year. My mind also returned to the dozens of trashy, nearly forgotten American action movies I'd learnt about in my own research—*Out of Control, Hollywood Cop, No Dead Heroes, L.A. Crackdown 2, No Hard Feelings AKA Kick or Die*, too many more—that had nearly indistinguishable rape scenes deleted by their own distributor to secure a more permissive classification. I even thought of the animated film *The Hunchback of Notre Dame* from 1996, which had its PG-rating challenged by Disney despite featuring a scene in which 'a gypsy mother (with baby in arms) is pursued by [male villain] Frollo on a ferocious looking horse … flung on to the cathedral steps, hits her head and dies,' and another in which 'Frollo grabs Esmerelda in the cathedral, sniffs her hair, and says "I'm imagining a rope around your neck".' Disney ultimately cut these moments in Australia—and more—to get a G-rating. All of these instances occurred across different eras, long after the period covered by *[CENSORED]*. I too wondered, like Sari: was there *that much* being lost by them not being seen? But then again, I'd prefer for that debate to occur in the open, held by a trusted, film-literate public. Plus, a blanket rule that banned scenes of sexual violence would be unwise, and that's not what *[CENSORED]* calls for either. Take 1992's *Man Bites Dog*, a defining Belgian mockumentary that specifically—and mercilessly—satirises the nature of violence we crave in cinema. It was initially refused classification for its depiction of a gang rape. Once the rape was deleted, the movie received an R-rating. But by softening the movie for the public's perceived temperament, they were softening the rotten characters at its core too. It has not been re-assessed since 1993, meaning Australians cannot legally watch the uncut version of this significant historical document.

At least one of the excisions highlighted in *[CENSORED]* was worth salvaging from the cutting room floor. *Persona* was re-evaluated by the board in 2004 and received an M-rating for a 79-minute cut, making it still a few minutes shorter than Bergman's original, unhindered vision. It was nonetheless released by Accent Film on DVD, though that's now out of print. Could it be that *Persona* was never made whole in Australia? I revisited it on the Australian streaming service Stan and confirmed that its controversial (in the board's eyes) sequence was at least reinstalled online. Legally? Seemingly not. But thank goodness. Besides being a stunningly delivered monologue by Bibi Andersson, it contains the key to unlocking basically any and every interpretation of Bergman's otherwise baffling art-horror film, with its explanation of the past abortion of Andersson's character, Alma. The section below includes a transcript of Alma's soliloquy, with the three minutes excised by the Australian Classification Board in bold:

> Karl-Henrik and I had hired a cottage by the sea. It was in June, we were all alone. One day when Karl-Henrik had gone into town, I went to the beach alone. It was really nice and warm. There was another girl there. She lived on an island nearby but had come over as our beach lay to the south and was more relaxed. So we lay beside one another completely naked and sunbathed. We slept a little, woke up, and put on some oil. We wore these hats on our heads, you know, those cheap straw hats. I had a blue ribbon around my hat. I lay looking out from under the hat, glanced out at the landscape, the sea and the sun. It was so curious. Suddenly I saw two figures jumping about on the rocks above us. They hid and peeped out occasionally. 'There are two boys looking at us,' I said to her. Her name was Katarina. 'Well, let them look,' she said, and turned on her back. It was such a strange feeling. I wanted to run and put on my costume, but I just lay still, on my belly with my bum in the air, totally unembarrassed, totally calm. All the time I had Katarina beside me with her breasts and thick thighs. She just lay there, giggling to herself. Then I saw the boys had come nearer. They just stood looking at us. I saw that they were terribly young. Then one of them, the bravest one, he came up to us and squatted down beside Katarina. He pretended to be busy with his foot and sat poking between his toes. I felt totally strange. Suddenly I heard Katarina say: 'Aren't you going to come over here?' Then she took his hand and helped him take his jeans and shirt off. **Suddenly he was on top of her, and she was helping and was holding his behind. The other boy simply sat and observed. I heard Katarina whisper in his ear and laugh. I had his face directly in front of mine. It was all red and swollen. Suddenly I turned and said, 'Aren't you going to come with me as well?' Katarina said, 'Now go with her.' So he pulled out of her and fell over me, completely hard. He grabbed one of my breasts. God, how it hurt! And in some way, I was ready and I came immediately. I was going to tell him, 'Be careful so I won't be pregnant,' when he came. I felt ... I felt**

something I had never felt before, as he poured inside me. He grabbed me by the shoulders and arched backwards. I came again and again. Katarina laid beside us watching, holding him from behind. When he was done, she embraced him and finished herself off with his hand. As she came, she gave a shrill cry. Then we all three started to laugh. We called the other boy that was sitting. His name was Peter. He came down, all confused and looking like he was completely frozen in the sun. Katarina unbuttoned his pants and started fondling him. And when he came, she accepted it into her mouth. He bent forward and started to kiss her on her back. She turned around, grabbed his head with both hands, then she lay down and put her breast in his mouth. The other boy got so aroused, that we both started again. It was as good as the first time. Then we swam and said goodbye. When I returned home, Karl-Henrik was home. We dined together and drank the red wine he had bought. Then we slept together. Never had it been that good, not before or after.

Persona is a hard nut to crack even in its reinstated form; I pity the audiences who weren't privy to this morsel of information that would've added context to Alma's terminated pregnancy, and at least indicated what Bergman was going for here: a commentary on motherhood, oedipal and Electra complexes, womankind's societal-imposed division of self and the cannibalisation of female personhood to make way for children. Without that monologue and its key reveals, *Persona* could be (mis)read as being about mad women gone wrong. And that's to say nothing of what Andersson conveys in her delivery here, which looms over the rest of the film.

'It's such a great scene, right?' Sari agrees over the phone in 2020, a year after *[CENSORED]* has screened at film festivals around the world. (It otherwise remains unavailable for viewing in Australia due to clearance issues with the clips.) 'Some people, when they've read [my] film, they've sharpened their memory of it and think I go through this dance of pro-censorship and hating films. In fact, the purpose of [showing] *Persona* is [to say] there's just some amazing stuff in here. Both are true: the censors cut the best of cinema and also some really troubling reoccurring things that filmmakers do. And the archive actually revealed those patterns to us accidentally. They weren't trying to show us the archetypes of misogyny, but they just did.'

[CENSORED] is not the movie Braithwaite initially set out to make. In fact, she tells me after the fact, 'I didn't expect to be this filmmaker.' She explains that she was set on this path after making the short film *Smut Hounds* about David Stratton's involvement in the *I Love, You Love* 'argy-bargy'. 'I felt like I was more looking at [the clips for *Smut Hound*] through a lens of sexual liberation, and that Australia was prudish and this was part of this transformation that would happen in the '60s in the US and the '70s in Australia. I wasn't expecting to find those clips [that feel more misogynistic].' It was the sheer volume of those troubling excisions that changed her perspective. 'When I think about the first compiled reels that I watched, it's all in there, but it wasn't in such a great quantity where it felt like a problem to me,' she explained. 'I thought, a bit of boobs and arse is just a bit of fun.'

Her perspective shifted, though not immediately. 'I like to think that my feminist eye revealed itself very quickly, but in fact I just was like, "Ugh, filmmakers are gross,"' she laughs. But the toll of visiting the National Archives for months on end, several days a week, from 10am to 5pm each day, with her own VHS player in tow, watching these context-less cuts in chunks of mere seconds or minutes at a time, on a near ceaseless roll, ultimately shaped *[CENSORED]*. 'I was finding the process not particularly fun, and a bit gross, and I couldn't quite understand why,' she says. 'Mostly I was underwhelmed and unimpressed by everything I was watching. But I also had this experience that I didn't really remember anything. I would spend this whole day just watching clips and I was writing notes as I was going, into a database. It was rare that something would stand out as unique or interesting. It was all blurring.' For a time, she hoped the process would reveal patterns, and that those patterns would yield beauty, so she could eventually compile a collage that celebrated cinema, like the conclusion to *Cinema Paradiso*. And sometimes she saw exactly that. Other times, the patterns revealed something she describes as 'darker and complicated'.

'It's obviously such a huge archive and I narrowed my lens as I went through it, and I came out with a particular perspective,' she says. 'I feel like I've got all the empirical research and evidence to feel confident in the thesis I put forward in the film, but I also think someone could make a totally different film with that archive, and that's something that's true to any archive or medium or platform. Someone could navigate their way through that archive to only show the classic films and make something that is in the vein of *Cinema Paradiso*. It was just on viewing this whole archive, it was my point of view at the end that this was the most compelling and urgent thing that came out of my study of the archive.'

In horrible synchronicity, Braithwaite locked picture just as the #MeToo movement emerged, and the crimes of serial rapist and abuser Harvey Weinstein, one of the Hollywood's most powerful producers, became known publicly. 'The #MeToo movement and the focus on the feminist gaze hadn't been at the top and front of centre of public discourse [before then],' she says. 'Of course, it was there in film theory and of course I was aware of it, but I wasn't looking for it. It took me a while to sharpen my gaze and be willing to see it. I spoke to a number of women filmmakers as soon as I saw it and understood what I had collected and what I was looking at; they saw the patterns and made sense of it and organised it. Then I couldn't step back from it.' Arguably, besides the censors of the day, no one has gotten closer to this once-incendiary and still-troubling footage than Braithwaite. And yet, she suggests that getting so close to what was previously deemed unsuitable for audiences has unfortunately complicated the issue further in her mind. 'One of the things I really felt is true in all of this research is, it's not helpful to be like "I'm for or against censorship", because censorship in some form always is and always exists as an expression of power of who gets to say what to who, and the question is kind of dissecting how it's working and how problematic it is. It's a very difficult area to have an answer that doesn't exist in the grey. I think that's where I came out of it. I started thinking in this space of "censorship is wrong" and then where I emerged is "this is far more complicated, and what do you mean by *censorship*?"'

For that reason, she appreciated hearing from the New Zealand Censorship Board that they had 'real debates' over what to rate her film, and whether or not under-15 audiences should be allowed to see it. They decided to restrict it to an over-15 audience, not because of the specific content, but 'because of the unrelenting tension in the work'. Braithwaite likes that 'it wasn't about breasts or a vagina or the actual actions' for them: 'It was about the tonal quality of the work, which is something fundamentally different to how censorship used to function.' At least, you'd hope. In Australia, though the checklist of classifiable elements is still key to how the board hands down their decisions (or, you could argue, washes their hands of them), there remains a foggy cloud over the moral frameworks they're applying when dealing with more extreme content, shielding, in the board's mind, audiences who are not equipped to recognise when confronting material is contextually relevant. As Sari puts it in the movie, 'No one in Australia saw sex and violence on screen before 1971. Censors may have thought they were protecting the nation from the outside world, ensuring Australia would thrive as a friendly island of harmonious virgins. But weren't they just in denial? Purging the screen didn't purge it from people's lives.'

EFFED UP FACT:

I don't know if it's fair to ever accuse a movie of 'asking for it' from the censors, unless it's *Can Heironymus Merkin Ever Forget Mercy Humppe and Find True Happiness?* starring writer-director Anthony Newley in the role of Merkin, opposite *Playboy* model Connie Kreski as Humppe, and real-life wife Joan Collins as Polyester Poontang. In David Stratton's biography, he specifically recalls seeing it at a special screening for film reviewers, by which point the censors had already stripped away the film's many gratuitous nude scenes. Though the film was now 'a pointless and singularly unamusing shell'—Stratton's words—distributor Universal and publicist Hans van Pinxteren had a bold idea to curry favour with the critics: inviting male reviewers on a boat trip to Goat Island in Sydney, where a stripper performed before the screening. Unfortunately, the projector ultimately 'sputtered out' before the film finished, so everyone was taken back to Circular Quay, including the stripper, whom Stratton offered a lift home.

CHAPTER 11
THINK OF THE CHILDREN

We know films can be refused classification. They can be banned. They can be censored. They can be self-censored. They can even be uncensored (eventually). But does it count as censorship if they're *uninvited*? Maybe it depends on what they're uninvited from, but having your RSVP rescinded from the Melbourne International Film Festival (MIFF)—following a scandal over your film's controversial content—seems like enough to warrant a mention in this book (if anywhere).

MIFF is the main rival to the Sydney Film Festival as far as eastern state cinephilic superiority goes, and though it has no significant history of having battled the censors—as David Stratton did in NSW—it is where I've personally seen some pretty challenging material. That includes Markus Schleinzer's *Michael* (not to be confused with John Travolta's 'horny angel' movie; this one is about a paedophile keeping a pre-teen prisoner in a bunker) and Sion Sono's necrophilic true crime black comedy *Cold Fish*, neither of which was ever released widely in Australia after their screenings (for maybe obvious reasons). Unfortunately, MIFF stuck their foot in it during 2020's streamed-at-home schedule by unprogramming Sandra Wollner's Austrian flick *The Trouble With Being Born* when *The Age* contacted some experts to evaluate if it was 'masturbatory' material for paedophiles. The experts, unfortunately for the film, said it was. There's no such thing as bad press, but still, I wouldn't recommend plastering that pull quote on your posters.

The film takes place in a semi-futuristic setting in which AI androids are commonplace, often used as replicas for humans who've died (or, as we see, are perhaps no longer contactable for legal reasons). The first and most troubling part of the film involves an adult man, played by Dominik Warta, and the uncanny replica of his ten-year-old daughter, Elli, played by a pre-teen actor credited as Lena Watson, which is a pseudonym to protect her identity. (The young actor also wears a silicon mask to obscure her visage, and to resemble another actor who plays the real, older Elli that turns up later.) Though the relationship between father and faux-daughter at first seems ordinary to the point of banal, it becomes apparent that the man has taken to using Elli for sexual purposes in their remote estate. Elli has also seemingly been programmed to fawn lovingly—lustfully?—over her owner-father. At one point she's seen lying on her stomach, naked, chin in her hands, staring adoringly at dad as he tinkers with an iPad—or is he tinkering with her operating system, adjusting memories, feelings and intentions? Such is the discomfiting headspace director Wollner puts us in. This is one of two 'nude' scenes; later, the man dispassionately removes a mechanical part from Elli's pubic area and washes it out—itself highly disturbing—leaving the android sitting naked on a shelf, with its black cavern of a crotch completely visible. Both scenes were achieved with the assistance of CGI.

Descriptions of the film's content were provided to the Classification Board by MIFF in their application for an exemption to screen unclassified features at the 2020 festival. 'Extensive notes are available as to the safe and responsible production methods used on set when working with the underage actor in the production,' MIFF's submission to the board reads. 'The film was the recipient of an award at the Berlin Film Festival's Encounters section, and had been selected for the prestigious New Directors/New Films screening series at the Lincoln Centre in New York before its cancellation this year.' Indeed, this was enough to satisfy the Classification Board's then-director, Margaret Anderson, who wrote in her ruling, 'I have now considered all of the information in the written application, and have decided to exercise my power under subsection 6H(1)(b) to grant a declaration to approve the MIFF 68½ showing 110 unclassified films, as per the conditions contained in the attached Declaration,' even after acknowledging that these movies would be screened at home. None of this helped Wollner much at all.

'[MIFF] already had printed the program, included a big trigger warning, and everything in a way seemed fine,' Wollner tells me in late 2020, just a few months after the fiasco unfolded.

> And then I had this interview with *The Age* Melbourne, where I already had the feeling, 'Ooh, this could be in a way a clickbait article', even though the journalist [Karl Quinn] was really interested. I had a very nice talk to him as well, but yeah, you never know. Then they asked me—I don't recall if it was the festival; probably it was the festival—if I could send the [screening] links to two forensic psychologists, which I did. I also thought, 'Okay that's good, because I can give them some additional information about what were our safety measurements for the

kid, what we were thinking about.' And then one of them did not watch it because she said it would be illegal to watch it, without having seen it. And the other one watched half of it and came to the conclusion that it's a danger and a trigger for potential paedophiles to see that at home.

It was at this point that MIFF rescinded the invite; before the article had run, but after Quinn sought comment from the festival based on the expert's responses. In a postscript published on the Film Alert 101 blog defending his original article, Quinn said he believed that the board not needing to see the film to provide an exemption (despite getting a brief on the film's contents) is what caused MIFF such grief in the end. 'One psychologist—responding to my detailed but neutral descriptions of scenes in the film (which she declined to view)—asserted that they likely constituted Child Exploitation Material,' he wrote. Quinn continued,

> Personally, I think this is unlikely, but I'm no expert. But if she is correct, screening that material—let alone distributing it over the internet—would be a criminal offence in this country. Had the Classification Board asked to view the film, that matter could have been definitively settled. The fact that no one at the board did so ultimately left MIFF in the unenviable position of having to play censor to its own programming.

The suggestion here is that the board might have refused granting an exemption to *The Trouble With Being Born*, saving everyone the headache (except Wollner, and fans of thoughtful, complex cinema). But Stratton, from the sidelines, did not mince his words in an open letter, saying it was 'galling … to witness MIFF's apparently craven response to a film they themselves selected. If, in the future, the Government wants to censor a festival film, the festival will no longer be in a position to protest; they've done it to themselves'. Stratton elaborated on his points in a later conversation with me.

> I am convinced somebody from Melbourne [International Film Festival] had seen that film, and had deemed it worthy enough to screen in the festival. Now, once you do that, I think you stick by your decision, and you stand by the filmmaker whose work you've considered sufficiently excellent to warrant programming in your festival. I understand the nuance of [at home] streaming; I understand that that could have had

a somewhat different complexion, although that never really seemed to come out in the argument. [But] if you see the film and you see it in context—the whole film from start to finish—then, although it certainly has confronting elements to it, I think it's a very moral and serious work. So, I am absolutely—still, now—puzzled and a bit shocked that Melbourne did what they did.

I wrote to [MIFF's artistic director] Al Cossar after I saw the film to say to him, in the nicest possible way, that I thought this was setting a very bad precedent, because if you invite a film and then, under some pressure from a newspaperman who's trying to write a sensational story, and he's got a couple of so-called experts who have not seen the film in its entirety, and on the strength of that you withdraw the film, then I think that's outrageous. That sets up the possibility that in the future, censors might say to you, 'Well, you did it yourself so we're perfectly capable and willing and eager to censor you.' So, I thought that was pretty bad.

Wollner has no beef with the experts. 'Fair enough that an expert on this subject thinks that [way], and I think that's a legitimate way of seeing it,' she says. '[But] I really did not expect that a festival that invited the film in the first place, after they had seen it at the Berlinale, would withdraw the film after a psychologist has seen half of the film,' she adds. 'It just never occurred to me.'

To play devil's advocate, the trouble with *The Trouble With Being Born* playing MIFF was that 2020's festival was a solo experience; punters could only buy tickets for synchronised home screenings, a compromise for Victorians stuck indoors during the government-mandated COVID-19 lockdowns. MIFF acknowledged, when they withdrew their invite, that this particular film would be better suited to the in-theatre experience, as private viewings could indeed prove too tempting for the unsavoury types who might get off on it. However, their explanation raises a further conundrum: Couldn't *any* film featuring children be used as 'masturbatory' material by paedophiles in private, even if those films—just like Wollner's movie—didn't actively try to instigate it? 'That would have been enough reason for me if they would have said, 'Okay we withdraw the film because this film obviously—and it is obvious—is made for the cinema; that would have been a reason to withdraw it,' Wollner says. 'But stating that they had to withdraw the film to make sure that their community is safe, and make sure, how did they say it?' she asks herself, looking for the wording published by the festival. While we talk, she finds it: '"The safety and wellbeing of the MIFF community and broader Australian public is of paramount concern to the festival. With this in mind, we have made the decision to withdraw Sandra Wollner's film *The Trouble With Being Born*."'

'And that I found really a little problematic because it went along with other people who thought this is the danger; that this film *is* dangerous,' she says.

†

It takes just one (full) viewing of Wollner's film to realise it would need to be actively misread to consider it dangerous, much less an endorsement of paedophilia. As Wollner describes it, her movie tries to capture the 'weird energy of a dream', and in its second half, we see the Elli doll repurposed into a young boy to remind an elderly woman of her deceased little brother Emil, and soothe her decades-long grief. Instead, the android only exacerbates it. The provocations that precede this second act are intentionally structured for squirm-inducing effect, Wollner explains. 'I really wanted to tell this as an anti-Pinocchio story, where this object only wants what it is programmed to want, whether it is an unbearable dynamic like we see in the first story, or whether it's an understandable story of loss like we see in the second story.

'But the particular order was very important for me also in the writing process. So, we as an audience could get over the scandal and deconstruct her android— let's say, *see* the object behind it—but also see how we as human beings hold onto emotional attachments, and how that is also the stuff that makes life so painful, because unlike machines, we of course have limited time on earth and the people we love and eventually our memories tend to slip away. That really is, basically, the trouble with being born.'

Once Wollner and her co-writer Roderick Warich arrived at this structure—for what she calls 'the linear medium called cinema'—she accepted that she needed an actual pre-pubescent actor in the role of Elli. 'The original idea always was to tell the story of this child android with the appearance and also the physicality of a child, and all which goes along with that, because the audience reaction and my reaction to what we see would just never be the same if we tried to sidestep the issue by using an adult actress or CGI,' she explains. 'But then we started thinking how shooting this film with an actual child would be possible at all, and which kind of safety measures would we have to take.

What would it mean for the kinds of scenes we would shoot, and also for the mood of the scenes? Then I also realised, all the scenes we have in this film where sexuality is implied were created in post-production. So, the context and set were completely different and quite harmless.' Wollner found 'Lena', a young actor up to the challenge, and insists the girl had a supportive family to explain 'in an appropriate way, the subjects of the film, and also about the dangerous relationship between this man and the android.' This would be key for the sequences in which Elli's nudity would be realised in post-production. She also reiterates that the scene in which we see naked Elli being cleaned 'was not only important to show the sexual aspect of their relationship, but also to really show that this is an object that has changeable parts and it's not a real child that we're talking about. That was the core scene to show both, at the same time, but to also show to our audience, clearly, that this is the story about a machine, about an object.'

This logic and critical reasoning, presumably employed at first by the selection team at MIFF, eventually went out the window. 'The thing is, they chose the film, and they assured me that it was an incredible discovery, and one of the best they saw at the Berlinale, and, what did they say?' Wollner wonders aloud, eventually recalling, 'They liked the "subtle exploration of grief, identity and memory".' Nonetheless, she is not suggesting a free-for-all when telling stories of a sensitive, even incendiary nature. She too believes filmmakers must be held accountable, and that 'the line' of what is and isn't acceptable isn't just a theoretical demarcation point for academic discussion. 'I certainly think that there is a legal line, which experts would have to judge based on the respective laws of the country,' she says, adding,

> I do think that freedom of art is incredibly important and a pillar of our society, as perhaps you can maybe see in the ongoing debate about Muhammad's caricature in France [referring to the controversies regarding illustrations of the Islamic prophet]. Our Western idea of art includes the depiction of horrendous acts, because that's what reality is. I really think that art needs to be able to reflect that. But of course, there is also the responsibility of any filmmaker, writer or artist not to glorify acts of violence or abuse. I do think that in striking the right balance there, intentions matter. I really can say we certainly did *not* want this film to become masturbatory material for paedophiles, and frankly, I think the way this film depicts a psychologically deeply disturbed relationship should make it actually almost impossible to see it in that way.

She then adds, half laughing, 'Of course, I think one should see the whole film before reaching a conclusion. I mean, that would be my idea of common sense. But it's really also a sign of our times, to quickly jump to conclusions; to make sure not to stand on the wrong side, without ever taking the trouble to investigate further. Sometimes I have the feeling that people enjoy the idea of a scandal. But those are mainly people who have not seen the film and who probably would never have watched it anyhow.'

Those kinds of viewers, Wollner believes, would rather cinema forbid the depiction of human darkness as seen in her story. 'I think that's a little problematic. I really, truly believe that it is important not to only show the best humans can bring out but also the abyss. Everything else would just be a lie and would never show life or humankind in a full picture.'

Religious groups let this particular scandal through to the keeper—or were presumably oblivious—but didn't miss a beat the following month, when the Classification Board published an MA-rating for the French Netflix film *Cuties* from debut director Maïmouna Doucouré. (Technically, Netflix had self-classified the film using a specialised tool, which we'll discuss in Chapter 15.) The Australian Christian Lobby decried the decision, fixating on a sequence in which the main character, an 11-year-old girl called Amy, is ostracised from her dance troupe after sharing a graphic photo of herself on social media in a confused response to a public humiliation. ACL chief political officer Dan Flynn said in a statement the board should have banned the film and also accused the picture of grooming young girls to upload child pornography. However, the Classification Review Board upheld the MA-rating in October of 2020, saying the 'depiction of how young people can be influenced by the internet and social media today to their possible detriment is real'.

If the religious groups' censorious influence was waning, it at least garnered them the same headlines they regularly earned in previous eras: effectively, the kind of easy wins where even a 'loss' (i.e. the film isn't banned) still counts as a victory ('isn't secular culture perverse?'). A cluster of these so-called spiritual associations had coalesced behind a call to ban Gregg Araki's *Mysterious Skin* in April 2005, citing similar reasons as that provided by the psychologists who'd viewed/half-viewed/read descriptions of *The Trouble With Being Born*.

Mysterious Skin stars Joseph Gordon-Levitt and Brady Corbett as two young men who, in their childhood, were both sexually abused by their baseball coach, drastically altering the trajectory of their adulthoods accordingly. The Classification Board nonetheless passed the movie with an R-rating, calling it 'a serious and legitimate exploration of a disturbing and confronting theme.' This declaration spurred a concerned letter writing campaign in Queensland, which alerted Queensland Parliament to the picture. The Australian Family Association (AFA) and the Festival of Light followed up by asking the OFLC to waive a reclassification fee, which would have allowed them to challenge the initial decision at zero cost. When this was denied, they contacted the South Australian Attorney-General, Michael Atkinson, who encouraged Federal Attorney-General Philip Ruddock to appeal the rating, later telling the ABC, 'I don't think a how-to manual of sexual abuse against boys ought to be screening in our cinemas.' A spokesperson for the Australian Family Association even told the *Sydney Morning Herald*—shortly after the film's screening at the Sydney Film Festival and ahead of its debut at the Melbourne International Film Festival—'Being able to get hold legally of a DVD where they can play the [molestation] scene over and over again, showing the adult baseball coach fellating an eight-year-old boy... could prove very helpful to some pedophiles.' (Sound familiar?) Margaret Pomeranz made a bold counter, saying *Mysterious Skin* 'could be a paedophilia-curing film because they're confronted by the damage they do'.

The Classification Review Board announced they would reassess the film in August, and Araki, who had been in the country for the festival screenings, told ninemsn how surprised he was by Australia's reaction. 'The fact (is) that the film has opened already in so many other countries with no incident, no problem with censorship or anything,' he said. 'I have always thought of Australia as a very sort of progressive, sophisticated, cosmopolitan place. So to run into this roadblock is surprising.' The AFA, appearing as an interested party, had gone all-in with their written and oral submissions for the review, suggesting films (yes, *any* films, documentaries included) that featured a description or depiction of child sexual abuse likely to cause offence to a reasonable adult must be classified RC. It took 12 hours for a six-member panel of the review board to uphold *Mysterious Skin*'s R-rating, conceding only to change the consumer advice to 'high level child sexual abuse themes, high level sexual violence, paedophile themes.' A media release further explains their reasoning: 'In the Classification Review Board's opinion, *Mysterious Skin* warrants an R18+ classification because of the general character of the film in its treatment of child sexual abuse from a victim's perspective. The educational merit in this treatment means the film is such that it contributes to the understanding of the consequences of this horrific crime.' In making their decision, they too had consulted an independent child psychologist—though Dr Robin Harvey actually watched the whole film before presenting her evidence that 'developmentally and clinically the film is very accurate [and] the portrayals are certainly not gratuitous or over the top from the point of view of (the boys') psychological being'.

Several decades earlier, a similar controversy had unfolded on the other side of the world in Canada. Director Volker Schlöndorff's acclaimed feature *The Tin Drum* was banned by Ontario's censorship board in 1980 for what they called 'child pornography'. This was despite the fact that Schlöndorff's sprawling German feature had already claimed the Palme d'Or at Cannes and the Best Foreign Language Film prize at the Academy Awards. The problematic sequence at issue involves physically stunted 16-year-old Oskar—played by then 11-year-old David Bennent—licking sherbet off the finger, from the palm and ultimately out of the naval of 16-year-old Maria (actress Katharina Thalbach, aged 24 at the time). Moments later in the film, while getting undressed, Oskar pounces on a nude Maria and appears to perform (completely static) oral sex on her. It culminates with Maria pulling what we'll conclude is a pubic hair from Oskar's mouth. Watching it today, there is no denying it is off-putting—in a way that *The Trouble With Being Born* and even *Salò* aren't—knowing the discordant ages of the performers. (It is actually one of three extremely disconcerting scenes; the other two involve Bennent in bed with older female actors as they vaguely simulate sex.)

However, in an interview included on the most recent Australian Blu-ray release, Schlöndorff goes to great length to articulate how Bennent was protected on the set of *The Tin Drum*. It apparently began with Bennent's 'enlightened' parents reading the original novel to him before shooting commenced. 'Whenever there was a graphic situation of that kind occurring, the parents explained it to him,' Schlöndorff says. 'He saw it was all fake anyhow. It's actors, they pretend to be naked, they pretend to make love. It's a playful way for a child to learn.' It turns out that the more nervous parties were the women Bennent starred opposite, and that Thalbach was only convinced to participate once Schlöndorff showed her detailed storyboards on how she would avoid being naked in front of her 11-year-old co-star.

Schlöndorff describes how they utilised the same tactic he learnt on the set of director Alain Resnais' *Hiroshima mon amour* with Emmanuelle Riva: using black velvet material to cover up Thalbach's breasts and a 'black triangle so no one could see public hair', as Schlöndorff puts it. He continues: 'It was very much in a similar way that every other scene was solved. I was in close complicity with the boy but also he was well protected, also by his parents and the actors.' As such, upon first application to the Australian Classification Board in 1980, *Die Blechtrommel* (*The Tin Drum*'s German title) passed with an R-rating. However, four years later, for its VHS release in Australia, an edited cut was submitted to the Classification Board—the R-rating was upheld, but eight minutes were now missing (perhaps because the distributor was considering the aftermath of the Canadian controversy and anticipated pushback). It would take another 26 years for those eight minutes to be reinstated in Australia, and it's not just the Canucks' fault. You can blame the Okies too.

In 1997, the director of the religious advocacy group Oklahomans for Children and Families (OCAF), Bob Anderson, led a crusade to ban *The Tin Drum* in Oklahoma after hearing it described on a radio show. Anderson didn't watch the film, or even the troubling scene, before commencing his campaign. He didn't need to. After complaining to the police, they passed it along to the county courthouse to seek their opinion. State District Court Judge Richard Freeman declared that the film breached Oklahoma's obscenity laws because it included—according to his oral decision—scenes of children under the age of 18 having sex. (Freeman only needed to see a few scenes to make his ruling, which is still more than Anderson saw.) The OCAF celebrated victory by publishing a threat on their website, warning all makers of literary, artistic, educational, political or scientific works that not even an Academy Award could spare them from being designated as 'contraband'. Judge Freeman's ruling was passed down on 25 June 1997, and the very next day, the head of the Oklahoma chapter of the American Civil Liberties Union (ACLU), Michael Camfield, was visited in the night by three police to ask him about a recent rental from Blockbuster Video. He was informed that, by having in his possession a VHS of *The Tin Drum*, he was now holding onto child pornography, and had to surrender the tape. Police had in fact been visiting all the local video stores to recall *The Tin Drum* and receive all the names and addresses of customers who had rented it.

Camfield subsequently sued the City of Oklahoma alleging violations of his constitutional rights to free speech and due process. Following a jury trial, he won 'declaratory relief and statutory damages' (for approximately $US2,500). One year later, a federal judge overruled Oklahoma's ban on *The Tin Drum*, noting that—despite its inclusion of an underage actor in a sexualised scene—it is protected as a work of art. 'While the state has every right and duty to prohibit and criminalise such a profound evil as child pornography ... the court concludes that the film in issue is not one that violates the law as claimed,' the ruling stated. 'While many viewers may find the three scenes at issue objectionable, and while they are inappropriate for young viewers, the theme of the film, taken as a whole, is not sexual ... Applying the bona fide work of art exception to the statute will not affect the state's ability to attack hard-core child pornography, it will require only that the exception be considered before material may be subjected to the law,' the judge added. (Schlöndorff acknowledges in the DVD's special features that the detailed storyboards outlining how the nudity was obscured from Bennent was likely the film's saving grace, having been later utilised as part of the film's defence.)

Of course, as all this played out in public, Australian punters presumably didn't even realise that *they* hadn't been able to see the theatrical edit since 1980. Thankfully, DVD re-releases by Umbrella Entertainment in the year 2020 and a 2022 Blu-ray included the deleted scenes. The film was even accompanied by a documentary titled *Banned in Oklahoma*, though the adjoining short doesn't mention its Aussie watering-down. That documentary goes into detail about the legal quagmire encountered by Camfield, but, frustratingly, never really engages with the movie itself. Reflecting on *The Tin Drum* with a modern-day lens, it is hard not to find the deployment of young Bennent in overtly sexual sequences distressing; I can't even agree with the Oklahoman federal judge who believes the 'theme of the film ... is not sexual.' In actuality, *The Tin Drum*—besides being a critique of war through a magic realist lens—is alert to its characters' sexuality during the most trying of times. Oskar has a mild lust for his mother, insists on his nanny reading to him about Rasputin's orgies, and witnesses (with jealousy) his parents engaged in various sexual acts. The orgasmic delight in Maria's expression as Oskar licks sherbet out of her hand (and elsewhere) is also not meant to be read as ambiguous. But the picture is a towering achievement of black comedy and sad irony, regardless. Bennent's performance is remarkable for an actor of any age. There must have been an understanding that he's playing a somewhat wretched and perverse creature; a pubescent and recalcitrant teen who refuses to grow his body any further. The film achieves Schlöndorff's artistic intentions, as well as those of the Pulitzer Prize-winning author of the source novel, Günter Grass. It also features an 11-year-old actor in several disturbing scenarios (no matter how 'responsibly' shot). What do we do with these conflicting ideas? All I know for certain is that the debate cannot be reserved solely for those whose perspectives are situated on the fringes of moral puritanism, and who haven't even seen the thing they're critiquing.

Back in Australia, there are more examples of the governments of the day attempting to limit paedophiles' access to independent art cinema, for reasons of moral inexactitude. In 1978, the Harry Hurwitz erotic comedy *Auditions* was refused classification on the grounds of 'sexual exploitation of a minor', for it included naked 20-year-old actress Linnea Quigley playing a 16-year-old. A few years later, the SA censor banned Melvin van Peebles legendary 1971 blaxploitation film *Sweet Sweetback's Baadasssss Song* from the 1980 Adelaide Festival, for what it also called 'sexual exploitation of a minor', referring to an opening sequence in which a 13-year-old Sweetback mimes having sex in the nude. (Never resubmitted to the board in Australia, it is technically still banned.) And in 2004, Jonathan Glazer's *Birth*—starring Nicole Kidman, in a Mia Farrow pixie cut, as a widow convinced her husband has been reincarnated in the body of a child—was accused of being a tool to teach adults how to groom children. That same year, the Australian Family Association argued that Catherine Breillat's R-rated 2004 picture *Anatomie de L'enfer* (*Anatomy of Hell*) featured child sex abuse. However, the review board found that the aggravating scene in question—where the arm from a pair of spectacles is inserted into a child's vagina—didn't count as child sex abuse, as the 'insertion' took place off camera and the 'child' was a prosthetic dummy. At least the Classification Review Board's convenor, Maureen Shelley, addressed the complexity of the issue in in the board's 2004 – 2005 report: 'Films that have the issue of paedophilia or underage sex as a central theme, such as [Todd Solondz's R-rated] *Palindromes* and *Tras el cristal* (*In a Glass Cage*), are challenging to classify. Yet there must be some way that society can examine and discuss issues of paedophilia and under-age sex via the medium of film.' I'm not sure future classifiers heeded that call. By the end of the decade, Australian Sex Party's founder Fiona Patten was calling the board out for suggesting imagery of naked women with A-cup sized-breasts was too reminiscent of an adolescent's body.

'The Classification Review Board determined in the case of *Anatomie de L'enfer* (*Anatomy of Hell*) and *Palindromes* that the depictions—whilst some adults may take exception to some scenes—were acceptable,' Shelley continued in 2005. 'However, in the case of *Tras el cristal* (*In a Glass Cage*) the Classification Review Board unanimously determined that the combination of sexual references and torture of children was such that the film should be refused classification [again in 2005].' It's in the conclusion of her point that Shelley reveals the contradiction of the Classification Review Board's approach: 'Of the three titles, it is my view as Convenor that *Tras el cristal* (*In a Glass Cage*) had the most artistic merit and the highest production values. However, artistic merit alone is insufficient to ensure classification if the classifiable elements are such that the matter should be refused classification.' The art of the film ultimately didn't matter at all.

†

There's a strange, unexpected coda to *The Trouble With Being Born*, which was achieved by the temporary eradication of COVID-19 throughout much of Australia in 2020 (and well before the rest of the world). Cinemas reopened, in WA first and eventually in the eastern states, including Victoria. And so, on 3 December 2020, *The Trouble With Being Born* was released theatrically by indie distributor Potential Films, now officially rated R18+ by the Classification Board, for 'high impact themes'.

Potential's email announcing the release even came with a description of the MIFF controversy, not shying away from the irresistible sales angle. And so, Wollner, ever the optimist (though that's not necessarily apparent from her motion picture) couldn't help but redirect my questioning about Australian censorship in our interview ahead of this wide release: 'Australia is now the first country where the film has a theatre run, so let's concentrate on that.' *The Trouble With Being Born* earned $13,748 in Australia, according to Box Office Mojo—apparently 100 per cent of its worldwide cinema takings.

EFFED UP FACT:

The cover for The Wiggles' G-rated 2015 DVD *Rock and Roll Preschool* features the playmates Emma, Lachy, Simon and Anthony (as well as special guest Lou Diamond Phillips) positioned around a toddler dressed as Bruce Springsteen. Sounds harmless. Who'da thunk 12 minutes had been deleted from it by the ABC after the first cut received a PG-rating for 'mild themes of grief and loss'? (Do the Wiggles *kill* Lou Diamond Phillips?) Turns out a special feature called 'Grief Counsellor' was meant to be included, but by the time the re-rated G edition wound up in shops, the extra had been excised. I'm not sure of the content in 'Grief Counsellor', but it was clearly too much of a bummer for the ABC. I guess that's why they call her Dorothy the Dinosaur and not Dorothy the Death Doula.

CHAPTER 12
NO ORAL, PLEASE

Nine tonnes (that's 9,000 kilograms) of prosthetic penises, harnesses and vibrators arrived in a Canberra warehouse in June of 2002, and it wasn't because of an unfortunate typo on one punter's order form. This was Sydney-based adult business Sharon Austen Limited not so much attempting to aggressively corner the sex toy market in Australia, but dominate it through volume. That same month, scandalous French flick *Baise-Moi* set tongues wagging upon its release into cinemas in its home country. *Baise-Moi* (which translates to *Fuck Me*) wouldn't front the Australian censors until October of 2002, though when it eventually did, it faced serious opposition down under, setting off yet another battle between anti-censorship campaigners and those who would see the film banned. The experience might have not been so contentious if David Haines, the disenchanted deputy chief censor from 1988 to 1996, had still been on the Classification Board, given his commitment to championing challenging works during his tenure. Unfortunately, he was busy at the time. Specifically, he had just helped orchestrate that Sharon Austen Limited deal to become the exclusive local distributor for US sex toy manufacturer Erostar Erotic Novelties, having become the company's chairman in 2001.

In 2003, the newly renamed Gallery Global Networks Limited (GBN) would sign an exclusive agreement to distribute *Playboy*'s programming. Soon after, GBN would partner with GoConnect Limited to launch 'The Adult Channel', a video subscription service intent on delivering high-quality video clips direct to mobile PCs, as was the parlance of the times. In 2004, GBN launched the benignly named DVD mail-rental arm TheDVDCompany.com, which charged $8.95 a week to allow customers access to what they pledged was basically every legally available adult film in Australia (in discreet packaging, of course). In the space of a few short years, GBN had a virtual monopoly in the adult space, as X-rated material could only be supplied from its premises in Canberra. Yes, the one with nine tonnes of dildos in stock.

Former *Penthouse* Pet of the Month and pornographic actress Tera Patrick was on hand to launch TheDVDCompany.com that July, and it would probably mark the heady, high point of this burgeoning business; the bloom before its untimely autumn. For Haines was on a quixotic mission all the while, seeking to convince the government to allow X-rated films to be distributed beyond simply the ACT and the NT; a bureaucratic quirk he likely identified from his time on the Classification Board. 'For 17 years Australia has been subject to the absurd situation whereby it is legal to own X classified films, and legal to obtain them from the ACT either in person or by mail order, yet it is illegal to sell them from retail outlets in NSW and Victoria,' he wrote in the company's 2003 annual report. 'Legislation of the sale of X films in NSW would allow the Company to expand into retail outlets within NSW, and to extend its wholesale business. We are optimistic that the Government will support this Bill.' Spoiler alert: they didn't.

By March 2005, GBN had divested the adult side of the business, 'necessitated by the negative impact of political decisions by State governments, and particularly by the failure of the NSW Government to support a Private Members Bill to legalise the sale of adult product in the State,' as Haines wrote in his Chairman's Address to the AGM that November. 'Such inaction has allowed the development of a thriving illegal market in adult product four times greater than the legitimate market. This has been exacerbated by piracy and the ready availability of adult product on the internet.' So began the evolution of the company—eventually renamed, many times over—into one that just focused on the perfectly staid and smut-free world of marketing and lead-generation. Its latest iteration, Impelus Ltd, was delisted from the ASX in 2022.

Haines had spent 14 years in the OFLC mines (eight of those as deputy chief censor), delivering his judgment on sex in cinema, only to emerge seemingly disillusioned with how the government perceived (and banned) actual sexual activity on film. This was not simply limited to pornography either. Plenty of 'legitimate' movies that featured actual sex were threatened with an X18+ or refused classification entirely. And then there were the 'inbetweeners': hardcore pornos like *Deep Throat* or *The Devil in Miss Jones* that were initially banned by the board, subsequently re-rated as X, and then ultimately given R-ratings in slightly more enlightened times once they became considered important documents of their era. However, a few years after Haines left the board in frustration (to produce the pornos *Buffy Down Under* and *Revenge Aussie Style*, which were both shot in the ACT), they handed down what might have been their signature landmark decision: granting a release (and R-rating) to Catherine Breillat's *Romance*, and consequently opening the floodgates—relatively speaking—for films with unsimulated sex, with previously banned films applying (sometimes successfully) to get their scarlet RC brandings scrubbed. Though censorship fights of the future would see the board focus (perhaps more concerningly) on a film's ideology and potential for misuse, this decision on

Romance brought actual sex into the mainstream. Take director Ben Hozie's 2021 release *PVT Chat*, which scored an R-rating that boasts 'high impact sexualised nudity and actual sexual activity' for scenes in which star Julia Fox simulates masturbation and co-star Peter Vack does it for real. Before *Romance*, the threat of actual sex in cinema meant movies could be deemed pornographic and banned; made notorious even. After *Romance*, many movies with actual (heterosexual) sex barely warranted a shrug. Have *you* ever heard of *PVT Chat*?

Romance may have been a watershed moment for the Classification Board, but it was business as usual for Breillat, who spent the years prior to its release producing sexually explicit works—both written and cinematic—designed to prod and provoke audiences. This infamous picture, released in its native France in 1999, tells of a 20-something teacher named Marie (played by Caroline Ducey) who is driven to nymphomania by her model boyfriend Paul (Sagamore Stévenin). He refuses to sleep with her, so she seeks out other willing suitors, including Paolo (played by porn star Rocco Siffredi) and eventually her boss Robert (François Berléand), the latter of whom introduces her to sadomasochism yet is the most emotionally engaged of all her partners. Upon my first watch, I realised that *Romance* is explicit twice over: firstly in its long, unbroken takes that culminate in unsimulated sex, including shots of fellatio, masturbation, ejaculation and penetration; and secondly, in Ducey's droll voiceover outlining Breillat's exact thesis on 'romance', from its impossibility to its shameful and demeaning physical manifestation in those sex acts (and other fetishes) being depicted. The point is made—and made, and made, and made—well before the picture reaches the end credits, but Ducey's unmannered, uninhibited performance carries the viewer through. Of course, one can only make that critique—or challenge it—if one can see the film, and in January of 2000, the OFLC nearly made that impossible for Australians by refusing it classification. Distributor Potential Films appealed the ban that same month, and the Classification Review Board capitulated, giving it an R-rating for high level sex scenes, deciding that offence was not enough to negate the value in its artistic aspirations. 'The Review Board found that the graphic depictions of sexual activity would undoubtedly offend some people,' they wrote in their report. 'However, a majority of the Review Board also found the film to have serious intent and artistic merit. This majority also found that, with appropriate consumer advice, the film could be accommodated within the guidelines for the legally restricted R18+ classification.' As their report continues—and the National Classification Code explains—for a film to be refused classification, it must depict, express or otherwise deal with matters of sex, drug misuse or addiction, crime or cruelty, violence or revolting or abhorrent phenomena in such a way that they offend against the standards of morality, decency and propriety generally accepted by reasonable adults to the extent that they should not be classified; or b) depict in a way that is likely to cause offence to a reasonable adult a minor who is or who looks like, a person under 16 (whether engaged or not in sexual activity); or c) promote, incite or instruct in matters of crime or violence.

Potential Film's first successful defence was that Breillat, the provocateur herself, had been behind the camera. 'For a film to depict a person in a demeaning manner,' the report reads,

the guidelines require that the depiction must be either indirectly or directly sexual in nature and must debase or appear to debase the person or the character depicted. In the Board's majority view the film is a serious study from a feminist viewpoint of one woman's journey from emotional subservience to the man she loves who physically rejects her, to personal independence and fulfilment. As such, it is anything but a demeaning portrayal. The film does not depersonalise her nor does it invite hatred or ridicule in the viewer.

The board therefore deemed *Romance* 'of serious intent and considered by many to have artistic merit ... not exploitative or gratuitous ... generally a thought-provoking discourse on the role and experience of a woman in a couple relationship from a radical feminist perspective and that it contains few popular entertainment values [and] likely to appeal to a relatively sophisticated section of the public with some familiarity with the issues it raises.' They added a pat on the back of Australian punters, saying: 'In reaching this conclusion the Board was influenced by the belief that the Australian community is more accepting of a film containing controversial elements that are sexual in nature, are not violent or exploitative of women, are placed in a serious artistic context, and are unlikely to cause harm to an adult viewer.' But more accepting than whom? Other reasonable adults from the UK, apparently, as the British censors cut out a single second of visible semen, which survived our local release. The Australian decision wasn't unanimous, of course; a minority of the review board insisted the high-impact sequences were 'exploitative' and therefore 'could not be accommodated in the R18+ category'. But a minority is just that, so the R-rating was carried.

The overturned rating wasn't just a win for *Romance*. In fact, another paragraph in the board's report ended up changing the classification game entirely by effectively allowing real sex in R-rated features. 'In the R18+ Restricted classification, sexual activity may be realistically simulated; the general rule is "simulation, yes—the real thing no,"' they wrote, perhaps not foreseeing the deluge that would soon befall them after these next sentences:

> For the most part the sexual activity depicted is simulated albeit at times very realistically. 'The real thing' possibly may have occurred in the fellatio scene, and certainly in the masturbation scenes. The 'rule' referred to above is expressed to be a general rule, implying the possibility of exceptions in a limited number of instances. After careful consideration the majority of the Board decided that the limited discretion implicit in the application of the rule should be exercised in this film's favour.

This meant a precedent had now been set for films with actual sexual activity, allowing them to be potentially rated R18+ rather than classified X18+ or even refused classification. So came the sex avalanche. As reported by Refused Classification (the encyclopaedic website tracking Australia's censorship history), about 57 films released between 2000 and 2014 managed an R18+ certificate despite featuring unsimulated sex acts. That includes films of high (albeit provocative) art, such as Michael Haneke's *The Piano Teacher*, Lars von Trier's *Antichrist* and John Cameron Mitchell's *Shortbus*; much-maligned misfires, such as Vincent Gallo's *The Brown Bunny*; and then some miscellany, including the collected videos of German metal band Rammstein (specifically, their clip for 'Pussy'). Most fascinating, however, are the banned or censored films that were re-evaluated (and restored) post *Romance*, such as 1998's *I Stand Alone* from Gaspar Noé and Lars von Trier's *The Idiots*; Paul Verhoeven's 1985 effort *Spetters*; 1981's *Taxi zum Klo* (which boasts a golden shower, to boot); 1976's *In the Realm of the Senses* (justice for PIFF!); and 1978's *1900*, in which Robert De Niro and Gérard Depardieu are both visibly masturbated by the same sex worker at the same time (the scene made it to cinemas, but not videotape in 1985, until it returned on DVD in 2005).

In the year 2011, a coalition of religious right groups—including Melinda Tankard Reist's Collective Shout; the Australian Christian Lobby, founded in 1995; the now-defunct anti-gay collective Salt Shakers; and who else but Fred Nile's FamilyVoice Australia?—addressed an inquiry of the classification system chaired by conservative Tasmanian senator Guy Barnett, decrying the decision that awarded *Romance* an R-rating and subsequently so many other films with unsimulated sex. They felt that 'actual sex' was the clear dividing line between R18+ films and those that should be rated X18+ (or not at all). The Christian groups found themselves to be odd bedfellows with Australia's adult film distributors, who were also upset with the *Romance* classification, albeit for different reasons. As the latter group argued in their submissions, since X18+ films were not legal in most states, they had to have their 'hardcore' scenes scrubbed to warrant an R-rating. This effectively meant they couldn't include 'actual sex'. Those that did were immediately rated X. But if *Romance* could earn an R-rating with actual sex, this meant the goalposts had been moved for everyone but adult filmmakers and distributors, who faced stricter guidelines in the X18+ category. Once again, the government didn't budge.

But back to the early 2000s. You can imagine the frustration of the distributors of the big budget (at $US450,000) porno *Dream Quest* in October of 2000, who learnt it was refused classification by the OFLC for simply featuring PG-level violence, mere months after the *Romance* ruling. 'Under the Guidelines for the Classification of Films and Videos, material containing consensual sexually explicit activity cannot contain depictions of violence, sexual violence, sexualised violence or coercion ... In the Board's view this film contains depictions of violence which warrant an 'RC' classification,' the finding for the film reads. Fair enough. Or is it? Because here is the description of violence from the board's same report:

> [At] 98mins – This sequence commences with the heroine (Sarah) and another woman, who is her guide, riding on a horse up to a statue on which there is a warning about venturing any further. The guide tells Sarah to ride off, saying that she will take care of any difficulties regarding the warning. The statue then comes to life. In the Board's majority opinion the clashing of their swords that ensues constitutes a depiction of violence as the swords are weapons and they are used with an intent to harm. This is further indicated by the dialogue exchange between them which refers to, for example, 'it would be a shame to slay one so magnificent' and the fact that one of them will 'not live to see the dawn'.

Uhh, okay, maybe the next cited example is a little more graphic:

> [At] 102mins – In this sequence Vladimir tries to convince Sarah to stay with him, offering to set Fantasy free if she agrees. She vows never to give in to his request and is taken away protesting 'no!' repeatedly as Vladimir tells her that she and Fantasy will both remain his prisoners forever. In the Board's majority opinion her protestations combined with the two guards pulling her towards a cell constitute violence as there is force used against an unwilling participant with the threat of further force if she does not accede to Vladimir's wishes.

Perhaps the third and final example of 'violence' will clarify its unacceptable intermingling with sex:

> [At] 103mins – Feet are seen walking in the darkened corridors of the dungeon cells as a male walks up to a guard and implicitly hits him on the head from behind, rendering him unconscious. He takes the guard's keys and goes in to rescue Sarah. In the Board's unanimous opinion the hit on the head constitutes an act of violence which is not permissible in a film containing consensual sexually explicit activity and thus warrants an 'RC' classification.

Hmm. So it turns out, you simply can't have violence in a film with sexually explicit activity, even if the sex acts themselves are consensual in context. Distributor AXIS (a division of adultshop.com) appealed the decision, saying, 'It does not offend, in our view, against the stricture that X films should not contain violence or sexualised violence as the construction of plot, narrative, sets and filmic representation allows for the types of contretemps portrayed to fall within the visual lexicon of the reasonable adult with no suggestion of or incitement to violence or sexualised violence.'

Though they should have earned some brownie points by using 'contretemps' in a sentence, their conclusion may have rubbed the board the wrong way:

> To suggest that *Dream Quest* is part of a greater narrative on violence is so laughable as to make a complete mockery of the classification process in trying to unclassify offensive titles. As an industry great investment is

being made to comply with the guidelines with little in the way of actual benchmarks or definitions, with severe financial detriment to the industry. In cases such as this where film[s] of significant artistic and erotic merit are being released, providing the adult viewer with material that is wholly accessible to women, couples and singles which presents all parties in a decent and respectable fashion are being refused classification on such spurious terms, the board seems to be in breach of their charter of care to the community of reasonable adults they purport to represent.

In their submission to the review board, AXIS specifically called out the *Romance* decision: 'Without the OFLC guidelines being at all detailed or specific, the industry has regulated along an understanding of what is permissible in R18+, a category which hasn't changed its guidelines for content in the recent amendments. All attempts are made by AXIS to submit films that comply with guidelines, and in the light of recent decisions on films such as *Romance* which contain very explicit sex to be housed in the R18+ category, the denial of *Dream Quest* with its partially clothed and art house style filmic techniques to be denied this rating smacks of hypocrisy and discrimination.'

'I vehemently argue that this film is well and truly housed within the R18+ guidelines, and to refresh your memories on the recent benchmarks, I have for you some shots from *Romance* juxtaposed with the supposedly offending material from *Dream Quest*,' their appeal continued, and seemingly a presentation followed. 'If the rule is "simulated yes, real no" for classifying R, then I would pose the question that if a man and woman are engaged in what appears to be actual sex, it stands to reason that a viewer happening across the scene may actually interpret that scene as a graphic representation of consensual sex,' they added.

> It is not that they know the couple on the screen are doing it, it is rather that they have no proof that they are not doing it except their understandings of the classifications such as they are. The simulation is then really for the benefit of the OFLC's peace of mind and moral code, not the viewers. Sex is a part of our society, on every level, it has become the essential commodity of our time, for better or for worse. Films like the R-rated version of *Dream Quest* are so tame, so nice, so vanilla as to make the RC classification totally laughable.

AXIS saved its most cutting lines for its final paragraphs:

> Cannibalism, penetration but no oral please, we're censors. It is a pathetic joke that the industry which is treated like pariahs is more accountable and dedicated to benchmarking and sanitising unsafe images than the bureaucrats who condemn us. *Romance* is a film that portrays sex as a dark, dirty and violating experience that is tantamount to rape and abuse. *Dream Quest* portrays sex as an experience that is fun, sensual, uplifting and liberating. The brief snatches of what I argue are just as easily simulated scenes are nowhere near as explicit as others that the board has classified with an R.

The review board didn't blink. AXIS trimmed *Dream Quest* until it earned its R-rating in 2001, at a total appeal cost of $30,000. They also failed to get clemency for fellow RC films *Codename Ecstasy*, *Private Superfuckers 7* and *Euro Angels Hardball 6: Anal Maniac*, wherein 'a flexible long (say 25cm), black sausage shaped, with bulges like golfballs, device was fed into the anus', per the review board's decision report. (At least the 138-minute sequel *Euro Angels Hardball 11: Analholics* managed an X-rating in 2002.)

†

Reading about this exchange, I was reminded of a recent example that may have caused a similar stir ... had the local distributor let the board see their film upon its debut. Following Travis Mathews' earlier recommendation, I watched 2021's *Violation* (from directors Dusty Mancinelli and Madeleine Sims-Fewer) on the horror-dedicated streaming service Shudder, as it debuted mere weeks after our chat, and as Mathews had insisted, the sequence featuring a visibly erect penis was contextually relevant but undeniably taboo-busting.

Violation centres on two sisters holidaying in Canadian cottage country with their husbands. After Miriam (Sims-Fewer) is raped by her sister's partner, Dylan (Jesse LaVercombe), she summons him to a secluded location and flirts with him until he strips naked and performs a blindfolded autoerotic act. She then knocks him unconscious and commences a graphic dismantling of his body. Masturbation, by the board's book, counts as unsimulated sex (see also: *PVT Chat*), so I was especially curious why the board had decided to let it fly, considering it occurs in a sequence that also culminates with violence (first, a bashing of the head, and eventually, the draining and dismembering of a dead body, in unflinching detail). However, upon investigation, I discovered it wasn't classified by the board at all. In fact, it was marked as 'Not Rated' on Shudder, despite it being a legal requirement in Australia—under the National Classification Scheme—for films to be classified before going on sale or becoming available for hire (except those exempt from classification, of course). And no, it's not just because it's on Shudder, which is owned by AMC Networks in America: the scheme includes content that's available on streaming services to the Australian public too. Narrative dramas like *Violation* wouldn't be considered exempt. But it turns out the onus is on publishers to have their content classified, and the current Classification Board doesn't have enforcement powers in relation to publishers granting Australians access to unclassified films. It's the perfect crime: you can only be caught if you hand yourself in, and by that point, it's no longer technically a crime. It's not a legal loophole, per se, but it meant I could watch *Violation* without the board actively seeking it out and slapping it with an RC, which could have been the case if the local publisher decided to submit it first. As Mathews asked: 'People manage to see these films in Australia, yeah?' Yeah.

I asked film scholar and author of *Violent Women in Contemporary Cinema*, Dr Janice Loreck, if she thought *Violation* would have been passed by the board with an R-rating. 'I think ultimately, probably no,' she tells me. 'I think they probably would have asked for some cuts. Just because of the length of time that certain images are on screen.' And just as Mathews initially pointed out, Dr Loreck felt that the penis' state of arousal was a key issue: 'That's just a signifier of hardcore pornography and therefore that's what would have been the problem when it came up against the censorship board, because certain images get associated with certain genres.'

I wondered if the fact that this film had been co-directed by a woman, much like *Romance*, might have earned it a pass; not for some reason of gender inequity, but because the perspective of the female lens challenged its potentially exploitative reading. 'I rewatched *Romance* a couple of weeks ago,' Dr Loreck countered, 'and that type of [full frontal male] nudity is not on screen for very long at all. It's actually only a couple of seconds. Whereas in [*Violation*], it is on-screen for quite a long time. It's also in addition to intense violence and very graphic violence, and so I do think that does change the context.'

'[*Romance*] was very clearly positioned as an arthouse film,' she adds.

> It was very intellectualised. It has lots of voiceover and there's no mistaking the earnestness of its intent, because it's literally presented

in the voiceover dialogue. She's literally talking about sexuality and the difference between men and women, so I think that framing is really key in *Romance* and changes the way in which people view it. I think this film, *Violation*, is also very earnest; however, it articulates its earnestness very differently, which has to do with presenting the troubling [nature] of violence. And also, look, yeah: I do think it has to do with the fact that it's a genre film, not positioned within this arthouse milieu, and I certainly think that would have affected how it was perceived by a censorship body.

For what it's worth, she notes, 'I've seen worse, I will say that straight up. *Salò*, for example, is harder to watch than this film.' Dr Loreck also adds to the list the aforementioned *Baise-Moi*, which has 'a rape sequence that is incredibly intense'. 'I think you can screen it in Australia, you just can't distribute it,' she wonders aloud. If only it was that simple.

In October 2001, a 77-minute edit of *Baise-Moi* was passed by the OFLC, though the full uncut version has been refused classification four times since. That standing R18+ version was at first protested by usual suspects Fred Nile, Brian Harradine, Trish Draper and De-Anne Kelly, along with the feeling-hard-done-by porn lobby group Eros Association. It is nevertheless easily available on streaming services today. Written and directed by women—Virginie Despentes and Coralie Trinh Thi—*Baise-Moi* concerns a part-time sex worker and an occasional porn actress (played by Karen Bach and Raffaëla Anderson, respectively) who go on a killing spree after they are gang-raped in a garage. Comparing the cut and uncut versions of *Baise-Moi* is not the same as comparing the edited editions of *Romance*, which comes down to one added second of semen. *Baise-Moi*'s shocking rape sequence initially included a close-up shot of real penetration, which Despentes defended as being vital to demonstrate the violation of the body in the act of rape. But now, the rape in the Australian version of *Baise-Moi* is half the length of the original, with no penetration or genitalia shown, though its unpleasantness is not diminished. There are other sex scenes in which the 'sex' has been removed. During my own viewing, I wrote in a notepad that the Australian edit has 'no fellatio, no genitals, no penetration'. But worse than that are the scars left on our local version: awkward cuts in music and obvious edits hardly bandage over what is clearly the handiwork of the distributor's excisions to make it fit an R-rating. The merits of *Baise-Moi* are worthy of debate, but the value of seeing this shredded collection of sequences is effectively nil. The review board agreed, saying in their decision report that the original uncut feature had 'a strong plot, good characterisation, compelling and believable performances by the actors Bach and Anderson, an outstanding musical score which enriches the visual elements and entertains the viewer/listener with rich melody, rhythm and beat, and some integrity of cultural purpose.' Still, they slapped it with a ban.

As our conversation winds down, Dr Loreck raises the hypothetical question that has been flitting around in the back of my mind as I write this book about the extremes of cinema; it's also the practical question I would want the board to consider each time a film winds up under their microscope: 'My question whenever I watch a film is: "Is this ethical?"' she explains. 'I think that [*Violation*] is an ethical film in what it's aiming to do, and so I am glad that it's available to be seen. And frankly I really do believe that adults should be able to watch media and should not be infantilised by censorship bodies.' She continues:

> I think some people may object to the execution of how it's done in *Violation*, simply because it is so uncompromising in terms of what it shows, and one could argue you didn't need to show as much as the film shows in order to remind you that killing a person is awful and not redemptive. [But] I believe that cinema, like other art forms, is interested in the extremes of experience, so this is interested in an extreme of human experience, therefore it is extreme.

The late film critic Roger Ebert, in his review of director Marco Bellocchio's scandalous 1987 release *Devil in the Flesh*, made the clarifying observation that when actors get naked and start having unsimulated sex, a movie shifts into documentary mode. In that political drama, leading lady (and mainstream Dutch star) Maruschka Detmers goes down on her male co-star for a few seconds of fellatio. Ebert had this to say of the unsimulated sex act: 'The fellatio scene is not very erotic, but then the political scenes are not very political.' Perhaps he had it twisted: maybe the fellatio was the political part, forcing the audience into making a value judgement not only of the character, but the filmmakers themselves, and therefore reflecting the perspective of 'prude' or 'pornography apologist' onto themselves. (In Australia, *Devil in the Flesh* went unreleased; we got an M-rated Australian production by the same name and based on the same source novel a couple years later instead, directed by Scott Murray of *Cinema Papers* renown.) Our Classification Board was primed to make the distinction between 'porn' and 'the rest' on behalf of cinemagoers until the *Romance* ruling. From that point on, everyone from David Haines, the Australian adult film distributors, AXIS and Shudder to the wowsers of Collective Shout, the Australian Christian Lobby, Salt Shakers and FamilyVoice Australia came to the agreement that the Board needs to clarify the circumstances around R18+, X18+ and RC-ratings. To this writer, the distinction has become clear: it's no longer about degrees of sex or nudity; it's about morality.

With their rating of *Romance* in 2000, the board may have been perceived as becoming more open-minded from an outsider's perspective, but actually, they were perhaps applying a moral bias more explicitly; moving away from the model—as Dr Loreck describes it—'Oh, this particular body part is on the screen for this particular amount of time, therefore we can't allow it to be shown.' Instead, their decisions in the early 2000s seemed to be largely based on the ethical assessment of its Board, which casts the bans of *Ken Park*, *A Serbian Film* and *I Want Your Love* in a new light. It suggests little patience for either unsimulated gay sex or sex acts that are in proximity to violence, no matter the artistic intent (or the conditions under which the acts were filmed). That indicates the classification process is not as transparent these days as believed, with some kind of further evaluation occurring behind the scenes, and between the lines of the legislation. The checklist of classifiable elements was apparently a smokescreen, to the frustration of those aforementioned distributors, no doubt. As I said earlier, this is actually what I thought I'd wanted from a Classification Board. But then, it really depends who's on the board.

In a 2001 column for *The Guardian*, Alexander Linklater—then-boyfriend of New Zealand actress Kerry Fox—reflected on the experience of witnessing Fox take her co-star Mark Rylance's erect penis into her mouth for the solemn Patrice Chéreau film *Intimacy*. The article—weirdly fixed on the jealousy of Fox's partner, rather than Fox's viewpoint—sees Linklater ultimately justify the unsimulated act as legitimate artistic expression. 'So why, if it's an illusion, the need to go as far as the film does? Why the need to show real oral sex, even if only briefly? And why the need to show, more often, Mark with an erection?' he asks rhetorically. 'It is to take the internal logic of a work of art to a conclusion; that is its integrity. In this case, it is to take a story that deals with sex as far as the actors can allow, without compromising their personal lives, and to elicit from them the most powerful performances of which they are capable.' That 'integrity' allowed *Intimacy* to escape the clutches of the Classification Board with an R-rating for 'high level sex scenes', nearly two years after *Romance* earned the same. Much like 'morality', however, 'integrity' is in the eye of the beholder. For confirmation on the 21st-century practice of classification, there remained only one body left to ask: the censors themselves.

EFFED UP FACT:

When Sacha Baron Cohen followed up *Borat* with *Bruno* in 2009, most critics agreed that the film didn't quite reach the heights of his (Oscar-nominated!) previous flick. The censors, however, definitely felt it hit a new low. They gave the picture an R18+ classification, so Universal Pictures decided to cut the most extreme scene and resubmit it for a softer rating. They succeeded in getting an MA15+ classification, but viewers missed out on an absurd sex montage between Austrian fashionista Bruno and his boyfriend. The scene was added back to the film's R-rated Blu-ray release in 2009, titled 'UN-CUT EDITION, BULGING WITH UNSEEN EXTRAS'. They weren't lying.

CHAPTER 13

IN THE REALM OF THE CENSORS

In the opening scene of Prano Bailey-Bond's 2021 horror-satire *Censor*, a bespectacled prude called Enid watches a gory VHS tape with her male colleague, declaring which part of this video nasty needs to be excised: 'It's the eye gouging. It's too realistic.' Her fellow censor tries to reason with her, though his tongue is placed firmly in cheek, perhaps knowing that he can't salvage the sequence given the film's early 1980s context, at the height of the UK's moral panic over violent cinema: 'See it less as an eye-gouging, more part of a grand tradition. It's no worse than the Cyclops in Homer. It's Gloucester in Lear. It's *Un Chien Andalou*.' But Enid doesn't see the joke; only a tapestry of compromise. 'I salvaged the tug of war with the intestines. Kept most of the screwdriver stuff. And I've only trimmed the tiniest bit of the end of the genitals. But some things should be left to the imagination.'

Such is the conundrum of the censor: they need a strong enough stomach to endure with clinical banality whatever horrible imagery filmmakers dare to conjure for them, but a moral sense (and even maybe a conservative bent) to edit for the sake of 'community standards'. Basically they need to decide what we shouldn't see even though they seemed to see it fine.

Margaret Anderson—who served as deputy director of the Australian Classification Board from 2013 to 2017, acting director in 2017 and director from 2018 to 2020—does not, unlike many of her predecessors, seem like the kind who needed to retire to a chaise longue to recuperate at the end of a long day in the classification trenches. Nor does she relish the idea of censorship—like Enid in *Censor*—but she too is a strong advocate for the need for classification, even declaring her adoration for the *Classification Act* when we spoke in 2022. Where she and Enid intersect is in their 'detachment' while viewing both horror movies and also real footage of incredibly violent acts. 'Detachment is very much what [we] were aiming for,' she tells me. 'Having said that, you have no concept of what it is to stone a human being until you see it done,' she continues, reminding me that horror films have nothing on the real-life depravity she was required to classify.

Bailey-Bond's film finally morphs into the kind of graphic 'video nasty' Enid's been watching (too much of, it turns out), and the female director reclaims some ownership of the genre's historic trend towards violence against women with some pointed sleazy-dude slaughtering. (After watching a graphic rape scene that's been submitted for censorship, a female colleague of Enid's asks, 'What is it with these directors?' Enid doesn't have to hesitate: 'Male inadequacy revenge catharsis.') Of course, besides being a wicked throwback to Margaret Thatcher's puritanical reign—with a phantasmagorical colour palette that would make Dario Argento proud—*Censor* could even be accused of priggishness itself, given that Enid slowly goes round the bend and turns murderous after watching one too many nasties, including a snuff film that may or may not have starred her once-abducted sister. In that sense, Bailey-Bond's almost suggesting what the censors of the time argued as well: movies with troubling, violent, depraved content can turn its viewers into troubling, violent, depraved consumers. Anderson, for her part, acknowledges the contradiction of participating in passive observation of content you believe should be banned. 'You sit there thinking, 'whoa', and you do have to have that reaction, because to not have that reaction is subnormal,' she says. 'In a funny kind of way, you're doing this funny combination of not being affected by it, yet you do all need to acknowledge that it's putrid, weird shit, you know?'

In *Censor*, Enid insists, 'We can't afford to make mistakes', when it comes to leaving offensive content uncut, so gravely does she feel the responsibility of her duty. However, the film does offer a counterargument, with one character intoning to Enid, 'violence is an inherent part of human nature and it's important that we find a cathartic outlet for it.' Another says humans are equipped to self-censor when confronted by challenging imagery: 'You'd be surprised what the human brain can edit out when it can't handle the truth.' Perhaps censors, by definition, are in the business of evading social catharsis, editing out the truth in favour of a shinier reflection of society.

Of course, Anderson was not a censor. She makes that clear. Set aside the fact that assigning the RC classification effectively bans movies in Australia. She never slashed and re-edited submissions to make them more palatable to an imagined audience. She was a 'classifier'; one who 'loves' the National Classification Code. 'I love it because it starts from a position of saying that classification decisions give effect that adults should be able to read, hear, see and play what they want, and I love that. I think that needs to be enshrined in stone. That should never ever waver.

That should be the starting point for classification.' But she also came to the Board with a steelier resolve than most, having begun her career in the criminal justice sector, classifying prisoners for maximum, medium or minimum security. 'When you're classifying a person, whether they're on remand or been sentenced, you ought to be giving them the lowest possible classification that you can so that you are affording them the rights and protection that you are affording others, be it staff or other prisoners,' she explains. 'You are [also] making sure that you're not giving them such a low classification that you're bringing into disrepute the whole criminal justice system. By that I mean, can you imagine: someone commits a murder, gets sentenced today to 15 years with a non-parole period of 12 years. You'd be really pissed off if you were the judge, a member of the community or the victim's family if that person next week got classified minimum security. You'd think: "You've gotta be kidding me."' She adds, 'The classification of media is exactly the same legal concept. You've got some kind of a structure. It needs to be interpreted. And it needs to be applied ethically and with consistency. And I like that intellectual challenge.'

Anderson had long dreamed of getting into film classification, spurred in retaliation to Fred Nile. 'I remember saying to my parents when I was about 15 that I wanted to decide what people were going to be able to see at the movies and on TV,' she laughs in recollection. 'I knew there was a concept of a chief censor back then, and I reckon there must have been some kind of contentious issue ... I dunno, Fred Nile got his knickers in a twist at some point; *The Last Temptation of Christ*, I think, was the film ... There was some contemporary issue that caused me to go to my parents, "That's it, I'm going to be the chief censor one day!"' In time, though, the appeal of bucking 'censorship' had been supplanted thanks to her experience classifying prisoners: 'What I really liked about what had happened since I was 15 and now decades later as an adult looking at a potential job for me to do, was that the concept of censoring had long and truly gone.' This avowed fan of arthouse cinema (who nonetheless cops to seeing *Bohemian Rhapsody* four times in theatres, even after sitting through it for classification purposes) was sold on the job thanks to the introduction of the *Classification Act* in 1995. She explains:

> What that says was: censorship is out. Not interested in having a cuts list. Not interested in the government of Australia or one of its instrumentalities telling creatives what they can or cannot have in a film or a computer game or a piece of literature. What we are going to do is set up

a system whereby whatever is submitted for classification gets classified. If it exceeds what can be accommodated in that G to R18+ [range] and it's not an X18+ film, then it will still get a classification, but that classification will be RC, for Refused Classification. There are guidelines sitting there in that legislation but there is nothing so prescriptive or boring that is saying to you, for example, 'Oh well, five lots of fuck equals an M.' There's no formula in classifying inmates or classifying media.

Most filmmakers and artists would agree that there are such things that should be banned in our new audio-visual paradigm, such as the footage of the Christchurch massacre that was livestreamed onto Facebook and could have remained available for posterity without the intervention of a classification board to render it illegal. (It was during Anderson's tenure that this was viewed and refused classification.) Is there a moral line that can be drawn to help us differentiate what should and shouldn't be banned? Well, not according to Peter Greenaway, director of *The Cook, The Thief, His Wife and Her Lover*, who was asked in the *Sydney Morning Herald* if the absence of 'moral imperative' in his films disqualified them from consideration as art. 'Good God! Australia must be the last moral nation on Earth, if that's any indication,' he argued. 'What is morality in art anyway? I thought that whole concept had well and truly died by now, or at least since the 1920s. Post-modernism doesn't even recognise the concept of morality, it's just an irrelevant concern.'

There are indeed models of reasoning that can be applied to help the Classification Board find a middle ground between thoughtful, contextual analysis and emotionally detached box-ticking. Dr Ralph Potter of the Harvard Divinity School developed what would become known as the 'Potter Box' in the 1960s; a diagram that includes four dimensions of moral analysis. Picture a grid of squares, with arrows pointing clockwise from the first square to the second, from the second to the third, and from the third to the fourth. A user of the Potter Box method begins by 'defining' the situation, or as we'd apply it here, the content of the film that has raised the board's hackles. Definition is followed by a consideration of the 'values' that might see that problematic content cut (if not banned outright) or kept, requiring the evaluator to weigh up the social benefit of upholding freedom of artistic expression against protecting the public from seeing it. Next, 'principles' are considered, and these may be the not-usually-negotiables the board relies upon ('cunt' not being allowed in an M-rated film, for example). Finally, the board would outline their 'loyalties', which is when the board might consider whom their decision benefits most. The latter is perhaps most important: while a decision might be made in the 'principles' quadrant, the consideration of 'loyalties' would force the board to acknowledge why they really made that specific call. Perhaps they came to a conclusion that most benefited themselves, banning a movie that may have generated controversy if released and drawing greater scrutiny upon themselves. Maybe they gave a pass to a larger studio film because they knew the studio had the resources to advocate for an appeal to the Classification Review Board (and generate public sympathy) anyway. Maybe they decided to ban a film because it offended them personally, if not in ways that were clearly defined by the Board's principles. The 'loyalties' quadrant won't always change a decision, but it would make the Board more considerate of their allegiances, their deficiencies, or, ideally, their sound reasoning.

'Rarely does a distributor, certainly of a major film, object to a few seconds being cut out of a film for a word or something like that,' David Stratton tells me, hinting at where 'loyalties' stood in decisions by censors and distributors alike: the financial bottom line. 'I remember back in [the late 1960s] being on television with the then-managing director of Hoyts,' Stratton continues.

> I was promulgating the idea of having an Adults Only classification, as happened in the UK and other places. He said, 'I would rather cut 15 minutes from a film than have my staff decide the age of a patron.' That was the attitude, and soon after that's what happened to *Bonnie & Clyde*. I don't know if 15 minutes was cut, but a lot was cut out of *Bonnie & Clyde* on its original release, and the same with *The Wild Bunch* and quite a number of other films before the censorship reform happened and the R classification came in. A lot of films were banned altogether; a lot of significant films. Distributors would tend not to scream about a ban; not to publicise it, because they didn't want to upset the censors. When *The Night of the Hunter* was banned in 1955 on the grounds of blasphemy, of all things, did United Artists complain? No of course they didn't. They thought, 'Oh well, it wouldn't have made any money anyway' and chalked it off to experience.

'This of course has always, always happened,' he adds. 'It's reprehensible, but it's [the distributors'] film, so I presume they get permission from the producer; probably not the director. I know a notorious case was the *Men in Black* films, where the distributor routinely reduced them to get an M-rating. That I think happens more than we know.'

David Roe of the defunct Perth International Film Festival—who certainly has no reason to offer much sympathy to the classifiers of the time—concedes it wasn't always censors who were doing the cutting. 'I think sometimes it was the distributor trimming the sails to suit the winds before they even submitted it to the censor,' he tells me. 'It could well have been the distributor not appreciating what they would see as an overlong film and the limitations that placed on the number of sessions they could run per day. It was shocking.'

The Potter Box model isn't foolproof; as mentioned, it may not change anything except how the Board looks at—or justifies—itself. It wouldn't have spared *Men in Black*, which was cut down by its own distributors several times in pursuit of a lower rating, which meant removing *just* the right amount of alien-on-human violence, including the disposal of an empty skin bag in a crater and the sound of a thud after an extra-terrestrial walks off a rooftop. But there are other moral guidelines to consider. Aristotle argued that 'moral virtue is a middle state determined by practical wisdom' (or, as Confucius put it centuries earlier, 'moral virtue is the appropriate location between two extremes'), suggesting morality was found in some kind of community 'mean'. The application of this ethical model would make little room for challenging art, no matter the nuance Aristotle or Confucius might have intended in its usage. Eighteenth-century German philosopher Immanuel Kant believed we should 'act on that maxim which you will to become universal law'. It may sound utilitarian, but Kant was conveying that we should be wary of how we *apply* universal laws; if you want to ban a film for *this* reason, you better be ready to ban all relevant films for the exact same reason. Perhaps, if Kant's maxim of categorical imperative was applied, there'd be no banned films at all. But here in the real world, Kant's unbreakable deontological ethics do not have the requisite wriggle room we're looking for. Even more functional was John Stuart Mill, the 19th-century Brit who sought 'the greatest happiness for the greatest number'. Yet again, there's an obstacle in its application: what if the happiness of the mainstream cinema-watching public was prioritised over the tastes and appreciations of the arthouse regulars who might enjoy or have a meaningful experience with *Romance* or *Baise-Moi*? Not all films are for all people—that should be the point of classification—but applying Mill's principle of utility to censorship could cause widespread havoc for any filmmakers or film fans on the fringes. We see how attaching ethical models to classification can result in roundabout, purely academic conversations, and few results. Still, to quote Walter Sobchak from *The Big Lebowski* (another great fount of philosophical reasoning), 'At least it's an ethos.'

Of all these models, the National Classification Code can be most neatly squeezed into a Potter Box. It does, after all, clearly outline its values: 'a) adults should be able to read, hear, see and play what they want; b) minors should be protected from material likely to harm or disturb them; c) everyone should be protected from exposure to unsolicited material that they find offensive; [and] d) the need to take account of community concerns about: (i) depictions that condone or incite violence, particularly sexual violence and, (ii) the portrayal of persons in a demeaning manner.' Section 12 of the *Classification Act* then outlines the principles to take into account when evaluating films: 'importance of context; assessment of impact; and the six classifiable elements—themes, violence, sex, language, drug use and nudity.' There is, however, one non-negotiable under Section 9A: 'a film that advocates the doing of a terrorist act must be classified RC.' On any published Classification Review Board evaluation, we can even read which applicants challenged a rating (such as the Australian Christian Lobby against Netflix's *Cuties* in 2020) and if there are any interested parties who submitted letters or videos to help the board come to their decision. Even if the board's specific 'loyalties' may be kept private and unspoken, at least we have a shortlist to speculate about. But ultimately, it's a moot point. As Anderson explains, the process of classification was more 'instinctual' than Ralph Potter may want to hear:

> Did we apply the Potter Box method? No, we didn't. Did we bother about Aristotle or anybody else? (And I love Aristotle.) No, we didn't. Or Socrates? No, we didn't. One of the things I would very much say to people when they started was, 'I truly sincerely am not interested in what you personally think. What I truly, sincerely require you to do is to understand what the legislation is requiring us to do. And what I need you to understand is the framework that has been built around the six classifiable elements; so the themes through to sex, violence, nudity, drug use, coarse language. I need you to understand the frameworks that sit around those six classifiable elements for each of the classification categories.' I would also say to people, 'I need you to understand that

there will be material that you would not choose to watch. There are genres and films that you may never watch as an individual member of the community but you are going to be watching those here, and I need you to keep going back to the legislation, and consult your peers, but that's what you're here to do. Apply the legislation. You are not here to apply any kind of moral code.'

'Having said that,' she adds, 'the National Classification Code, particularly when it's talking about Refused Classification, refers in part and in passing to morality and to standards of morality, decency and propriety.' Anderson continues:

I think that's appropriate and the board didn't have any problems with understanding what that meant. I think it was really applying all of those common-sense things that largely people understand simply as a result, if you like, of the criminal laws of this country. Most people walking around the streets have got their own moral framework. We don't, generally speaking, walk around killing one another, because we know that killing is not acceptable and murdering someone is not something we want to embrace. Same with child sexual assault and all of that. Can you still have a dramatic film that deals with topics like murder or child sexual assault? The answer is yes. Of course you can. What becomes interesting is then saying, what happens when I've got a film that I'm being asked to watch and it is in fact not a dramatic film but is in fact a real piece of life where there is a child being sexually assaulted? You've got your own instinctive moral code around that. You sit there thinking, 'that eight-year-old is not an adult and has no adult frame of reference; that eight-year-old should have been protected; that eight-year-old should have never been subjected to that sexual abuse and if that sexual abuse had taken place, at no point would that eight-year-old have consented to it being filmed and being out there for all and sundry, potentially, to be gawking at.'

I have no problems at all—and I think it's actually a really important part of the National Classification Code—to reference morality, and I personally, from my time on the Board, don't have a problem with the concept of morality not being defined. I think everybody who was appointed to the board was capable of having a common person's understanding of what reasonably could be considered moral as opposed to amoral.

Our earlier suspicions about the board were both right and wrong. The board sticks to the legislation as rigorously as possible, while still applying a moral framework based on their individual values, principles and loyalties. So, the code—and the boards—are only flawed when they're operated by flawed people. And yet, we're all flawed people. There's no legislating away that particular problem.

Are there better models elsewhere in the world? There are certainly more convoluted systems, if you were already managing a stress headache trying to keep the different Australian classification boundaries straight in your memory. Some nations use censorship as an arm of state control of its people; others vary in letting government departments of Culture, or Child Protection, make the final calls; a few even outsource classification to private enterprise. Our friends in New Zealand have an Office of Film and Literature Classification, which demands that any film released in Aotearoa must have first been classified in Australia or Britain. They also are happy to 'cross-rate' anything that we graded G, PG or M. But even they have to complicate things: instead of an MA-rating, they have RP13, RP16 and RP18-ratings, with R standing for Restricted and P standing for Parent, as audiences are restricted to those respective ages (and older) unless accompanied by a parent or guardian. New Zealand features can also be rated R15, R16 and R18, which straight-up restricts anyone under the age of 15, 16 or 18, parental accompaniment be damned.

It was the original plan of this book to look beyond our shores to see who was doing it *right*, or at least better than Australia. Here's the thing: Australia's process of film classification is the most outmoded in the world, except for all the others. Perhaps the outlier is the Netherlands and their self-classifying 'Kijkwijzer' scheme, which is a questionnaire developed by scientists and academics measuring consumer habits, and is regularly reviewed to reflect the attitudes of parents and children. Complete the questionnaire and receive a rating based on a film's classifiable elements, which in the Netherlands are violence, fear, sex, discrimination, drugs and/or alcohol abuse and coarse language. The system—half-funded by government and half-funded by industry—has been so successful, it's been licenced to Belgium, Iceland, Slovenia and Turkey. So, okay, excluding Belgium, Iceland, Slovenia, Turkey and the Netherlands, maybe Australia's current system is best?

Well, not even Margaret Anderson would co-sign that conclusion. She is extremely forthright and open with me about the process of classification, its benefits, its failings and how it can be improved. She can even identify the ways in which the process of classifying prisoners is still better than classifying movies: 'Everyone's got a classification [in prison] and it gets reviewed regularly while they're inside serving their custodial sentence [unlike films]. And that's the problem. In so many jurisdictions, film classifications are set for life and that is absolutely foolish and stupid.'

'I understand entirely why films ought to be reclassified,' she says.

> There will be stuff that was classified back in the 1970s or 1980s in Australia. We didn't even have an MA15+ classification when those films were classified. So there is this unknown but extraordinary quantity of stuff that is sitting there today with an R classification, that you and I would roll around [laughing] on the carpet, and go, 'What the hell? That's not an R!' The classification act as it currently stands specifically prohibits you from classifying an already classified film. The only way to get around that at the moment is if you've got a film distributor wanting to bring out say the film on DVD or Blu-ray; you say to them, for God's sake, add something. I don't care what you add. Add bloopers. Add outtakes. One-minute intro of yourself going, 'Hi there, welcome to Madman or Umbrella or whatever film distributor, we really hope you like this 50th anniversary edition of *Rambo*.' The moment you add content, the film becomes unclassified. So, it means it's gotta be reclassified. And that is how we have regularly got around stupid, outmoded, old, irrelevant classifications.

She also confessed personal mistakes, saying 'every classifier has got one film that they got the classification wrong on.' Her great white whale was *The Secret Life of Pets*, which was rated G, even though, in her heart of hearts, she knew it should have been PG. 'I regret that to my dying day,' she says. 'The films that caused the most angst on the board are blasted children's films ... M/MA15+, nuh, that's clear. Nine times out of ten that is abundantly clear.'

Anderson even cites a children's film, specifically 2018's *Show Dogs*, as an example in which the Australian community became 'a bit vapid and hugely American', after a US woman got 'her knickers in a knot' observing that its scene of a dog getting its testicles waxed was tantamount to teaching children how to be groomed for sexual predation:

> For God's sake people, before you jump on the bandwagon, think about it and honestly ask yourself, do you really, truly think that a film directed at children would truly, honestly have included a scene that was intended for sexual predators to groom children? Dear God. Absolutely not. That scene was your standard kind of scene that is placed in a children's film that is there really for the adults so they're not completely bored shitless watching the film with their seven-year-old.

The American owner of *Show Dogs* nonetheless modified it and resubmitted to the board for re-classification the week of its release.

Anderson also noted that the job was, above all else, *fun*.

> Oh, God yeah, absolutely. It was fantastic fun. I think part of it was, there's an intellectual side to it as well as being a bit like on a treasure hunt. Because you're going into a film blind, you've got no idea what you're gonna be dished up, and so, it was absolutely the joy of sitting there going, 'surprise!' I loved it on multiple levels. And then just the conversations you might end up having with your colleagues about things and just seeing where people stood. And you very quickly worked out amongst your peers as to who was conservative, who'd led a shocking sheltered life [laughs], who had some very interesting, very relaxed attitudes to things, and it's not based on age or ethnicity. It's quite wonderful. I was quite surprised. I had two 25-year-olds, one I would have said was right out there, and the other one of whom I thought, 'oh my Lordy you're more conservative than I would have guessed', and it was quite fun because it challenged my own ageism [laughs] and expectations.

†

Censor wasn't the only 2021 release to turn a critical eye to the idea of censorship and the oftentimes hypocritical puritanism that takes root among those doing the censoring. Romanian filmmaker Radu Jude did just that with *Bad Luck Banging or*

Loony Porn (to include its full subtitle: *A Sketch for a Popular Film: No One Understands That the World Is Sinking on the Ocean of Time That Is So Very Deep and That Is Infested With Those Huge Crocodiles Called Decrepitude and Death*—emphasising the point that, maybe, a bit of on-screen nudity isn't humanity's biggest problem right now). If the flick's jokingly clumsy name doesn't make it crystal clear, Jude's picture hammers the point home over its 106 minutes: everyone gets worked up over pointless sexual scandals instead of worrying about the world's real ills (perhaps precisely because the world's ills are too multitudinous and overbearing to even comprehend).

Bad Luck Banging opens, without much warning or fanfare, to a graphic sex act (technically four sex acts) being self-taped by a couple. There's a blow job. Full frontal nudity (male and female). Anal sex (or maybe it's vaginal penetration from the rear, as is debated by characters in the final act). According to the Classification Board, which rated *Bad Luck Banging* R18+, this is 'actual sexual activity'. The British Board of Film Classification clarifies it further, referring to 'strong scenes of unsimulated sex, including graphic images of fellatio, cunnilingus, masturbation, and vaginal penetration' (I suppose that clears up the debate). The woman in the sequence is later revealed to be a schoolteacher named Emilia (played by Katia Pascariu), and her sex partner is her husband (whose face isn't glimpsed in the sex tape or the rest of the movie). When their video is leaked onto the web, she's hauled before her students' parents for a show trial in the school's courtyard. Filmed during the COVID-19 pandemic, everyone is masked and social-distancing, adding a layer of absurd irony to proceedings, not to mention additional tension, perhaps permeating from the reality of the shoot. As Jude says in the press notes:

> It was quite disappointing to have a few people every day taking off the mask whenever they could. I see it as a lack of respect for their colleagues, a kind of 'Fuck you, I don't care about anyone else, I want to feel good even if I can infect you.' This sometimes made the atmosphere on the set tense, but that's it. I felt relieved when the shooting ended, and we were all healthy.

Jude spends a good chunk of the film's first act following Emilia as she walks around Bucharest's shopping district, reeling from the humiliation, while the camera drifts towards provocations of the surrounding visual stimuli. Cinematographer Marius Panduru loses interest in Emilia's ordinariness (and the ordinariness of her 'scandalous' tape that, in essence, features a married couple having consensual sex), training his camera instead on real obscenities on public display: a window display of books about Jesus Christ; a giant cardboard standee promoting the anti-government, pro-militia cartoon *Paw Patrol*; a shelf of pregnant Barbies. (The most provocative involves a giant billboard advertisement featuring a woman soaked in milk, with the tagline, 'I like it deep.' It's selling chocolate.) Emilia walks past political and electoral signs, endures the noise pollution of ambulances and strides past a Pepsi-branded convenience store and a Coca Cola–branded kebab shop; she even briefly steps off the street to take a call in a chintzy sidewalk parlour full of electronic gambling machines. *Bad Luck Banging* claims 'pornografia' is derived from the Romanian phrase 'portrait of a prostitute'—and what else would you call these soulless vulgarities? Jude appears to suggest that the public exhibitions of our modern existence are more grotesque and pornographic than anything conducted behind closed doors. That includes the particularly modern sight of people with their masks pulled down around their neck, or under their nose, or not masked at all (see Jude's previous quote about the shoot—yikes). I spoke to Jude ahead of the release of the film in Australia, who indicated I was maybe predisposed to looking for vulgarity. 'Actually, there's a lot of beautiful, positive things [in that sequence]; things that are more neutral,' he explains.

> I didn't want only to show vulgarity. I wanted to show more complex things to invite the viewer to judge them and analyse the image. But of course, there's a lot of vulgarity because that's how this city is. Obscenity and classism; that was the idea of the film, to contrast the so-called vulgarity of the porn scene, of the sex tape, with real issues, real vulgarity, real obscenity, real depravity [which we've gotten] used to it that we don't even see it. But also, there are moments of beauty sometimes in all of this shit.

Regardless, there's no denying the underlying point: real life is way more R-rated than *Bad Luck Banging*. Yes, the opening sex is surprising in its frankness, but it does, after all, come contained within an R-rated movie (or, in the context of the film, as Emilia argues to the enraged parents: behind the veil of an adults-only website that parents should be shielding from their children anyway). We also see the vulgarities of existence Emilia endures each day without warning or classification: the decrepit abandoned buildings on her way to work; the woman causing a scene at a supermarket checkout; the passer-by staring down the camera and saying 'eat my cunt'. The final shot of the first act is of an abandoned cinema, out of action during the pandemic. Sitting atop it: five nude statues. As if the message hadn't been received, the picture's narrator relays the Greek myth of Perseus chopping off Medusa's head by only looking at her reflection, since beholding her directly would otherwise turn him to stone: 'The moral is that we do not, and cannot, see actual horrors because they paralyse us with blinding fear; and that we shall know what they look like only by watching images which reproduce their appearance. The cinema screen is Athena's polished shield.'

On the topic of 'actual sexual activity', Jude confirmed that the penetration hadn't been faked—but Katia Pascariu wasn't exactly the person engaged in it. 'In Romania, for many actors—less than in other countries in western Europe for instance—there's a kind of reservation, a kind of refusal many actors have not only to perform sex on screen or on stage but to appear nude sometimes,' he tells me.

> There are actors who say, 'Well I would never undress in front of a camera.' I'm not judging. I can understand them. No problem. Everybody has his or her own limits and we must respect that. But I still feel it's a little bit of ridiculousness because to be an actor means to use your body for expressing things; expressing the life. Being naked is a part of life. Sex is a part of life. I'm not speaking about real sex of course, that may be too far. Katia is not like that.

He continued:

> The first meeting we had, before me saying something, she said, 'Don't worry, I don't have any problem with nudity. I don't have any problem with performing sex on screen if necessary. I don't have any problem with a blow job. I don't have any problem with that.' I said, 'But Katia, at least the penetration scene we should get a body double.' She said, 'Okay if you can, it's good, if not, don't worry, I'll do it.' For the penetration scene we just replaced her with a porn actress. The husband [character] was a professional porn actor. His lack of erection in the scene is part of the [skill of his] profession, I don't know.

Filming the sex acts turned out to be one of the easiest parts of putting *Bad Luck Banging* together. 'We just did the scene. Very easy. I was much more stressed than [the actors] were. It was very easy to do in one hour, two hours. For the porn actors, they said, 'Only *that*?'

To the Australian Classification Board's credit, they did not take Jude's bait and ban the film outright for featuring unsimulated sex. Perhaps the flick fortuitously found an advantage in the board's 21st-century willingness to let actual sex acts remain uncut. Or, perhaps the board felt there was no need, given how there's no proximity to suggested violence in the acts, which are indeed performed as consensual between a heterosexual married couple, even though that may be a puritanical way to look at it too. ('In the board's opinion, the depictions of actual sexual activity are neither gratuitous nor exploitative, rather appearing to be part of a genuine exploration of sexuality and hypocrisy in contemporary society which are considered to be contextually relevant within the narrative of the film,' they wrote in their decision.) However, Facebook Australia was less forgiving. Mere days before the picture's release, an email from the local distributor, Potential Films, carried a warning to outlets that Facebook had deleted the picture's trailer due to it having 'porn' in the title (and, okay, because it had some nudity in it too), suggesting instead that all outlets refer to it simply as *Bad Luck Banging* on socials. The irony here is that Facebook has been historically slow to react when footage of live-streamed violence—such as the Christchurch massacre—or political and health misinformation is widely disseminated. But this Romanian art film's trailer, this, they catch.

Jude was surprised to learn about the censoring of his title on Facebook in Australia. I put to him that he had to have been aspiring for provocation by putting 'Porn' in the title to begin with. 'A little bit, yes,' he conceded,

> and a little bit more in the Romanian version of the title, which is the same but it has different connotations because the word for banging or shagging—that would be 'Babardeală'—is not only considered quite vulgar, it's also of Roma origin. So maybe people because of racism or internal racism wouldn't use that word because it's not only vulgar, it's of 'impure' origin.

Still, he was confused by Facebook Australia's decision. 'I wouldn't imagine it's so provocative [to be banned on Facebook], I wouldn't know that the world is so stiff towards these kinds of thing. I never imagined.'

†

Ultimately, Australia's Classification Board had bigger fish to fry than *Bad Luck Banging* as far as censorship and controversy was concerned, given *Nitram* was becoming a point of concern at the same time. Director Justin Kurzel's dramatisation of the events leading to the Port Arthur massacre hit a raw nerve in Tasmania—and wider Australia—before it was even released. Kurzel told the *Sydney Morning Herald* that he wanted to make the film upon hearing that the gun ownership laws introduced in the wake of the tragedy that cost 35 people their lives had been walked back in recent years: 'To hear that some of those reforms have been softened and there are more guns in Australia than there were in 1996 made me think about how these events are now being discussed and remembered … Australia has a real difficulty in looking at its history.' Upon the announcement of the film's existence, the community that was rocked by Martin Bryant's shooting spree two decades earlier was unequivocal in their denouncement of the project. Only the State Cinema screened the film in Hobart, prefaced by a lengthy message on their website explaining that they merely sought to provide for those who want to engage in the discussion, and a promise not to play its trailer before other sessions or place posters in the foyer. Indeed, the poster advertising the film on their website was simply a black sheet with the title, cast names and a few golden leaves to indicate its presence at prestigious festivals.

The picture itself is nearly devoid of violence, and the Classification Board awarded it an MA15+ for its 'strong themes'. 'While the shootings are not depicted on-screen, the overwhelming sense of menace imbued in the film's dispassionate depiction of events—and amplified by the viewer's awareness of the looming massacre—cumulatively generates a strong impact,' they wrote. But even if the board had wrung their hands over the content, the bounds of their classification guidelines denied them the opportunity to rate it any higher than MA15+. And though that's a win for fans of free speech and unlimited creative expression, experts have suggested films shouldn't be made about mass shooters, without exception, as this particular killer profile craves the fame—or infamy—a dedicated movie provides. Dr Glynn Greensmith, an expert in the field of mass shooting coverage, told ABC Radio Perth at *Nitram*'s release, 'It's such a complicated area. I'm far from being a censorship guy, and we are dealing with a piece of art, so I get very nervous.' Nonetheless: 'It's simple and it's surprising. My research involves Port Arthur as a case study. And there's a reason I'm using Port Arthur to try and talk to American colleagues about how we can potentially reduce the number of mass shootings, and that is the fact that the way we cover mass shootings is a big part of why they happen.' The counter-argument that we've always produced movies about real life tragedies—and its perpetrators—doesn't jibe with Dr Greensmith's particular academic assessment. 'If we change the way we cover mass shootings, we could stop quite a lot of them,' he added, noting how mass shootings increased from one every five years to 15 a year from August 1966, when Charles Whitman climbed to the top of the main building at the University of Texas in Austin and opened fire, and the media responded by uncovering everything about him in pursuit of an explanation.

> What the killers have told us is, 'When we commit this crime, we expect the news to talk about us a certain way', and the argument we're trying to make is, when we take some of those things that they're looking for away, they won't do this. We don't know what they'll do, it could be awful, but they won't do *this*.

'This film isn't just a piece of art; it taps into something evidence-based,' he continued.

> The way we have treated the killer of Port Arthur is a big reason why we haven't had another mass shooting in this country. It's not just about gun control. Something happened in Australia that day. We took from him what we know he sought. I've dealt directly with the psychiatrist who sat next to him in his hospital bed and said, 'Why did you do this? Tell me about yourself.' This isn't ethereal. We know what he was looking for. We know what drove him to this crime, as close as we can get there, because motive is difficult. We know that the shooting that happened a month before in Dunblane in Scotland was a major factor in turning this killer from suicidal to homicidal and suicidal. Something happened after Port Arthur. We as a nation said, 'No, you will not be what you seek. You won't be an anti-hero. You won't even be a monster. You'll be pathetic. You'll be reviled. And most importantly, you'll be forgotten.' We put him in a pit and we forgot him. I am of a belief and so is the psychiatrist who did the analysis that that is as important as gun control, because we changed the

script that day and told any potential mass shooter, 'You ain't gonna get what you're looking for.'

And yet, the board didn't make a moral call on the release of *Nitram*. They didn't step beyond the guidelines or go with their nervous gut and ban it. They left it to cinemas and citizens to debate the merits for themselves. In a way, it's an abdication of ethical duty. It's also exactly what this book argues the board should be doing: providing sound and safe advice to allow an educated and appropriate audience to consider works of art. Compare that to the real footage of the massacre, which was leaked in 2011 when a police training video containing footage of the aftermath landed online. The board gave it a Refused Classification rating on 30 August 2011.

†

Nearly 25 years before *Nitram*'s release, a similar fact-based drama incited a heated public debate—though that time, it indeed led to a stand-off with the Classification Board. The film, *Blackrock*, featured an 18-year-old Heath Ledger in one of his earliest roles, and like *Nitram* it dealt with dicey subject matter, having been based in part on the gang rape and vicious murder of 14-year-old Leigh Leigh in New South Wales. *Blackrock* was adapted by Nick Enright from his own play, which was commissioned by Newcastle's Freewheels Theatre in Education as a response to the 1989 crime. Though it changes the names of the real-life parties, it still concerns a gang rape of a girl, here called Tracy (played by Bojana Novakovic), and her subsequent murder. Directed by Steven Vidler and shot in the same Newcastle suburb of Stocktown as the crime took place, a *Sydney Morning Herald* report from 1996 captured the tense mood of the community. 'A former deputy lord mayor of Newcastle, Mr Frank Rigby, said the film would cause much heartache in a community that had managed to put the murder behind it,' Julie Delvecchio wrote, quoting Rigby: 'When are they going to stop torturing the innocent people of this world?' The report also included criminologist Dr Kerry Carrington of the University of Western Sydney, who said, 'I think that it is really important that this film does actually go ahead … I think that art has a very legitimate role to play in terms of making a social comment. [But] I can't imagine that it will heal the community. It will reignite the seething anger.' On 20 February 1997, the OFLC handed down an R-rating for the 102-minute flick, citing 'medium level violence', and it was this version that screened at the Sundance and Boston film festivals abroad. Despite earning some acclaim, no international distributors picked it up for release. Back at home, the filmmakers excised 12 whole minutes and resubmitted it for classification to achieve an MA-rating on 28 April. For its DVD release in 2003, the MA15+ cut stood.

Blackrock went on to gross more than one million dollars at the Australian box office in 1997, a significant financial benchmark that local films are still graded by today. Given the premise of the movie and its content, even in censored form, this is no small feat. It certainly appears to vindicate the decision to delete some of the more graphic detail from the rape sequence. But an excision of 12 minutes—more than 10 per cent of the whole picture—is a nearly unprecedented amount of movie to cut in the post-Chipp era of Australian film classification, or even the pre-Chipp era, frankly. Producer David Elfick justified the self-censorship of *Blackrock* at the Violence, Crime and the Entertainment Media conference held jointly by the Australian Institute of Criminology and the OFLC in Sydney that December. 'In writing the screenplay the decision is made by the producer, director and writer that the film should pull no punches but definitely should be seen by people 15 years and over,' he explained. 'Since the movie was about kids 14 to 18 years old, the 15 to 18-year-olds should not be restricted from seeing the film as it would defeat the purpose of making the film. So Nick had that in mind when he wrote the screenplay.' However, this is where the writer and the director differed:

> As the writer Nick perhaps saw the sexual act as being seen through the eyes of the observer Jared who didn't take part in the rape and Nick imagined the act to be somewhat more distant than in the film. When Steven Vidler the director, shot the movie (Steven is also the co-editor of the script) he felt that what he was trying to do was not show graphic violence but try to make the emotional content of the scene disturbing. He avoided nudity, but he wanted to show the emotional content of the act of rape and how it affected those involved. And when we took the film to the Censorship Board it was that scene, the rape scene, which in fact was the reason for the Board to indicate that the film would have an R-rating unless the rape scene was modified in some way.

According to Elfick, the censor had the following to say of their decision:

> The Board agreed that the depictions of the implied sexual violence were not gratuitous or exploitative. The scene is central to a narrative which carries

a message about the strength of peer group pressure on teenagers. It lacks titillatory details and has been carefully constructed to deliver conceptual strength to what is the key event in the film. The scene emphasises the ugliness of the violence, the girl's powerlessness and Jared's complicity during the attack. The camera focuses on creating a sense of fervent action rather than establishing detail, however depictions include some male buttock nudity during thrusting, and visuals range from full length distance shots of the attack to close-ups of the faces of the participating males, the victim, and Jared's reactions as he watches. Further into the attack, the boys hold the girl above the ground during implied rear entry penetration, and her bloody face is turned towards the camera and her hand is outstretched in Jared's direction in a powerless, silent appeal for help. Afterwards, the males let her drop to the ground and one stomps on her before they run away. She crawls, bent over, then gets to her feet pulling her skirt close around her thighs. Jared flees the scene. Also relevant to the classification of the film are impactful verbal references to the rape and murder at approx 76 mins.

Though the Board agreed the depiction of the rape was discreet, the majority insisted it could not be considered mild. More surprisingly, however, the majority felt that the unresolved nature of the ending contributed to the R-rating; that it was actually the artistic choice for ambiguity around the motivations and subsequent emotions following the crime that required a restricted rating. 'The majority noted the film does not present a fully resolved version of events, perhaps for the apparent purpose of encouraging viewers to contemplate the related issues,' Elfick said of the Board's ruling, which continued

> The ugliness of the violence is offset by the portrayal of the killer as a mate, hero and role model to his peer group. The victim is referred to by the males as a 'fucking slag' and a 'slut'. None of the perpetrators are shown to feel any remorse, and [murderer] Ricko's implied suicide could be interpreted as a heroic alternative to punishment for his actions. The fate of the characters, apart from the deaths of the victim and the killer, remain unclear.

Elfick was generous towards the board—whom he described as 'sympathetic' to *Blackrock*—but suggested Vidler was less appreciative of their perspective.

Steven Vidler ... pointed out to me that at the time *Blackrock* was going through the Censor, a CD-Rom [game] called *Road Kill* was available for people 15 and up. Basically it was a game where you went up and tried to kill people on the roads. Now it's amazing that that is available to 15-year-old people and yet *Blackrock* had to be modified to get an MA-rating. The director of the film, the person who created the film, has a very good point in wanting to present the film in the way that he conceived it. Films are often re-cut because of the sales agent, the distributor, the producer and the writer depending on their power and those decisions are made often for economic reasons and that's part of the filmmaking process. Not necessarily always a good part of it but part of the reality of it. But here is a film that had to be re-cut so that it could get the desired censorship rating and the director was not happy about it. And he has every right not to be happy because he conceived the film in a certain way and he believed that what was on offer was something that had a powerful message to the youth in our community. Watering it down and cutting some of the more stronger visual aspects of that message didn't necessarily make it more palatable to people aged 15 to 18.

Elfick concludes that the decision to edit the film to receive an MA-rating was 'a very bitter pill for the director to swallow', adding, as a button: 'The irony is now the film is out on video, viewers of any age can see the film.' What he couldn't have predicted, in 1997, is that the edited version would be uploaded unlawfully on YouTube some years later as well, its rights holders unaware or letting it stay there unimpeded. (In a further irony, video games today face the more widespread bans. More on that later.)

Nitram is also available to watch online, legally. The picture's box office returns were underwhelming, but being a Stan co-production, it was made available nationally to stream within months of its release. Though the barriers to entry dropped, the public debate has already been held. If anything, the model for *Nitram*—an absolutely incendiary film that is neither violent, sexually explicit or, in this reviewer's opinion, exploitative—is evidence of a Classification Board and community working in concert to decide and debate what our standards should be. The picture still resulted in real pain for actual victims of a not-so-ancient crime, and there's an argument that no film is worth that torment. But the citizenry, this time, was at least looking at Athena's polished shield to reckon with a real-life horror, and not to be diverted from it. The system, at least in this instance, finally worked. The End.

†

Just kidding! The system is still broken and actually got worse in the 2020s. Be warned, things are about to get *really* frightening.

CHAPTER 14
SHUDDER TO THINK

When there's no more room in hell, the dead will walk the Earth. Either that, or they'll end up on Shudder. After all these years of refused classifications, banned horror films are lumbering back to life on a streaming service that has found an ingenious—yet painfully obvious—censorship workaround: it's just ignoring the law ... and getting away with it too.

As with *Violation*, Shudder has perhaps realised that, by not sending films to the board for classification, movies that would otherwise tempt censors to whip out the 'refused' stamp are getting a stay of execution instead, being published online as 'not rated' and remaining untouched. It's not technically legal, but if the board isn't in the business of law enforcement, then who exactly is going to turn to vigilantism to bring this streaming service to justice? As we've discussed throughout this book, there has been no shortage of opportunistic politicians, religious fringe groups and moralistic superiors looking to make examples of (and careers out of decrying) 'obscene' art. If VHS or DVD rental services had tried this on in the early years of the 2000s, you could imagine Fred Nile sharpening the pitchforks; in the 20th century, wowsers of all stripes would have pulled out the placards. But by circumventing the classification approval process completely, Shudder is similarly avoiding the controversy that comes with being banned—or, even more scandalously for the wowsers, approved—by a government department. Who is there to get angry at—or, really, score points off—if the board has nothing to do with a violent or sexually explicit film's release? More likely: whom among these couch-fainters even *knows* what a Shudder is?

For those who celebrate freedom of expression (and especially horror), this is a victory, and you'll certainly get no complaint from me that challenging horror movies can become available to appropriately-aged adults (you must be 18 or older to register on Shudder) in a nation that would have otherwise likely banned them. But then, the censors have never really known what to do about horror anyway, and turning a blind eye to a broken law is just the other side of the same coin as banning them simply out of precaution. Never forget that former chief film censor John Alexander said in the late 1940s, 'horror films are neither entertaining nor cultural,' outlawing them by the imported boatload. That included *The Night of the Hunter*, a stone-cold masterpiece. But it also included a bunch of silly, goofy, gross-out movies too that, even in hindsight, can't be named among the greatest features ever made. So what? Then and now, one thing holds true: horror movies can be fun. They're amusement park rides. Often they are more successful than, say, uber-serious awards bait at accomplishing the aim of communal cinema. They elicit strong feelings and reactions from audiences, and they often give us permission to explore—yes, in disgusting detail—our valid curiosity about death and the extremes of human experience. They allow us to scream and laugh at it, together. That should be defence enough for horror movies. But Alexander's stance on the subject would largely be upheld by his successors into the 21st century.

In 2001, Victorian premier Steve Bracks banned *The Exorcist—Director's Cut* from being screened in cinemas on Good Friday, the holy Catholic holiday. At the same time, the Classification Review Board made the rare decision to overturn the Classification Board's more lenient rating of MA15+ when they decided to slap Ridley Scott's *The Silence of the Lambs* sequel, *Hannibal*, with an R18+. The reassessment was demanded by the Queensland Attorney-General and the Federal Attorney-General, who were responding to pressure from Fred Nile's Christian Democratic Party—who called it 'ultra-violent' and comparable to 'porn'—as well as the Australian Council of State School Organisations. Both organisations had been calling for yet another overhaul of the ratings system too, so it's hard not to imagine the heightened classification being a political distraction. By 2009, upon its Blu-ray re-release, *Hannibal* was back to MA15+ with the notorious scene of Ray Liotta being fed parts of his own brain completely intact. Here's the story of how our most banned genre somehow, and suddenly, came to be largely ignored by the censors in the 2020s.

†

James Whale's iconic *Frankenstein* was banned in South Australia in 1932, though its sequels *Bride of Frankenstein* and *Son of Frankenstein* were passed, with the claim—according to *Film Censorship in Australia*—that the original 'was more horrible than its successors' (when in reality it seems it's because the SA board did not want to challenge the decision of the federal Board). Another franchise-extension only somewhat inspired by the source text, 1936's *Dracula's Daughter*, was nearly banned in Victoria, but it was ultimately given the go ahead with two conditions: it be rated as 'Suitable only for Adults except the Highly Nervous' and that the rating appear 'as a subtitle at least fifteen feet long at the beginning of each screening of the film and in each trailer.' The definition of 'Highly Nervous' was never clarified.

The dawn of hardcore gore exacerbated the censors' firm grip on films that might terrify those nervous nellies. 1974's *The Texas Chain Saw Massacre* is perhaps our most notorious case of a horror film being savaged by the board. Tobe Hooper's brilliant, nasty feature—inspired by several real-life serial killers, with a dash of additional depravity for seasoning—was like nothing before it, courtesy of a washed-out look that made it feel like blood-spattered found footage. Featuring Leatherface and his family of skin-fancying cannibals, it plays like a snuff film starring the Marx Brothers (if the Marx Brothers were decaying from the hair down). Though pulled from numerous American screens due to complaints of its violence, the picture is actually pretty coy when it comes to on-screen gore. It's the tone and tension that makes it unbearable, in particular a seemingly endless sequence in which Leatherface's decrepit grandpa tries to kill a captive (played by Marilyn Burns) with a hammer as his family holds her head over a bucket, missing each time. *The Texas Chain Saw Massacre* nonetheless became a smash hit at the box office overseas. Locally, however, it was a different story. The picture was submitted for classification in Australia twice in 1975, and subsequently banned twice in the same year, with both appeals to the review board unsuccessful too.

After its first banning by the Board, the distributor submitted a new cut with six missing minutes, and yet even that wasn't enough. It was banned again when returned to the board in 1981. Finally, in 1984, the picture was awarded an R-rating, for a slightly edited 82:59–minute print (only 21 seconds hadn't survived this time around). We got the full uncut original in 1991. By then, the board had moved on, and by moved on, I mean they had moved on to ban *The Texas Chainsaw Massacre 2*, noting that the sequel's violence was 'infrequent' yet its explicitness and intensity was 'high', and that its purpose, amusingly enough, was 'gratuitous'. (How violence could be considered anything but essential to the plot of a motion picture titled *The Texas Chainsaw Massacre 2*, I have no idea.) So the ordeal began again in 1986, until the sequel was finally given an R-rating a full 20 years later. Only 33 seconds were of contention over those two decades: a few shots of steel-plated cannibal Chop Top hitting a victim with a hammer, and, more significantly, a moment of suggested sexual violence as Leatherface, waggling his tongue, slowly moves a (non-operational) chainsaw up the open legs of radio DJ 'Stretch' (Caroline Williams), thrusting until he nearly climaxes as it presses against the crotch of her cutoff jeans. (She questions him: 'Really?') Both sequences were restored for the DVD release in 2006, and for the writing of this book, I only needed to pull the aforementioned sequence up on easily accessible YouTube to refresh my memory, highlighting just how tame it's considered today. Several disappointing sequels still followed, but the original holds its place as a stone cold classic, while the deranged and inspired second instalment deserves its own appreciation as a freaky black comedy, separate from the guttural terror of the first. For the sake of the gnarly second chapter—in which Dennis Hopper has a chainsaw duel with Leatherface—I'm grateful this is one franchise that didn't die from 1,000 cuts.

The Texas Chain Saw Massacre wasn't the only bona fide horror masterpiece to be disregarded by the board. George Romero's defining *Dawn of the Dead* may not be as bone-chillingly potent as its predecessor *Night of the Living Dead*, but it would come to form the template for the decades of zombie cinema that followed in its wake, and reverberates today. However, this colourful critique of consumerist culture was first refused classification in November 1978, and then again in October 1979. An appeal by distributor United Artists failed, and a reconstructed 'soft' version with a minute of missing footage was resubmitted in December, yet refused again. A second, even softer version was put forward in February 1980, but even that wasn't cut down enough; it was only after 23 further seconds of 'excessive violence' were spliced that the board awarded it an R-rating—now it was two minutes shorter than the version first proposed. The distributor capitalised on newspaper listings blandly promoting session times with the tantalising declaration that they weren't *allowed* to show any stills from the feature. They also provided guidance in the press notes for cinemas to activate their entrances with hunting rifles and camping equipment, given how the mall-stuck survivors in the film have to stave off zombies using items from the surrounding sporting goods stores. It was an ingenious way to get punters into theatres. But at what cost? Compared to the American and Italian cuts of the film, the Australian edit was missing the moment in which an unsuspecting tenement occupant has his head blown up by a trigger-happy SWAT team (projecting 'food scraps' across the room, such was the special effects ingenuity of the time); a bunch of zombies tearing into tenant flesh in the high-rise basement; a zombie tragically having the top of its head lopped off by an escaping helicopter; David Emge's character Flyboy getting mauled in an elevator; effects artist Tom Savini—as the bikie Blades—thrusting a machete into a zombie's head; and the zombies getting back at the raiding motorbike gang by ripping out one of the crew's intestines. It would take until 1985 for the uncut version to get an R-rating in Australia, when it was released to VHS in all states except Queensland (becoming one of the notorious films to wear a 'Banned in Queensland' badge on its cover). A year later, you could see the film in Queensland legally. That was a better result than received by Wes Craven's formative urtext, *The Last House on the Left*, a schlocky rape-revenge flick with highfalutin stimulus, having used *The Virgin Spring* as a springboard. Australian distribution wasn't even attempted until a full decade after its initial 1972 release in the States. It was retitled in 1982 as *Krug and Company* upon submission (nice try), but that didn't fool the censors, who slapped it with an RC. It finally got an R-rating—and its original title back—in 2004. In the meantime, however, customs officers would arrest Rod Williams—then editor of Queensland horror fanzine *Skinned Alive* and now the administrator of the Media Censorship in Australia page on Facebook—for trying to import banned films into Australia, *The Last House on the Left* among them.

When the arrest was made in 1991, he indeed had a copy of *The Texas Chain Saw Massacre* on his person too, but as that video had already been 'examined by the Film Censorship Board', it was allowed to be released. Other items weren't so lucky: *Cannibal Holocaust*, *The Driller Killer*, *The Evil Dead*, *S.S. Experiment Love Camp* (not to be confused with the similarly-titled Nazi exploitation flick *Love Camp 7*, which was banned in 1974 but released that same year in modified form; or *Nazi Love Camp 27* AKA *The Swastika on the Belly*, which seemingly passed without issue in 1977). He also had the asking-for-it-in-retrospect title *Violent Shit*. To commemorate the 30th anniversary of the confiscation, Williams shared a picture of the customs report alongside a copy of the 'Deluxe Collector's Edition' DVD of *Cannibal Holocaust*, which was finally released for purchase in Australia in 2005. 'Banned in Australia since the early '80s, for years reviled as one of the most repugnant and morally questionable films ever made, and possibly the most horrifying ever,' reads the slip cover, continuing, 'A very original piece, later to be stolen by the writers of *The Blair Witch Project*, *Cannibal Holocaust* stands the test of time as the most brutal film ever made.' 'Stolen' is a strong word, but there's no denying that Ruggero Deodato's 1980 feature was a template for the makers of *Blair Witch* and the numerous found-footage mockumentaries that followed. Centring on a documentary crew that gets lost in the Amazon rainforest—and falls victim to a cannibalistic tribe—it was accused of being a snuff film shortly after its premiere. The courts investigated whether or not the on-screen murders were legitimate, but even after the production was cleared of, ahem, literal cannibalism, it remained banned across much of the world, with the actual animal slaughters captured on camera a key reason for the refusal of classification. (It was among the notorious 'video nasties' in the UK, too.) In 2005, *Cannibal Holocaust* was granted an R-rating for high level sexual violence, high level violence [and] animal cruelty'. The DVD was still banned in NZ, however. In 2013, the flick aired on Australian television, and the following year it was given the Blu-ray treatment, though it did not shy away from its reputation. The distributor's website, while promoting the presale, nevertheless added a warning in all caps: 'THIS IS A CRUEL PICTURE, NOT FOR THE FAINT OF HEART.'

†

Williams was far from the only Australian horror fanatic to have their door darkened by the law in the early 1990s. Except, in the case of teenage *Skinned Alive* contributor Joe Kapiteyn in WA, it was his mum who opened the flyscreen to the federal agents. 'We kinda had an underground tape-trading system via fanzines where you'd contact people in other states, and someone might have a copy of something, and you might have a copy of something, and organise a swap of a really-badly-multiple-dubbed version to each other,' Kapiteyn recalls. 'I was very interested in seeing *The Texas Chainsaw Massacre 2*, being a big fan of the original, and I think the other film I ordered was a delightful German film called *Nekromantik*. So, I ordered those two thinking nothing of it, because we'd done this kind of exchange before with various things.' Neither title arrived in the mail. Instead: 'I was awoken one morning by my mum telling me the federal police were at the door and wanted to search my bedroom.'

As best as he can remember, having been a bleary-eyed first-year uni student, 'they were really fucking heavy. They were in suits. One of them looked like a bouncer and was super serious.' But the feeling of the 6am raid has not dimmed: 'The tone was definitely, "You're in deep shit." I was terrified to be honest, and mum was beside herself.' Kapiteyn learnt that the federal agents had gained a search warrant by intercepting his correspondence to order items that had been refused classification, but really, they were looking for snuff films.

> They said, 'We know you've got this material, it's somewhere in the house, so make it easy on yourself and tell us where it is.' It was like something out of a movie. I said, 'Look, apart from some horror films, I don't really have much else.' They said, 'What about pornography, do you have

pornography?' And so I said, 'Oh look, I do have something.' [They said] 'Alright, show it to us.' So I lifted up my mattress and pulled out a copy of Playboy magazine, and that was the point they realised I wasn't a threat to national security. I saw them look at each other and lighten up at that point. They still turned the room upside down. I said, 'This is all I got,' and they said, 'Okay', and they proceeded to rip everything apart basically. And didn't clean up after themselves either. Just everything tipped upside down, stripped the sheets, that kind of shit. It was full on.

The agents not only confiscated his video collection and his fanzines, but also his personal artwork. Mum, miraculously, took it well. It may even be the first recorded case of a mum awash with waves of relief at the reveal of her son's porno mag. 'She was obviously mortified but she was pretty good considering the circumstances,' Kapiteyn says. 'I don't know how I'd deal with that situation now being a parent myself if some heavies came to the door. Given that context, she trusted me, I think, and she knew even though my interests were a bit macabre, it was pretty normal.' He wouldn't see *Texas Chainsaw Massacre 2* until happening upon it by chance on Stan in 2019. 'It was just weird watching it, because I found it to be more of a black comedy than a horror film; it was this kind of absurdist, surreal splatterfest and I'd seen things that were far more disturbing in the interim.' As for *Nekromantik*: 'That one I wish I hadn't seen.'

Before the dawn raid on the Kapiteyns, the board had been wrestling with director T.F. Mou's historical exploitation flick *Men Behind the Sun* (sometimes called *Man Behind the Sun*), which claimed to serve an educational purpose by re-enacting the medical experiments inflicted upon Chinese and Soviet prisoners by the Japanese biological weapons experimentation unit during World War II. Upon application in 1989, the board balked at the claim of its educational purpose, cuffing it with a Refused Classification rating. The chief censor of the time, John Dickie, explained the board's reasoning in an interview with *Tabula Rasa* in 1994:

> It showed women being left out overnight in freezing temperatures, and buckets of water being thrown over their hands and fingers being snapped off in the morning, because their hands had iced over. There were sequences of people being put into compression chambers, to the extent that their insides were blown out. Now, according to the material

that came with the film, this was a recreation of some of the horrible things that were done in terms of experimentation, or just in terms of torture. We knocked that back on the basis that, even though this was, I suppose, an accurate portrayal of what happens if you put someone into a compression chamber and increase the pressure, it really was exploitative material. Exploitative violence for its own sake; it was not necessarily part of the progression of telling the story. That's where it becomes a bit subjective, I agree, and there aren't too many films that are like that. But if [Steven Spielberg's holocaust drama *Schindler's List*] had been a film where they tried to recreate the full horror of the actual execution in the gas chambers, and things like that, you would have to look very carefully at the scene and say, 'Is this absolutely necessary to the thing or is it just a gratuitous scene to appeal to some violence freaks?' And that's something you can only really judge in the context of the film. But they're the principles that tend to guide us.

Within a month, the rating was reassessed at the request of Yu Enterprises—who had paid to distribute the film upfront and was at risk of losing the money completely without a different decision—and the Classification Review Board gave *Men Behind the Sun* the lesser R-rating, accepting 'the filmmaker's claims in good faith' as far as Mou's educational intentions went. 'The Board of Review was divided on this appeal,' they acknowledged.

> The guidelines for film classification prohibit 'unduly detailed and/or relished acts of extreme violence or cruelty'. That the violence in *Man Behind the Sun* is both detailed and extreme cannot be denied; whether it is 'unduly detailed', and whether the acts can be said to be 'relished', is open to question. *Man Behind the Sun* is ostensibly, and at least in part, a documentary. The question therefore arises: what constitutes undue detail in a documentary about war and its atrocities? The Board took the view that the word 'unduly' in the context allows—and was intended to allow—a certain flexibility in the interpretation of the guidelines, particularly in cases where the presentation of violent acts may be thought to be justified by the intentions of the film and the circumstances in which the act is committed. A majority concluded that in a film specifically

concerned with documented instances of atrocities and inhumanity, depictions of extreme cruelty can be justified, and may indeed be necessary to the filmmaker's purposes. In considering *Man Behind the Sun*, the majority took account of the film's strong anti-war message and the reaction of most of the characters in the film to the experiments they are forced to witness. Far from suggesting 'relish', the film provokes—and depicts—a powerful sense of revulsion.

Nonetheless, the version rated R in Australia—and advertised as 'uncut' on VHS—was four minutes shorter than the initial submission.

†

Now, no one is going to accuse the 2011 feature *Father's Day* of being as classic (or iconoclastic) as *The Texas Chain Saw Massacre*, *Cannibal Holocaust* or *Dawn of the Dead*, but it holds a rare distinction of being one of the few horror movies to be refused classification in the 21st century. Made by the collective Astron-6 as an intentionally lo-fi tribute to the works of Lloyd Kaufman and its distributor Troma Entertainment, *Father's Day* concerns a demonic being known as the Fuchmanicus, whose sole purpose is to rape and kill dads. The uncut film first debuted in Australia at Sydney's Dendy Newtown on 24 March 2012 without much protest (in fact, it picked up four awards at the Night of Horror Festival). But when Bounty Films later put the 99-minute feature forward for a DVD release, ahead of a session at Monster Pictures' Monster Fest, the Classification Board promptly struck them down. 'The film contains actual sexual violence and sexualised violence that exceeds a high impact including depictions of rape, sexualised torture, sexual activity with body parts and cannibalism,' their decision report reads. (In the report, received through a Freedom of Information request, a description of the scenes in question was redacted.) 'While some of the depictions of violence, which include viscera, generous blood detail and gore, are mitigated by unsophisticated production values and could be accommodated at an R18+ classification, scenes of sexual violence and sexualised violence are more realistic and result in a very high impact.' The scheduled Monster Fest screening was canned, and festival director Neil Foley came to its defence by calling it 'actually one of the sweetest films in the Monster Fest program', criticising 'the draconian censorship in [Australia]'.

It was an interesting gambit by Foley, considering how an earlier attempt the previous year to generate controversy for *The Human Centipede 2: Full Sequence* had unfolded. That sequel to the ingeniously disgusting cult classic—about a mad scientist who joins three victims, mouth-to-anus, in a sort-of, well, human centipede—was initially rated R18+ by the board in May of 2011 (it's worth noting the extremely meta *Full Sequence* follows a tollbooth operator named Martin played by Laurence R. Harvey, who is roused after watching the first film into creating a 12-person centipede). In my published review of *Full Sequence* from the time, I tried to tie it to a cinematic legacy. 'From *Oedipus the King*, to *Dante's Inferno*, to *Titus Andronicus*, there is a long lineage of great texts regarding the poetry of human (and inhuman) suffering. Director Tom Six would like his *Human Centipede* films—in which strangers are abducted and operated on until they share a single gastrological tract—to be a part of that disturbed family tree. It's hard to take them seriously however when they have this many fart noises. Instead, they'll probably be best remembered for their creative poster art and evocative, flatulent sound design.' Basically, this wasn't exactly the second coming of Dante Alighieri, but these flicks got their exceptionally specific jobs done.

While *Full Sequence* was banned in the UK that June, the Australian Classification Board shared in their Annual Report a month later that the 'film is ... appropriately located within the R18+ classification with consumer advice of "High impact themes, violence and sexual violence".' It was a surprising enough decision for Monster Pictures' acquisition manager Ben Hellwig to openly exclaim to the *Sydney Morning Herald* that their film dodged a bullet: 'We were so concerned that it might not pass that we made an unusual deal with the film's sales agent to submit the film for classification before signing the contract, thus protecting ourselves should the film be rejected.' He concluded by saying—somewhat ironically given what would pass—the board has a 'sound grasp of the sensibilities of the general Australian population'. Within days, the conservative Australian Family Association called on members to write to their state Attorneys-General challenging the R-rating, with NSW Attorney-General Greg Smith eventually applying for an appeal. Of course, while the appeal date loomed, the film was given the go ahead to screen at the Brisbane International Film Festival in November, and several other Q&A screenings with Foley and Harvey in attendance across the country. I was fortunate enough to host the event in Perth at Luna Palace Cinemas Leederville on 25 November 2011, with 500 people in attendance. Controversy has its perks. 'Recently we've had a complaint from the NSW Attorney-General, who's reacting to pressure from Christian groups or whatever to have it changed,' Foley said in the preamble to the film screening, as the packed-house booed in response. Three days later, the Classification Review Board would refuse the film classification. On that fateful night, though, Foley—who had provided *Human Centipede*–branded barf bags to each attendee—promised them an evening they wouldn't forget: 'This film is fucking crazy.'

The review board ultimately decided that 'the film must be refused classification because it contains gratuitous, exploitative or offensive depictions of violence with a very high degree of impact and cruelty which has a high impact.' They elaborated, in excruciating detail:

> The violence is perpetrated in a realistic, sadistic and often prolonged way with an unrelenting sense of fear, violence and despair. Martin's victims are aware of his intentions for them and can often see and always hear what he is doing to others in the Human Centipede, thus anticipating their own agony. The graphic images, in particular the scenes depicting Martin stapling people together, are accompanied by brutal sounds, screams and cries of pain, fear and despair, adding to the sense of violence, degradation and desperation. The music is also low and menacing and serves to emphasise the sense of fear and despair. The display of blood, gore, ligaments, flesh and bodies and body part[s] is very realistic and frequently shown in graphic detail. This very high-level impact violence cannot be accommodated under the R18+ classification.

They continued:

> The Review Board considers that some viewers of the film, particularly those familiar with *Human Centipede 1*, may expect to be shocked and repulsed, but this does not preclude a finding that the film contains high level and frequent depictions of cruelty, violence with a very high impact or revolting or abhorrent phenomena that offend against the standards of morality, decency and propriety generally accepted by a reasonable adult, which is a required consideration under the Code. Thus the film must be Refused Classification. The Review Board also considered the requirement in the National Classification Code (d) (ii) that in making

its decision the Review Board must take account of community concerns about, inter alia, the portrayal of persons in a demeaning manner. The level of humiliation and degradation, involving forced bodily functions, imposed on Martin's victims, deprives them of all aspects of their dignity and would, in the opinion of the Review Board, be sufficient to raise community concerns about the demeaning portrayal of men and women being reduced to a brutalised animal state for the sexual gratification of another person.

The Tribal Theatre in Brisbane soon after claimed on Facebook that a woman from 'the board of classification' came to inform them that they had to remove *Full Sequence* from their schedule following the banning. (The same theatre had to previously chide attendees of the screenings for defecating in the foyer.) Members of Collective Shout and FamilyVoice Australia jointly claimed credit for the result, even though it was revealed that neither cheerleaders Melinda Tankard Reist from Collective Shout nor Ros Phillips from FamilyVoice Australia had even viewed the film prior to making a complaint. Monster Pictures resubmitted a new cut with 30 seconds shorn, removing a close up of Martin's bloodied penis as he masturbates with sand paper and a few moments from a rape scene involving barb wire. Approximately 1,500 adults had all witnessed these moments in cinema screenings the prior month.

Of all people, Cardinal George Pell, then Archbishop of Sydney, wrote about the decision in December 2011, congratulating the board and the minister on the outcome and calling it a win for common decency and common sense, while diminishing those complaining about censorship. (Pell was found guilty of child sexual abuse charges in December 2018, though the verdict was turned over on appeal to the High Court in 2020.) Days before Pell blogged about *The Human Centipede 2*, the Sydney Archdiocese had published an article celebrating Collective Shout for its grassroots campaigns and directed people how to join their ranks.

The edited version of the film was reclassified as R18+ on 14 December 2011. The distributor had changed its tune about the board by this point: 'Monster Pictures feels that this decision highlights the absurdity of Classification Review Board's decision to ban the film in the first place.' Bounty Films, the UK distributor, ended up briefly making the uncut version available for download online for Australians. (As of this writing, the uncut version is still available via Troma Entertainment in the US on Vimeo.) The following year, a reflection on the ordeal was posted to the

Monster Pictures blog: 'No it didn't last long and in the end it amounted to sweet fuck all but yes it is true, in this country, in this day and age, a film made by a group of consenting adults for the entertainment of consenting adults was banned—why? Because God ordained it so! Yes that's right, God, as represented by whacko fringe members of this countries [sic] Christian right, made a stand, he cast his gaze down upon us and declared "Get that fucking obscene rubbish from my screens now you pack of heathen cunts" and so it was, *THC2* was ripped from our screens.' The post continued wryly, 'What a pain in the arse you say? Well yes it would appear that way, but all honesty the publicity generated from the banning could not have been better—we're a small company with not much dough to spend on advertising, we can't pay for coverage in the mainstream media but that's exactly what we got, and at the end of the day, the film returned with very little removed but with a lovely dose of notoriety hanging off every frame—a big thank you to Ros, Melinda and the kind ladies of the Classification Review Board.'

In the present day, I caught up with Foley's Monster Pictures co-founder Grant Hardie to reflect on the experience of cutting *The Human Centipede: Full Sequence*. 'We made minor changes to it, which in my view made absolutely no difference to the film as an experience. It was a couple of close-ups of things you wouldn't want to see anyway,' he laughs. 'Sometimes with film, you don't have to see everything. It made no less of an impact.'

Hardie and Foley initially founded Monster Pictures in 2010 with the intention of learning the intricacies of the film distribution business, having been left somewhat dejected by their little-seen first effort as filmmakers, *Bigger Than Tina* (a mockumentary about a delusional man obsessed with—and hoping to supersede—singing star Tina Arena). '[Neil and I] sat down for a couple days and went through all of our plans and thought, "look, let's be a specific film distributor, let's aim for a very specific market"', Hardie explains. 'We clearly saw that horror films are a very lucrative and well-established sector of the market. Neil and I are massive horror film fans ourselves, so we thought, "let's do it".' They opted to make a splash by launching in the market with a viral sensation, waiting in the shadows to pounce on just the right acquisition. That's when the trailer for *The Human Centipede* emerged.

So, clearly, picking films that'll potentially rile up wowsers is a calculated risk in the Monster Pictures model, but only to a point. 'The hardest part of releasing any film is, firstly, establishing that audience,' Hardie says. 'Secondly, how do you reach that audience? If there's a film that you know will cut through all of that, because it's either going to have some controversy or some hype or will be divisive as far as the audience is concerned, or is really going to speak to that audience, then yeah, we always look at that as a factor.' Those kinds of acquisitions carry as much risk as reward—and as Hardie says, 'It's a commercial process so you can't do it all the time, but it always helps to have those films in your catalogue and those sorts of films bringing a profile to you as a company.' Of course, in the instance of *The Human Centipede 2*, the roiling controversy impeded their initial release strategy and also incurred recutting and reclassification costs. 'The hope is that there'll be a discussion, but then nothing comes of it, and then controversy is created by the audience reaction once you've been able to release it,' Hardie says.

> Generally with film you get one go and then you lose your audience. Luckily with something like *The Human Centipede 2* or the *Human Centipede* franchise as a whole, it has a long life. But you know, there's always a window where you'll make the most amount of money, and that window is generally one to two weeks, especially theatrically. When it gets interrupted, it's stressful. [Plus] it's more prevalent these days but something was emerging back then; if your version in your territory is the 'cut' one, people just circumvent you and go elsewhere. That becomes a factor also where you're looking at all of those things. Momentum lost, extra cost. It's stressful but when you make a decision to get involved with a film like that, you know what potentially can happen. I don't have a particularly negative view towards censorship. I just have a healthy combative mentality to it. They've got a job, we've got a job, let's go.

That was likely the mentality when Hardie and Foley worked to generate perverse interest in *Father's Day*; interest that may not have existed prior. In fact, Hardie admitted to me that they 'may have manufactured a bit' of the controversy in 2012 for that very reason. (Their peers at Potential Films had a similar crack at generating a salacious appetite for Catherine Breillat's 2004 picture *Anatomie de L'enfer* (*Anatomy of Hell*), with ads in the cinema listings offering the tantalising prospect of seeing something mere days before it gets inevitably banned. Turns out the Board just gave it an R-rating advising 'actual sex, high level sex scenes, high level themes'—the first time a film included the 'actual sex' classification advice in Australia.)

But *Father's Day* could not benefit quite as *The Human Centipede 2* did, for one simple reason: it never got widely screened (save for the one exception in Sydney) in full uncut glory to capitalise on word of mouth, nor did it get initial pushback from Christian groups to further the argument of rating hypocrisy, since the board beat them to the punch. This despite the fact that the picture has a priest receive another priest's decapitated head in the post, and then imitate God at the pulpit, saying, 'Look at me, I'm God, I sit on my fat ass,' before loading a pistol and running past his parishioners to exact revenge.

After the initial 99-minute version was banned in Australia, a 98-minute version was submitted in February 2013, yet was still refused classification. Later that same month, *Father's Day* was finally given an R-rating for a different 98-minute version, albeit with around 40 seconds worth of further excisions. They include a list of some truly horrendous (on paper) sequences, documented by those at refused-classification.com who compared the pair: the Fuchmanicus biting a victim's penis; a 'naked rear shot' of the Fuchmanicus raping a victim; a close-up of the victim's bloody buttocks and the Fuchmanicus' erect penis; and the Fuchmanicus injecting his penis with a syringe and then slicing the tip off with a knife. 'In the view of the Board this version of the film has been suitably modified with all depictions of explicit sexual violence removed,' the Classification Board's final decision report for *Father's Day* concluded (while acknowledging a minority of the Board still thought it should be banned). 'As such, this film can now be accommodated within the R18+ classification with consumer advice of 'high impact violence, blood and gore, themes and sex scenes.' Imagine my surprise when I scanned through the version on Shudder in Australia and found that it contained each of those surgically-removed shots. This, I realised, was the banned cut, now available in Australia, seemingly without the Board's knowledge.

So what happened? How did one of the last contemporary releases to receive the Refused Classification stamp in Australia suddenly wind up in uncut form on a widely accessible streaming service, without any ceremony or public consternation? Can we really just attribute it simply to the passage of time, the changing of the guard at the board, and the evolution of our mores?

After *Father's Day*, the next major film we might have expected to be banned (if history is any indication) would have been *Raw*, by director Julia Ducournau, in which the ravenous sexual awakening of a young woman is metaphorically realised as the development of a cannibalistic taste for flesh. There were numerous reports, from its screening at the Toronto International Film Festival in 2016, of paramedics rushing to treat at least two members of the audience who had passed out. But unlike *The Human Centipede 2* or *Father's Day*, critics felt the extreme gore was creatively justified. It was rated R18+ for 'high impact blood and gore' on 12 April 2017, months after the TIFF tiff. Five years later, Ducournau's follow-up *Titane* won the Palme d'or at Cannes, an even greater critical endorsement, yet it inspired even more gut-churning reactions, with 13 patrons at a Sydney Film Festival screening in November 2021 reportedly fainting, while another had a panic attack, one vomited and numerous others simply walked out. Stories of chaotic screenings such as these are often worn as prized promotional badges of honour for horror films, yet not even that could rustle up much complaint from the same bodies who argued against visceral films in the past. (To be fair, in the 1970s, chief censor Richard Prowse told *Cinema Papers* he was unwowed by similar stories emerging from Melbourne screenings of Brian De Palma's *Sisters* after giving it a permissive M-rating, although the National Archives of Australia have itemised audiovisual records of 'censorship cuts' from the flick, so perhaps he had already used the scissors on *Sisters*.) *Titane*'s story of a serial killer who has sex with—and is impregnated by—a souped-up hotcar was rated R18+ for 'high impact themes and violence', with the Classification Board's website noting that it's a 'surreal French drama' that contains 'an implied sex scene between a woman and a car as well as an implied sex scene between a woman and a fire truck.' Honestly, I'm still surprised that didn't rile up the usual suspects. Is there something to be said about the fact that *Censor*, *Violation*, *Raw* and *Titane* are all directed or co-directed by women? Has the shifting of horror's lens affected how it's being received, both critically but also by the classifiers themselves? And is that why groups such as Collective Shout and FamilyVoice Australia have failed to gain ground with them? Was I wrong in my earlier assertation about the classification system's seemingly laissez-faire view of horror in the 2020s, and has the board instead intentionally course-corrected?

The answer to all these sunny hypotheticals is ... of course not. There's no denying that mores have evolved, that women have a more prominent role in defining cinema's formerly (though still primarily) masculine and misogynistic gaze, and that the goalposts have shifted in terms of what's considered permissible for an 18-and-older audience, further pushing the boundaries for that which might be banned. But we cannot underestimate the damage wrought by decades of censorship, its financial ramifications, and the cultural implications that have expanded far beyond film classifications. I suppose we could today celebrate the diminishing power of 'moral' figures like George Pell—who died in 2023—and Fred Nile—whose Christian Democratic Party was forced into receivership in 2021—as a reason for this change in the tide, but the fact is public-panic bodies such as Collective Shout and Festival of Light simply turned their attention away from film, and with even greater efficacy. Collective Shout's first few battles involved protests against overly-raunchy and problematic billboards before setting its sights on *A Serbian Film*. Since that headline-making move, it now counts victories against businesses as large as Instagram, Kmart, Big W, Target, Woolworths and more—including Pornhub—on its website, under the banner 'Wins'. FamilyVoice Australia's website, meanwhile, lists ongoing and recent campaigns to protect Christian schools, halt the Northern Territory's abortion bill, stop children from accessing 'trans drugs' and to keep Mosman Council from 'cancelling' Christmas, among other such expected bugbears for the Christian right. Obscure horror films and challenging art flicks are small potatoes compared to these larger, existential crises, but one should never forget where and how these groups made their bones, recruiting common sense parents in the process.

Though the wowsers have turned their attention elsewhere, now armed with cultural cachet earned during these encounters, self-censorship has become largely normalised, particularly among large studios submitting films for classification and wanting a more box office-friendly rating. Meanwhile, Shudder is doing precisely what once terrified those same wowsers—sharing unclassified horror films (and occasionally even those that were refused classification)—to literally zero complaint. Now, don't mistake this chapter as a complaint against Shudder. I'm actually pretty tickled by the fact they're not even remotely concerned by our stringent local regulations, given the history of horror censorship in Australia. You might argue Shudder gets away with it because it sits on the fringes of the streaming service landscape. But in fact, it's far from alone. Most streamers are actually defying classification law in Australia, with one of the world's most prominent distributors, Netflix, occasionally doing it in a completely different (but still not legal) manner. Except in that case, they're not loosening the standards for what Australians can hear and see, but in fact tightening them, maybe even returning our classification system to its original puritanical form. How's this for a horror story: they're making us more *American*.

CHAPTER 15
'NETFLIX CLASSIFIES MANBOOBS AS NUDITY!'

'In Australia, at least, censorship appears to be a somewhat dead issue.' Is this statement a fair assessment of today's social reality? The average Aussie's feeling towards the current state of film classification? Or is it the opening line from a 1974 article published by *Cinema Papers*? How about all three? Fifty years ago, that notable film journal wondered if the issue of censorship had been settled in Australia. Clearly, it was not. So it's possible that those who claim the same in 2023 might also be unaware of the censorship and suppression occurring just out of public sight, even by, say, global streaming behemoth Netflix.

Due to the simply enormous amount of content it was publishing on a weekly basis, Netflix was granted permission by the federal government to trial a self-rating Netflix Classification Tool in 2016, one year after the streaming service formally arrived in Australia. This tool is operated entirely by Netflix and allows them to classify their original content for Australian audiences, with their tool's decisions uploaded to the Classification Board database. A Netflix title—be it a feature-length movie or an entire series of television—need not ever be viewed by an Australian classifier to be classified for Australians. 'Developed in partnership with Netflix, the Tool generates ratings and consumer advice that aligns to Australian community standards and decisions of the Classification Board,' a government press release from the launch reads. However—almost in what would become the extreme opposite of Shudder's approach—the tool wound up re-evaluating previously classified films with harsher ratings. As I discovered in 2020, the tool gave M-rated movies *Moonlight*, *Blade Runner: The Final Cut* and *The Little Stranger* MA-ratings once they arrived on Netflix in Australia, and 2018's *Halloween* was upgraded from MA15+ to R18+. Once it was pointed out, Netflix corrected itself, and the Classification Board acknowledged that the tool should not supersede existing classifications, as it's not legal. Still, we were given an insight into how self-classifiers were acting even more austerely in private. The problem, I discovered, was not that the tool had been calibrated too stringently; rather, it was too American. A Netflix spokesperson shared with me that Netflix relies on the Classification Board's database to ensure they use previous classifications of titles where they exist, except when they're adding a different version or cut of a previously-rated film. 'If this is ever done in error and flagged by the Board, we update the rating on service to reflect the Board classification,' they said.

'It was all very secret squirrel's business,' Margaret Anderson recalls of the introduction of the Netflix Classification Tool. 'The Classification Branch [of the government] refused to disclose stuff to the Classification Board. They literally went on this frolic of their own.' She describes a 'former board member who hadn't done any classifications for decades at the time' being the one to train the Netflix staff in Australian classification standards. 'When you're classifying, you go, "Ah yeah, that's right, this is one of the things that you've always got to think about,"' Anderson explained. 'When do I mitigate, when do I not? When can I accommodate something? When can I not, or should not?' She suggested, however, that this 'former board member' didn't have that current experience under their belt, yet they were 'the one who the Australian government puts on a plane and sends to America to train Netflix staff'. ('Are you crying and rocking?' Anderson asked me after sharing that titbit.) When 'the mythical Netflix tool' was finally unveiled, Anderson discovered that it was 'literally a member of staff in California sitting there watching a film and then ticking up to 250 metatags and slapping those metatags on that film.'

In my years of researching this book, it was only during my chat with Margaret Anderson—near the end of this period—that my understanding of how the Netflix Classification Tool operates was shaken. I had all this time figured that the giant Netflix computer pumping out ratings was just a goody-goody. I should have known better: an algorithm is only as accurate as the data it's being fed by humans. And the humans were Americans.

Margaret Anderson's take on how the tool works was unsparing:

> All that happens with the Netflix Classification Tool is me, as a Netflix employee in California, I watch a film and then I go, 'Oh look, there's the word bitch. Oh well, I'll go put the metatag 'coarse language' on this film.' And then: 'Oh look, there's someone smoking a joint. I will put 'drug use' on this film. Oh look, someone's discussing buying a joint. Another verbal metatag for drug references as opposed to the visual metatag of drug references.'

And out of all of this, based on the training that they were given [the tool produces a rating]. And bear in mind there is no grid, no magic document that says, 'You can have up to 49 utterances of fuck language in an M-rated film, but once you get to 50 and above it's got to go MA.' There's no magic number. The point about having human beings classify is that when you're looking at a film, and you might think, 'My lordy there's an awful lot of fuck language in that film,' if it's not being said aggressively, and if there's not a whole lot of motherfuckers or whatever else—if it's just 'fuck this', 'fuck that' and you're thinking 'ah yeah, tiresome, boring but go on'—you could have maybe 100 uses of fuck language and that film will still be M. You may only get 20 uses of fuck language; it could be so aggressive and interrelated with violence that its suddenly sitting at MA15+. That would be an exception, can I just say, but that's the whole point about context and the fact that there's deliberately no magic number with anything. It's the same with themes; there's no moment you get five characters crying, [and you think] 'well, that's a bit of an impactful scene, isn't it, so maybe we should take it from PG to M.'

A Netflix spokesperson challenged Anderson's assessment of their rating process. 'For each region or country where we display ratings, a team of Ratings Specialists craft rules based on a variety of inputs, in this case the ACB guidelines,' they told me in a statement. 'These rules are applied to individual titles by a dedicated, global team of trained content assessors.'

One of the biggest issues Anderson finds with the Netflix classifiers was nudity, or, what they defined as nudity:

It took us ages to work out what the hell was going on in Netflix, because we literally would be getting films that would say PG or M, and it would say 'nudity'. And you would go, 'What the heck?' There's a film called *High Flying Bird* from 2019, rated M by Netflix. We literally were told that it had nudity in it. There are two screenshots that I used in a presentation that I gave where I said, 'spot the nudity!' Both scenes are in a sauna. In one of those scenes, you've got a man lying down and he's got a white towel wrapped around his waist. All you are seeing is the white towel from his side up to his head. You are literally just seeing a man's waist with nothing on; you then have that same man coming out of the sauna and he's front on to camera and he's got his manboobs showing. Netflix classifies manboobs as nudity!

Not just any manboobs, either. The man to whom the manboobs belong is Kyle MacLachlan, but surely this isn't what was meant by *Twin Peaks*. 'Never—to my knowledge of Australia—have we ever classified manboobs as nudity.' Anderson continues. 'We are sexists. Put our hands up to it. Yep, no worries. Women's breasts: nudity. Men's breasts: not nudity. Netflix went, "*Oh my God, it's a naked man!*"'

Of course, not even that topped the audaciousness of Netflix re-rating already classified features, like *Moonlight*. (Bad luck for André Holland, star of both *High Flying Bird* and *Moonlight*.) When I mention Netflix giving *Moonlight* a stricter rating, Anderson replied,

> Welcome to America. The most important thing you need to know about that is it is illegal—it is against the legislation. The board can't reclassify films that are already classified. Not only is it illegal under the *Classification Act*, but there is a separate piece of legislation [the *Classification (Publications, Films and Computer Games) (Netflix Classification Tool) Approval 2016*]. In that it very clearly says several things. Firstly, that the Netflix Tool has to produce decisions broadly consistent with the standards and expectations of the Australian community, and most importantly it says, it must not produce classification or consumer advice for a film if that film has already been classified.

> [The Tool] literally would produce these illegal decisions left, right and centre. The problem was, when the Classification Branch set this process, they didn't ever resource it. They didn't resource the board to conduct audits. They certainly didn't employ staff to be watching and cross-referencing and auditing every decision that came in from Netflix overnight. And that's what they needed to be doing. I had one particular board member who probably hated the Netflix Tool more than I did, and he had very young twins, so while he was busily feeding twins at two or three in the morning, giving them a bottle, he'd be busily going through all of the Netflix decisions that had come in overnight, going, 'Nup, bastards, they've done it again.'

It was the Australian Government's strip-mining of board resources—specifically the compliance unit—that allowed other streamers to release features unrated, as on Shudder, Anderson insists. 'There are two exceptions, and that's Netflix and Disney,' Anderson clarifies. 'Everybody else has done it from day one.'

'When I started at the board,' she continues, 'there was still a strong compliance unit. They still visited every state or territory in Australia. They would go into the sex shops, they'd go into the newsagents, they would go into cinema complexes, et cetera. They were really good at making sure that the classification laws were being complied with.' After reading this book, your first response in regard to the decommissioning of the compliance unit may not immediately be one of sympathy. However, that depends on how willing you are to substitute the oversight of the Australian government for that of Big Tech, which largely operates beyond our borders. Seriously: *Are you crying and rocking?*

'Now, your problem is that under the national uniform classification laws of Australia, although the Classification Branch undertook the compliance component, any prosecution for breaching the laws is the responsibility of the states and territories,' Anderson continued.

> I understand there was a nice little gentleman's agreement, and we all came together and agreed to have a national uniform code. What is troubling is that successive governments, including [Scott Morrison's Coalition] commonwealth government, have done absolutely nothing about addressing that gentleman's agreement and revisiting it and saying we need to do something that is workable and consistent everywhere.

Well, maybe not nothing. In December 2019, Morrison's Minister for Communications, Urban Infrastructure, Cities and the Arts, Paul Fletcher, organised a review of the classification system to be undertaken by Mr Neville Stevens AO, who worked as Secretary within the Department of Communications throughout the 1990s. The public was invited to share their thoughts on the classification system, be they major corporations or concerned individuals. Submissions to 'the Stevens Review' closed in February 2020. Then a pandemic happened. Though the review was concluded, it remained shelved while the country got on with the problem of COVID-19. The federal government changed hands 26 months later, but the review continued 'collecting dust' despite it addressing the problem of 'streaming services blatantly and deliberately not getting their stuff classified—because they know no one's coming after them', as Anderson puts it. (The Stevens Review would eventually be released in March 2023, though as of this writing, none of its recommendations have been instituted, but more on that later.)

'Most of the streamers are large American [corporations] or have multinational corporations behind them, and they just sit there going, "Come and get us", she continues. For instance, Amazon Prime Video desired a tool just like Netflix's, but Anderson had to inform them that no such Amazon Classification Tool was on the cards, and that they'd have to submit to the Classification Board instead. Amazon has since declined to submit anything to the Board, and uses its own global rating system: All, 7+, 13+ 16+ and 18+ or 'Not rated'. This brinksmanship was less like a game of three-dimensional chess and more like one player picking up the chessboard and flinging it into the ocean. Anderson certainly doesn't feel like we need to squint to see Amazon's point: 'This is Amazon's way of saying, "Screw you, Australian government. We told you when we were coming—before we landed in the [Australian] market—we told you we wanted to classify just like you let Netflix and yet you haven't let us do it."'

The Board was among the concerned parties who put in a submission to the Stevens Review, where they went into further detail on Amazon's flagrant treatment of Australian classification guidelines:

> It has been of particular concern to the Board that when Amazon Prime commenced streaming in Australia, it utilised the Australian classification markings including the CTC (Check the Classification) marking. This projected a false expectation upon Australian consumers that Amazon Prime would be undertaking an Australian classification process, when it did not and continues not to do so.

They also named and shamed yet another streaming service playing fast and loose with the rules—though this one is homegrown: 'The Board also notes that between 2015 and 2020, Stan Entertainment Pty Ltd submitted only 11 film titles to the board for classification purposes. These 11 titles are not indicative of the total number of unclassified films that have been available for streaming on Stan, which also utilises the Australian classification markings.' Furthermore, the board submissions highlights that 'the primary applicant for pornographic films ... has declined to submit content for classification. This highlights the current lack of compliance with classification laws'.

Of course, Margaret Anderson believes the larger fault lies with Australian government complacency—at least under Morrison's coalition (which had not yet been displaced by Anthony Albanese's Labor government when we spoke in 2022). If they had been on top of things, there may have been an in-house tool just like the Netflix Classification Tool, except less squeamish and more keyed into Australian community standards. She continues,

> While I was deputy and certainly while I was director, I had extensive conversations with my colleague David Shanks in New Zealand and my colleague David Austin who is in charge of the BBFC [British Board of Film Classification]. The three of us absolutely and utterly were committed to the creation of what's called a SIMO, which means Single Input Multiple Output, and that's exactly what you have got with the computer games tool [a questionnaire designed by the International Age Rating Coalition or IARC]. There are about 35 countries that use IARC to classify computer games, and each of those 35 countries has sat down with the software programmer and made sure that the answers to the questions that make up the IARC classification tool are all tweaked to produce a classification decision for that particular country, and it works brilliantly well. Australia's a signatory to that. We've been using it since 2016 and we spent about 18 months with the computer programming people to get the right calibration, so that we would get the correct classification. So you can be a computer programmer anywhere in the world; you want to put your game on the Microsoft storefront or Google Play, they will say, 'Yep, that's all well and good, put it through IARC and get a classification.' [You] end up with a classification not just for Australia but for 34 other countries as well. And it works brilliantly.

Alas, Anderson says the government 'kowtowed to Netflix' when the streaming service, ahead of its launch in the Australian market, complained the board was taking too long to classify their thousands of hours' worth of material. She is emphatic that her board was up to the gauntlet thrown down by Netflix, having up to 15 permanent and part-time classifiers on staff at the time to get through the workload. But what she found most irksome was that the tool was a complete 'furphy', saying

> in order to be broadly consistent with the Australian classification decisions, the Netflix Tool had to produce the same rating or one higher. Now, I've got to say, 'one higher' is not consistent. It is a joke. It's more than a joke: it's an affront to the Australian public to say 'we, the Classification Branch who is, de facto, the Australian government, have decided, Australian public, that it is okay for your understanding of the Australian classification system to be turned on its head by this American corporation who can't be bothered paying the money to get their films classified, and, in the interest of reducing costs for them, have decided that they're going to hoodwink the Australian government and say, 'Oh, we can have this tool that is meant to have a level of accountability' but joyfully, the Australian government hasn't actually provided any staff to undertake and measure that accountability, and to audit those decisions. And the trouble with them overclassifying is that you then are destroying the Australian public's awareness and knowledge and confidence in its own classification system. And this is the old problem: it's a bit like reputation; reputations take a lifetime to be earned and can be destroyed in a moment.

Anderson believes digital classification tools are worthwhile, provided they're robust and held to account. But the Australian government is currently abrogating its duty to Australians and leaving classification—at least in one major instance—in the hands of Americans. The ABC, in their own submission to the Stevens Review, also flagged the conservative nature of Netflix's ratings, concerned that the Americans' modest interpretation of what should be classified 'M' in Australia would make 'M' titles on the public broadcaster appear positively flagrant. 'Now suddenly [the public is] being told that an Australian comedian [on Netflix] is R18+,' Anderson continues. 'Really? Why? Were they naked? Were they performing a sexual act on stage? No, blow me down, it was 15 utterances of cunt language. And the prudish Americans at Netflix had heart failure.'

As of right now, Australia is at the whim of largely American media companies, who are inspiring a drift towards more conservative ratings, when a SIMO was once well within our grasp. At the conclusion of our lengthy chat, Anderson peered into the crystal ball: 'Australia, I think, will wake up one day and go, "Oh shit, we sure missed that boat." And I'll go, "Yep, you sure did. Ship sailed long ago without you."' The board's submission to the long-tabled Stevens Review makes it explicit:

> It is inequitable to require Australian industry assessors to undertake ongoing training and not to have the same requirement imposed upon Netflix, particularly noting that in the year ending 30 June 2019, the Netflix tool made 1,923 decisions ... the board is of the opinion that, given the number of decisions already generated, the use of the tool has irrevocably shifted the Australian classification standard away from Australian cultural mores, to those operative in North America, which is reflective of those undertaking the Netflix meta-tagging and the values of the US-based Netflix corporation. This is particularly evident in relation to the classifiable elements of language, sex and nudity, where the American tolerance is less than the allowance made by Australian consumers.

Is a SIMO the ultimate answer for movie classifications? Well, despite the board today mostly holding back Refused Classification ratings for films, they've turned their piercing attention to video games with even greater ferocity—and it's the single input, multiple output process guiding them. In 2015, around the same time as the Netflix Classification Tool was put to work, the IARC classification tool was developed by IARC members to automate ratings for video games (including mobile and online games). 'The tool requires developers releasing games on participating storefronts to complete a multiple-choice online questionnaire about the content of their game,' reads a report on the Australian pilot program published in 2016. 'Based upon the responses, the tool generates a tailored classification decision for each member rating authority's jurisdiction.' In January of 2017, the IARC tool was approved for ongoing use, and it worked swiftly. In 2018, an incredible 90 games were Refused Classification. In 2019, a further 103 received the dreaded RC. In 2020 and 2021, an additional 100-plus games were banned. Counting those that the IARC tool retroactively reviewed and prohibited, the number of bans has grown beyond 1,600 total.

Putting aside the fact that vastly more games (including those for smartphones) are being produced at this moment in time than films throughout much of the 20th century, it's an undeniable fact that there are now more banned games in Australia than there ever were banned films. And though it's hard—based on titles at least—to go to the mattresses for games such as *Drug Mafia Grand Weed Dealer Simulator* or *Rooster Fighting Game: Kung Fu Farm Battle*, there's also no way of knowing what their artistic benefits might be. The 'think of the children' brigade barely needed to start a petition for this campaign. The pilot for the IARC was inspired by gruelling administration, not public demonstration. 'If applications for all mobile and online games were submitted, the board in its present form would be unable to cope with the workload,' the pilot report continues. 'Additionally, if compliance action were taken for all unclassified online content ... it would impose a financial burden on industry which could threaten the existence of smaller operations and encourage some to withdraw or limit their Australian market presence.' The pilot report found that the media outlets weren't kicking up a stink over their strict decisions: 'There was a level of interest (but very little criticism) in the number of games that had been classified Refused Classification by the tool.' There were just five complaints from the community relating to the IARC tool's decisions during the pilot. Maybe that means it didn't warrant much complaint. Perhaps every banned game deserved to be banned. This book isn't about the effectiveness of the IARC tool nor the classification and censorship of video games. Other critics could reasonably adopt the perspective that video games are indeed largely targeted at minors, and those that ask the gamer to engage in antisocial conduct or literal gambling via the purchase of lootboxes need strict classification or censorship. But we now face a future in which the boards— flawed as they might be—are circumvented entirely by tech solutions that evaluate content without context, opt for the more conservative rating, and teach creators to save themselves the expense of appeal and take the safest, most palatable route from the get-go—or, hell, just release whatever, whenever, for anyone without oversight at all. Film classification and censorship in the 2020s is a matter of extremes—too much or none at all. This tortuous, century-long game of snakes and ladders hasn't solidified our freedoms of art, expression or speech in Australia, nor has it earned the confidence of the public in the protection of valuable, challenging movies *or* our most vulnerable viewers. More than 100 years after *The Story of the Kelly Gang*, lawlessness rules the land again.

EFFED UP FACT:

In late 2022, Sony Pictures resubmitted *Lyle, Lyle, Crocodile*—about a singing crocodile voiced by Shawn Mendes—with one minute excised after it initially earned a PG-rating. The modified version of the family fable was rated G and released in theatres. Should we have stormed the barracks and demanded the reinsertion of *Lyle, Lyle, Crocodile*'s lost minute? Does it still count as censorship of the enraging variety if the government didn't do it and the copyright owners are okay with it and the offending minute was put back in place for the DVD and Blu-ray? I won't relitigate those questions here, partly because I haven't seen *Lyle, Lyle, Crocodile*, and you can't make me. For the purpose of this book I viewed some seriously rough stuff, but I cannot safely subject myself to a viewing of *Lyle, Lyle, Crocodile* as well. Wearied by years spent in the censorship trenches, I'm afraid I have to let someone else serve as *Lyle, Lyle, Crocodile*'s defender and champion.

CHAPTER 16
A COLLECTIVE FAILURE OF NERVE

In Martin McDonagh's 2003 play *The Pillowman*, an author of sadistic fairy tales is arrested under suspicion of committing a spate of child-mutilating crimes that mirror his published work. Katurian, the author, is actually pretty quick to cooperate with the police officers of his unnamed authoritarian state, while still insisting on his innocence. Later Katurian finds out—spoiler alert—that his brother, Michal, is the child killer, having been inspired by his grisly stories. Katurian is shocked and appalled, but Michal's logic is, in his mind at least, faultless.

> MICHAL: All the things I did to all the kids I got from stories you wrote and read out to me.
> KATURIAN: You said that to the policeman?
> MICHAL: Mm. Y'know, just the truth.
> KATURIAN: That isn't the truth, Michal.
> MICHAL: Yes it is.
> KATURIAN: No it isn't.
> MICHAL: Well, did you write some stories with children getting murdered in them?
> KATURIAN: Yes, but ...
> MICHAL: Well, did you read them out to me?
> KATURIAN: Yes ...
> MICHAL: Well, did I go out and murder a bunch of children? (Pause.) 'Yes, I did,' is the answer to that one. So I don't see how the 'That isn't the truth' comes into it.

Though that's the long and the short of Michal's motives, there's plenty more context to be considered: Michal was tortured as a child; Katurian's stories were derived from a youth spent listening to Michal's abuse in the adjoining room; there's even the underlying possibility that the authoritarian police have invented the murders—and influenced Michal's admission—to stymy Katurian and his subversive works. But McDonagh, a playwright and screenwriter who's never one to mince words, at least asks us to consider strongly that the murders a) did happen, b) were directly influenced by Katurian's creative writing and c) while tragic, shouldn't taint the stories themselves. (Katurian offers to confess to police in exchange for the promised protection of his texts.) In effect: sure, the criminal should be punished, the author should consider the repercussions of their creations and the state should protect the populace. Just leave the art itself alone please.

A modern Classification Board needs to hold these conflicting ideas in its head: that the creation of art may have unintended consequences, yet that art should still be available for public consumption. It requires a steely resolve, both from the board and the country. Will it ever be possible for our society to have the necessary public conversation about the value of challenging, subversive, literally-by-definition-illegal art in the face of all the hypothetical social ramifications feared by the authorities? There may be reason to believe that time will soon arrive, but it's not here yet. In March 2023, the Albanese government published the fabled Stevens Review into Australian classification regulation; a 145-page document that, amusingly, ends with the three words 'nudity is permitted'. (Context is everything, but still, funny.)

The Stevens Review pledged

> to update Australia's classification scheme to reflect today's digital environment and will cover delivery platforms including broadcasting services, online stores and services, cinema releases and physical media (boxed video games and DVDs). Led by independent expert, Mr Neville Stevens AO, it will include consultation on the National Classification Code and the Guidelines for the Classification of Films and the Guidelines for the Classification of Computer Games, which are used to make classification decisions. Reviewing the current regulation will help to develop a new classification scheme that reflects modern content and delivery platforms to meet the needs of industry while providing appropriate information and protections for Australians.

A review like that could clarify the grey matters this book has explored, particularly for all those features classified, self-censored or refused classification since 1995. Neville's report was submitted in May 2020, but as Margaret Anderson's successor as Classification Board director, Fiona Jolly, noted in October 2022's Annual Report for the board, 'The former government did not progress classification reform prior to the conclusion of its final term. I am looking forward to working with the new Minister for Communications, the Hon. Michelle Rowland, and the department, to keep the classification system evolving to meet the community's and industry's needs.'

The problem is not just that the Morrison government buried the Stevens Review; it's that the Albanese government published it unceremoniously, refused to provide a formal government response and committed to only a few reforms (most relating to the classification of video games that simulate gambling). This despite the fact Stevens uncovered what this book has argued and has been clear to most other observers who've been paying attention for the past two decades: this creaky classification system—last changed with any significance in 1995 and left to squalor by both Labor and Liberal governments—is ill-equipped for modern media consumers.

The issues raised by public submissions and reinforced by the review included the high cost of getting content classified by the board; the lengthy classification timeframes; the lack of clarity on what kind of content actually requires classification; the lack of compliance among content providers based on the aforementioned concerns; the disconnect between the Australian government and the roles and responsibilities of the states and territories; and the fact that classification guidelines are infrequently reviewed, which means they rarely reflect contemporary concerns or current community standards. So, basically, everything.

Stevens recommends a new classification framework that can adapt to the changing tides of technology and community sentiment, and even an update to the key principles of the National Classification Code. The bolded words reflect his additions and changes:

- Adults should be able to read, hear, see and play what they want, **with limited exception**;
- Minors should be protected from content likely to harm or disturb them; and
- Everyone should be protected from exposure to **content of serious concern to the wellbeing of the community** [replacing 'unsolicited material that they find offensive'].

His recommendation eradicates the fourth principle: 'the need to take account of community concerns about: (i) depictions that condone or incite violence, particularly sexual violence; (ii) the portrayal of persons in a demeaning manner.' That's because his review finds the use of 'demeaning' problematic, especially if it refers to someone demeaning themselves freely. Which brings us to the suggestion that might boggle the wowsers' minds into cranial contractions: No more kink-shaming please! 'For X18+ films, I recommend that the absolute prohibitions on fetishes, which are not illegal, and violence (where it is unrelated to sex) should be removed,' Stevens writes. That includes—yes, let's run it down again—body piercing, application of substances such as candle wax, "golden showers", bondage, spanking or fisting. He doesn't mention the men in nappies, but surely the sunlight of acceptance is peeking through that door too.

Stevens does, however, note the significance of context when evaluating movies that depict young people in sexual scenarios, allowing that it may be justified by a storyline, such as in a film that dramatises the 'coming-of-age of an adolescent [including] scenes of *implied*, consensual, underage sexual activity', or a film that deals with child abuse and its impacts on victims. 'However sexualised depictions of minors (whether real or animated) that are gratuitous, exploitative or offensive, and which sexually objectify children should never be permitted.' To figure out when a film crosses that line, Stevens suggests a Classification Advisory Panel (inspired by the system used in the Netherlands) made up of experts in child development or other related fields, to provide guidance on the classification guidelines every four years (or whenever they may be called upon for specific contentious titles).

Margaret Anderson and I spoke after her tenure on the board had come to an end. (One can only serve for seven years.) I asked her why the Stevens Review, initiated in her final year as director, had been so thoroughly ignored by the government after apparently warranting enquiry to begin with. 'Because it's not sexy, and it doesn't involve terrorists.' She continued: 'I do criticise mainstream media here, because it is equally responsible for not picking up and running with the broader social and cultural issues of the country. So as long as the Australian public is seen to be silent and not caring about classification, government's not gonna be motivated to do anything. And yet there are some really great solutions.' It could also be that the public, perhaps not knowing any different is largely fine with the status quo. A government-initiated 2022 research report into classification usage and attitudes found that '88% of respondents felt classification was personally useful and almost all felt it was useful to people responsible for children (97%) and to the Australian community (96%)', while '79% of respondents agreed that the [classification] system met their expectations'.

One of the many recommendations in the Anderson-led Classification Board's submission to the review includes the proposal of a PG-13-rating, similar to the one in the US, though here the recommended nomenclature would be YP (young person). 'Modern cinema and film streaming has evolved greatly in the past 25 years since the Code was developed and the Code no longer reflects the way in which society is categorised (adults, young people and children), nor does it reflect the vast spectrum of films and computer games that sit in the PG and M classifications,' their submission states. 'This same phenomena of exponential change was recognised in America in the 1980s, and it responded at the time by developing a PG-13 classification to address its then-deficit in classification categories.' Unfortunately, even before it has been applied this recommendation feels a day late and a dollar short, given that young people—a specific kind of vulnerable viewer—are more commonly relating to and harmonising with MA15+ and R18+ content; at least, in the way streamers have rated their output. (A by-product of Netflix bumping so many titles up by one classification tier means movies and TV shows that should be rated M—and would naturally appeal to younger audiences—are blending in with those that actually deserve MA15+ or R-ratings.)

Anderson raises the spectre of TV series increasingly gaining release without classification (on streaming services, specifically). In fact, she cited perhaps the rare piece of Netflix content that was perhaps self-classified too casually: *13 Reasons Why*, the high school series centring on a teen suicide that hit a global nerve, forcing the streamer to add a retroactive warning before episodes, and, years later, edit out the climactic suicide scene entirely. She says,

> Not everyone is old enough to deal with the material, and even people who are adults, they could inadvertently watch something which, if they had had consumer advice prior to watching that film—if they'd had a classification category prior to watching that film—they actually would have gone, 'Ooh, this might not be for me.' I think what's incredibly important is what's set out in the National Classification Code, in Clause 1, and I absolutely still believe that's relevant: that people ought to be informed about things before they watch, so they can make some

kind of a decision. They want to go off and do some more research, go to your favourite search engine, type it in and see what somebody else has written, and decide whether or not they want to watch. But I think it's really important with not just children but young people, and particularly if you think about that Netflix series *13 Reasons Why*. There were some shocking things that happened, worldwide, in terms of an increase in both suicide attempts when that first season screened, and there was a number of bits of research that were done after that first season, particularly in the United States, and one of them found that literally there was an increase in the first two and a half weeks following the release of Season 1 in searches on how to commit suicide.

Research also showed an increase in the suicide rate among 10 to 17-year-olds in the month immediately following the release of *13 Reasons Why*.

Anderson continues:

I just think, particularly with young people, those teenage years, early adulthood, you're really vulnerable, and I think for people who are parents or other carers or guardians of young people, you need help, and I think the classification process is one way of getting some preliminary indication about something you may want to make further enquiries about.

The current suite of ratings would remain if Stevens' recommendations were adopted. Stevens saw no need for the YP-rating. He also suggested that enforcing the legal restriction of MA15+ content online was basically impossible, so it should be left up to parents and technology solutions at home, though restrictions in the cinema should remain. As for Refused Classification, Stevens simply suggests renaming the category 'Prohibited', freeing titles from their Kafka-like prison of appearing both classified and refused classification at the same time.

'So, do you need classification?' Anderson asks me rhetorically. 'Yeah, we do. Because what's really, really important in this country—and sets us apart from places like England—is that we don't censor, and we do not have a cuts list. So, you classify whatever is put in. I think that's incredibly important and sets us apart from some of the western democracies.' She says, going forward, I would have a Classification Board continuing to classify theatrically released films. I then think the importance of the Board lies very much in doing what is not being done now, which is auditing what the Netflix Tool is doing, and the government needs to create a single input, multiple output film classification tool that all the streaming services can use. And that's an absolute must.

The last major movement for the classification board occurred in 2014, when the Coalition government, in an effort to reduce the overall number of government bodies, amalgamated the Classification Review Board with the Administrative Appeals Tribunal, the Migration Review Tribunal and Refugee Review Tribunal. What had once been a concern of customs was now being held at the same level of gravity as human movement. Prior to that was the review of the National Classification Scheme in 2011—yes, nine years before the Stevens Review—when the Senate Legal and Constitutional References Committee wrote,

> The National Classification Scheme is flawed, and cannot be sustained in its current form. This is primarily because the scheme has not been successful in achieving a uniform and consistent approach to classification in Australia. Further, the current situation where the National Classification Scheme is loosely paralleled by co-regulatory and self-regulatory systems is far from adequate, particularly given the increasing convergence of media.

And yet the industry today still moves on without clarity; self-censoring with an understanding of the costs and risks involved in sending a thematically tricky work to the board, or avoiding the censors completely by releasing the content online, unlawfully unrated. Take *Violation*. After its sneaky unrated addition to Shudder in Australia, the picture was eventually submitted to the Classification Board by RLJ Entertainment for its subsequent physical media release, receiving a rating of R18+ on 6 August 2021 for 'high impact themes, violence, sexualised nudity and sexual violence'. Despite Dr Janice Loreck's initial suspicions, the board said *Violation* could be accommodated as is in the R18+ category, and the movie was burnt onto Blu-rays unbanned. '[Dylan] spits on his hand before a close-up of his penis is viewed as he masturbates,' the board's decision report describes. 'As Dylan continues to describe his sexual fantasy, Miriam walks behind him and suddenly bludgeons him with a blunt object. The scene cuts and the camera spins in a blurred view of a forest before Miriam and Dylan are depicted talking as they lie on the ground next to a campfire. In the Board's opinion, given that the elements of sex and nudity are inextricably linked, consumer advice of high impact sexualised nudity is appropriate.' Would *Violation* have passed similarly if initially submitted by Shudder? Or, since it already existed unrated on Shudder, did the board feel compelled to give it a pass, lest it be considered negligent, or accept that Shudder had pulled a fast one on them? *Violation* will forever be the Schrodinger's cat of the Classification Board, with us simply left to speculate what the board might have said of it upon first glance. (In their 2022 Annual Report, they didn't even refer to the sexualised murder sequence while referring to *Violation* as a notable example of an R-rated decision, instead describing how its 'depiction of the sexual assault is limited to abstracted close-ups'.)

It turns out this isn't even the most egregious example of a streaming service disregarding the board's rule of law in Australia. Throughout the research of this book—especially after reading about how 'adults imitating infants' became such a point of contention in defining the parameters of the X-rating—my mind turned to the TV shows *Pen15* and *Euphoria*. The former is an acclaimed, Emmy-nominated comedy from Hulu in the United States, created by and starring thirty-somethings Maya Erskine and Anna Konkle as their 13-year-old selves alongside actual teens and pre-teens. It's an excellent and astutely observed show, navigating the sticky, awkward experience of teenagerdom through the prism of a conceptual angle that makes things even more discomfiting, particularly when the adult women Erskine and Konkle appear to make-out with 13-year-olds. (As the credits note—and is clearly apparent due to the stubble on the lips of those they're kissing in extreme close-up—adult body doubles are used for those sequences.) According to Stan, its Australian distributor, *Pen15* is rated MA15+, though I could find no official listing on the classification website; not even for the show's final batch of episodes released in late 2021, in which Erskine's character Maya conducts simulated fellatio on another teenage character, culminating in graphic detail (showing everything shy of the penis). I wondered: Did Stan avoid submitting the final season, suspecting it would not have been up to snuff for the Board, given what we now know about the incidents involving *Salò*, *The Tin Drum* and *The Trouble With Being Born*? I asked the board if *Pen15* was submitted for classification at all, and discovered, it wasn't; not its second season, and not its first season either. Stan seemingly decided to take their chance with the board—and the law—by illegally uploading the high-profile *Pen15* in Australia with an assumed rating, having never submitted it for classification. And they got away with it. As of this writing, they're still getting away with it. As mentioned, they only submitted 11 film titles to the board for classification between 2015 and 2020, and that did not include the second season of *The Girlfriend Experience* from 2017, which features numerous graphic sex scenes, including perhaps the most convincing simulated blow job ever committed to the small screen.

Stan isn't alone, either. Foxtel made the scandalous teen drama *Euphoria* available to stream on its subsidiary service Binge without having submitted it for classification, despite the program featuring nudity (often full-frontal male) and regular sex scenes concerning high schoolers (played by 20-somethings). In October 2022, *Euphoria*'s first two seasons finally received an R-rating when submitted to the Board by Roadshow Entertainment for a home entertainment release. This was more than three years after its June 2019 premiere on Binge and Foxtel. (The show carries an MA-rating on Foxtel, which is the highest rating available through the Australian Subscription Television and Radio Association (ASTRA) codes of practice. Foxtel, like the ABC, has their own classification guidelines for the content they broadcast, which is regulated by ACMA, the Australian Communications and Media Authority, but Binge has to play by the Classification Board's rules.)

On the matter of streaming services, Stevens concurred that they really should be classifying their films and shows, provided they're 'professionally produced ... distributed on a commercial basis [and] directed at an Australian audience' (to differentiate, say, *The Marvelous Mrs. Maisel* on Amazon from a Russian child's unboxing video on YouTube). This would also be the criteria for sexually explicit films requiring classification too. Those who failed to classify relevant content should face 'fines or other civil penalties'. He did, however, encourage industry to take greater responsibility for self-classification, using approved in-house staff, third-party classifiers or classification tools like Netflix, which, he argued, is 'achieving the requirements set out in the Classification Act'. That said, he also endorsed the idea of a classification tool developed by the Department that could be made available to all content providers free of charge. Stevens also recommended the allowance for content providers to reclassify titles after 10 years to better reflect the new community standards. 'To continue high levels of community confidence in classification, industry self-classification must be underpinned by a robust accreditation, audit, review and timely complaints mechanism overseen by the Australian Government regulator,' he adds.

That regulator, Stevens believes, should be ACMA. Giving ACMA sole regulatory powers would end the job-sharing it's doing with the Classification Board, the Classification Review Board, and whichever government department they happen to fall under at any one time (it's hard to keep up). But that would also cease the need for a Classification Review Board, with ACMA charged with reviewing any classification decisions upon appeal.

I am conflicted when it comes to blowing up the spots of *Pen15*, *Euphoria* and *The Girlfriend Experience*, believing that *Pen15* in particular explores the difficult subject matter of teen sexuality through a necessary adult lens, with seemingly responsible working conditions to protect the younger actors. But there is a fair assumption that its local distributor believes the current classification system could perceive it as pornographic. Wherever you draw the line on art and exploitation, wouldn't it be better to have some kind of reasonable regulation when it comes to depictions of sexual activity in which adults portray minors rather than letting the content creators distribute it directly to the masses simply to avoid our classification mechanism? Conversely, if either of these shows had been released on Netflix, and left to the mercy of its Netflix Classification Tool, who knows how high a rating they might have received? Would they have been released at all? (That raised another interesting query: Can the Netflix Classification Tool *ban* movies and TV shows too? Turns out: yep.) A thoughtful human—like Margaret Anderson—might have been able to identify the nuance and intent of *Pen15* and *Euphoria* better than the so-called Netflix Classification Tool or even an internally developed SIMO—and maybe Stevens' suggested Classification Advisory Panel could offer that necessary advice. In November of 2022, Minister for Communications Michelle Rowland announced the implementation of a third option: the Spherex Classification Tool. More than 100 countries have relied on Spherex, a Silicon Valley–based data company, to produce classification decisions for online content, Australia now among them. How does it work? You'd have to untangle the technogarble from their promotional spiel to figure it out:

> The number of titles released annually is growing exponentially, and it is impossible for humans alone to accurately and consistently assess content for cultural compliance and suitability. Spherex solves this problem using expert-in-the-loop artificial intelligence and machine learning with the

goal of understanding human language, emotion, and the cultural context of content. A title is screened by both machines and humans to detect and classify cultural events. The system then produces reliable and consistent age ratings for every country worldwide—saving significant time and cost—and enabling international expansion at scale.

Effectively, Spherex lets AI scan films to identify any potential problems based on the nuances of a nation's culture and classification system, with humans tweaking the machines and their algorithms as a sort-of controversy backstop. Just like the Netflix Classification Tool, Spherex must still 'produce classification decisions that are broadly consistent with Australian community standards and with classification decisions made by the Board.' It must also 'have the capacity to refuse classification to films that meet the criteria in ... the approval guidelines.' It also can't classify anything intended for public exhibition or physical distribution—same as the Netflix Classification Tool. Maybe Spherex, a tech solution with a human touch, will solve every conceivable issue when it comes to classification going forward, but this writer personally felt a chill reading the words 'machine learning with the goal of understanding human language, emotion, and the cultural context of content.'

This will nonetheless be welcome news to Amazon Prime Video, who had previously been called out for using Australian classification markings despite ignoring the local classification processes. (Guess what? They kept doing it long after the board made their disregard of the system public. Amazon's sexually explicit erotic thriller *Deep Water* from 2022 carries an MA-rating on their website and app but hasn't actually been classified in Australia at all.) According to the *Australian Financial Review*, all streaming services operating in Australia will be able to use the Spherex tool, which promises to provide a classification within 24 hours, compared to the board's standard 20 days (or five working days in the case of a priority application).

But what about unofficial online releases? In 1992, the board refused classification to *Dr. Lamb*, a Hong Kong horror film about a serial killer confessing to his frenzied crimes after a beating at police hands. Hong Kong censors awarded it a Category III classification, excluding anyone under the age of 18 from watching it. In Australia, it scored the equivalent R-rating two years later, but only after eight minutes had been excised. As to what was cut, critic James Mudge describes 'some outstandingly unpleasant sequences of Lam hacking away at the corpses with scalpels and power tools, including the frenzied slicing of one mercifully dead woman's breasts (this scene is shortened in the cut version).' Out of curiosity, I googled 'Dr. Lamb full movie' to see if I could watch it easily online. It had been uploaded in full, uncut, to YouTube, with the only impediment to my viewing the necessity to 'log in' as proof that I was over the age of 18. Again, I am not one to complain about seeing an uncensored movie that is otherwise unavailable (and illegal) in Australia. But this contravening of Australia's byzantine and century-old system was almost too easy.

†

Make no mistake: things are (mostly) better in the space of film classification and censorship in Australia these days. There is transparency, at the very least. The Gore Vidal-penned 1979 feature *Caligula*—which held the record for the longest continual ban in Australian history—was submitted for re-evaluation by Umbrella Entertainment in 2021, and it received an R-rating. (Umbrella nonetheless told me they have no plans for a release.) The guidelines for acceptable violence in X-rated movies were amended last decade, following the absurd *Dream Quest* debacle, spurred by the cheeky release structure of the big budget porno *Pirates 2* in 2008: in the ACT, it was cut into two features—one featuring hardcore sex and without violence, and one with the violence (which, it should be noted, was of the sword-fighting skeletons variety) but no hardcore sex—and sold together. The 'official but unpublished' guidelines for violence in X-rated films were apparently updated with these clarifications, per an unofficial document that was circulated among adult industry professionals. And scholar Catherine Schubert, in her thesis *Film Classification and Censorship in Australia: a filmic image response perspective*, reminds that 'no films have been refused classification under the current legislation for images of violence alone,' unlike in eras past. (The two exceptions, *Executions* and *Faces of Death II – IV*, contain at least *some* actual on-screen deaths.)

Organisations on the religious right—having parlayed their initial stoushes with the board into greater cultural battles for society's souls—don't appear to pay much attention to scandalous film releases anymore either. Fred Nile—who remained in NSW parliament until 2023, when he was in his late 80s—didn't say peep when Paul Verhoeven's blasphemous *Benedetta* was rated R18+ in September of 2021 for 'high impact sex scenes', including one in which its titular Mother Superior is pleasured by her lady servant with a sex toy fashioned from the bottom end of a Blessed Virgin statuette. (As a witness to the act describes it within the movie, the servant 'brings [Benedetta] to crisis.') Nile could no longer muster up a measly complaint against a scandalising erotic thriller that features multiple nuns exhibiting full frontal nudity. Two decades ago, he could dominate several news cycles by dunking on smut-loving arthouse elites. No longer. Perhaps his desire to fight minor culture wars was dead, having identified more heathenistic foils: chiefly, marriage equality and halal certification. Or perhaps Nile was subject to divine intervention. In May 2022, he announced himself as leader of the Seniors United Party of Australia (SUPA), pledging to stand at the 2023 NSW state election aged 88. It dovetailed with the introduction of a bill to protect Aboriginal culture; a collaboration with independent MP (and former Australian Marriage Equality head) Alex Greenwich. At the time, Nile openly stated that SUPA party membership was open to all (not just Christians), and the party's policies, according to its website, included a stunning stance on marriage equality; specifically, that they believe the union of marriage isn't dependent on any particular gender or combination of genders. However, one month later, SUPA was deregistered by the Australian Electoral Commission. (Was *that* the divine intervention?) By October 2022, Nile pledged to step down at the next election so his wife Silvana could represent his Revive Australia (Fred Nile Alliance) party in his place. In early 2023, he reversed course once more and decided to follow Silvana in second position on the same ticket. In a pre-emptive exit interview with Peter FitzSimons for the *Sydney Morning Herald*, he was steadfast: 'I can't think of any single belief or activity where I've had that feeling that I was wrong.' When pressed by FitzSimons, he at least apologised for praying for rain during Mardi Gras. At the time of his election loss in March 2023, he was the longest serving member of NSW parliament. That same month, Nile collapsed at a protest of Channel 10 program *The Project*, which had featured a queer comedian making a joke about Jesus.

†

There are and have been plenty of good people working in classification to achieve that difficult balance of allowing free speech while protecting vulnerable individuals (even if they've erred towards conservatism more often than not). Interestingly, at the time of *Salò*'s short-lived release in the 1990s, the argument was made that the new Classification Board (comprising journalists and writers, lecturers, teachers, counsellors and adolescent support workers) did not reflect the current community or their standards, a stunning contrast to previous combinations that did not rely on even a single academic or thinker of film. I maintain a board comprised of thinkers is preferable to the alternative.

The Classification Review Board has also helpfully stepped in to right some of the Classification Board's wrongs, as in the case of 1988's *Moon, Star and Sun*, which was banned by the board only to receive an R-rating the next year following an appeal. The Hong Kong–produced picture—which details the oftentimes degrading lives of four prostitutes—contains some rape sequences and was reportedly of 'little artistic merit' to those who re-evaluated it, but as the review board wrote in their decision,

> *Moon, Star and Sun* ... is not the sort of junk film or blatantly exploitative vehicle for which refusal might be warranted. It deals with an aspect of modern society that cannot be ignored; incidents of the kind depicted are inseparable from the lifestyles and experiences of the women portrayed. Moreover, although some of the subject matter is extremely ugly, the story is relieved by good humour and by a degree of sensitivity in its treatment of the relationships between the girls. While the film is not one which members of the Board would necessarily commend, neither is it one, in their view, which adult audiences should be prevented from seeing if they wish.

Some may wonder why, then, a book like this needs to be written. Is it just to publicise and plaster the board's mistakes or question their decisions when the grand majority of films are still seeing the light of day compared to the darkened era that immediately followed the birth of cinema? Those same people may wonder why numerous websites still track the Australian deletions—both minor and major—from films, be they censored back in the bad old days of the state boards, or edited down by distributors more recently. For instance, did you know the Australian DVD release of Jan De Bont's 1996 disaster flick *Twister* is missing two uses of the word 'fuck'? You can thank website *The Chopping List* for that revelation. *Twister*'s cuts may not seem like a big deal in isolation—and, truly, they aren't—but it's the result of the edited UK master print being used as a source for the DVD (since we share a PAL video format with Europe) rather than the Australian cut, because why would anyone check that the correct, unedited edition was in play? The same happened to the local DVDs of *GoldenEye*, *The Glimmer Man* and *Enter the Dragon*. Earlier in this book we lamented the fact that the censors of the 1960s and 1970s were slashing existing prints of movies ahead of their film festival berths, and then putting them back into recirculation, meaning Australia was guilty of cinematic graffiti and responsible for 'losing' films and scenes that previous generations had deemed in defiance of contemporary mores. Wither *Twister*?

The website refused-classification.com studiously tracks the cuts made to films by distributors as well, such as 2020's gentle Naomi Watts drama *Penguin Bloom*, which was mysteriously downgraded from M to PG, with its 'themes' reduced from 'moderate' to 'mild' by the magical reduction of 'blood detail' from a car crash scene. They also caught Roadshow Films snipping the use of 'fucking' from *Crazy Rich Asians*, which garnered the picture a PG-rating in cinemas after previously being rated M. The YouTube page 'Australia Movie & TV Censorship' also notes when censored films are played on Australian television, creating video montages to compare uncut scenes with their more palatable made-for-TV editions. They all understand that measuring the modern-day mauling of movies as sub-necessary as 2011's Nicolas Cage vehicle *Drive Angry* is as valuable as understanding the reasons why *Breathless* was so scandalous in the 1960s: if this whole censorship agreement is based on some vague definition of current moral standards, we need to know what assumptions are being made—or what instructions are being handed out—prior to any cuts. There is no better audio-visual representation of who we are and what we'll allow than the collated scenes, shots and lines of dialogue that made someone with scissors feel highly nervous indeed. Those sites—and this book—aim to prove that Australians, despite the lies we tell ourselves about ourselves, are terrible at holding our nerve and upholding what we consider our foundational values. What Stephen Murray-Smith wrote in 1970, in *Australia's Censorship Crisis*, holds true today:

> Censorship had and has an inbuilt accelerative component. Firstly, to censor you need a censorship apparatus, and such an apparatus is self-perpetuating and self-assertive. Secondly, for those who practice it, censorship is an extremely *efficient* means of raising political capital; it costs little in time, effort and money, but in favourable circumstances it denotes, in the governments which sponsor it, incorruptible moral standards and a ceaseless vigilance on behalf of the public weal. Thirdly, and at a deeper politico-psychological level, it is a cathartic exercise of power for the politician of the right stamp: it is the kind of authoritative, unambiguous, far-reaching and morally-righteous action which politicians would like to be taking all the time, but which in most cases the nature of

politics itself does not permit ... Indeed, more than this, for censorship has been the one way in which the typical anti-intellectualism of the Australian voter has been given legislative force. It has been the one effective way to hit at the egg-head so that it hurts. Most voters have seen it as a harmless, even a diverting, exercise.

We have seen the tool of censorship used in this way throughout each of the decades, establishing and reinforcing the special interest groups who have countered social progress until they find themselves among the nation's lawmakers, Fred Nile being just the mascot for a movement, and Brian Harradine just one instrument among many. Note that, after Harradine's retirement, Family First's Steve Fielding—described by David Marr as a 'happy clapper from Melbourne's Bible Belt'—happily stepped into the morally superior position in parliament, to be followed by Liberal Senator (and later Tasmanian Premier) Guy Barnett, who incited the 2011 re-evaluation of film classification laws under the short-lived Labor government that replaced Howard's Federal Coalition. Though Labor didn't play the morality card as much, they still took advantage of the cultural shift towards conservatism. This included a surprising return to raids of adult shops under Prime Minister Kevin Rudd, with the authorities seeking unclassified pornography that would otherwise be assigned to the RC category. It led to the imprisonment of one Sydney proprietor in 2010, marking the first jailing of an Australian for the reason of distributing porn since 1948 (though in the '48 case, it was author Robert Close who was sentenced to three months behind bars for his book *Love Me Sailor*).

Rudd's government had also put forward the proposal for an internet service provider (ISP) blocking policy that sought to filter the internet, block RC content from overseas, and empower ACMA to remove RC content simply under 'presumption', meaning they didn't have to actually check if the content had been refused classification with the Classification Board. Mistakes were made, resulting in Communications Minister Stephen Conroy ultimately conceding that some 'faceless bureaucrats' had blacklisted sites ultimately found to be housing completely legal R-rated material, and, most bafflingly, the homepage of a Queensland dentist. Conroy eventually backed down on the policy in 2012, following years of robust debate and complaint, but Labor's reign was months away from coming to an end anyway. The career of a shadow minister within the Coalition, however, was on the upswing: it was one Scott Morrison, a Howard acolyte, who had insisted the then-government was allowing minors access to R-rated material and that this was the equivalent to exposing them to pornography. Once he became Prime Minister, Morrison would rush the *Surveillance Legislation Amendment (Identify and Disrupt) Bill* into law, which the Human Rights Law Centre accused of providing 'unprecedented powers for the Australian Federal Police and Australian Criminal Intelligence Commission to monitor online activity, takeover accounts and disrupt data.' Morrison's Coalition government had already overseen raids on ABC headquarters and a Canberra journalist's home by the Australian Federal Police, claiming national security leaks. Those who blinked blankly at the detainment of Margaret Pomeranz probably wouldn't see any trouble with this jackbooted escalation among journalists.

'Creeping censorship in Australia can only be held in check by an unremitting counter-offensive employing every available device: ridicule, legalisms [and] publicity both internally and internationally,' Murray-Smith wrote in 1970. I hope this book can at least inspire a temporary halt of any further censorship-creep in this early stage of the 21st century, much as those previously cited texts did in their era. That requires vigilance on your end too. If you're reading this because you're a film aficionado, take advantage of the public classification.gov.au website and kick up a stink when it appears the board or Netflix or Spherex has rated a film too harshly, or hell, even when a distributor has resubmitted a trimmed version of their own product. The cuts I'm picking over might seem like small potatoes, but just like David Stratton wanting to protect literal cinema from being mutilated, your film fandom should extend to your desire to uphold film history in Australia. Don't resign yourself to offering last rites for lost films. And definitely don't give any more power to the fringe moral crusaders who used and abused the concept of 'offensiveness' to gain a foothold in the public sphere. Like Margaret Pomeranz standing up—and risking it all—for challenging artworks that may have few other champions, we're going to need to bring the fight to them after decades of letting them set the tenor and tempo of the culture wars.

I also hope the next generation of writers, critics and film fans will do the same when it seems a government is overreaching and filmmakers are being denied a reasonable avenue of expression, no matter how enlightened those future times may be. After all, over the past hundred years of cinema, we can clearly identify how periods of uninhibited expression were closely offset by a reactionary movement, and vice versa; when the buttoned-up values of the 1950s were defied by the 'free love' 1960s, which met its opposite in the late '60s counter-counter-culture. (Never forget that Nile's Festival of Light, later FamilyVoice Australia, was founded in 1972, the year of *Barry McKenzie*'s first cinematic outing.) There has always been an 'other' to fear—be it communists, foreigners, the LGBTIQA+ community, and who knows who's next?—and a body of reactionaries to scapegoat them accordingly. In 1970s Queensland, fundamentalist Christian organisations STOP (the Society to Outlaw Pornography) and CARE (the Committee Against Regressive Education) campaigned in favour of monitoring film, television, radio, children's books and state libraries for texts that challenged their moral beliefs. Its director, Rona Joyner, claimed then that communists and socialists deliberately used pornography—as they defined it—to undermine the Christian religion and social mores. They were among many who urged the conservative Queensland government to take a more reactionary stance than their national counterparts. In Melbourne, at the same time as Don Chipp was seeking to gradually nudge Australia away from state censorship and towards personal responsibility, a reactive book titled *Mr. Chipp and the Porno-Push* was published, in which authors R.A. and J.A. Strong unwittingly showed their hand at what horrors they felt a more permissive society might allow:

> The question, however, is not, naively, whether there is in some way in us our own censor; but rather on the one hand how it got there, and on the other its moral degree, its level of civilisation as it were. Mr. Chipp will surely not maintain for example that the 'censor' one might find in an untutored savage of New Guinea is characterised by the same moral sensibility, the same conception of human dignity, etc., as in the 'censor' of a responsible Australian editor. For naturally the savage's 'censor' is only appropriate to the primitive social and materials situation in which he finds himself... Your savage society will become a civilized society and will rise to high material standards only when the 'censor' in its members becomes a civilised censor. On the other hand you can *reduce* a civilised society in short measure to hippy or tribalist level by phasing in, through the developing young, inappropriate moral standards.

For them, the figurative fig leaf was the only thing standing between modern civilisation and savagery.

As history has proven, blaming on-screen sex and violence—or even transgressive themes—for social ills is usually just the first, easy step to gaining an audience for your right-wing brand. David Haines—the censor-turned-porn-producer—lamented this in his final days as deputy censor, speaking out at a Queensland University of Technology conference against the pressure groups pushing their fringe agendas, as well as the willing media that amplifies their flawed, skewed, unrepresentative views. Is the media being connived once again when it comes to the banning of video games?

Australian society needs to decide whether we can trust an independent arm of a government department to detachedly review and classify films by checklist, or if we want them to apply moral reasoning by thinking of each work's potential value to society, and its harm. Sex education advocacy not-for-profit Consent Labs would prefer the latter, especially as they've begun advocating for a 'consent' classification that would identify films and TV shows that misrepresent affirmative sexual consent (examples include *The Empire Strikes Back* and *The Devil Wears Prada*). Based on their campaign, launched in September 2022, they specifically call for such a classification to be used when a film or TV show normalises non-consensual acts by depicting them as funny or romantic. In this scenario, the board would be required to make an actual, honest-to-goodness value judgement on content. Though I doff my hat to Consent Labs' overarching campaign, I'm not convinced this kind of change will future-proof the board from reactionaries down the line who may want other, less nuanced, more dogmatic morality clauses inserted into classifications. To their credit, the current classifiable elements these days are, at least in theory, not yet value judgements. (However, the Stevens Review does flag that consumer advice should be as specific as possible, possibly replacing 'strong themes' with specific mention of 'suicide, incitement of racial hatred and domestic violence'. The Board adapted in May 2023 to include warnings for potentially triggering content such as bullying, suicide and self-harm, but not for scenes lacking in consent.)

While good intentions in media representation are one thing, there's an equally valid argument that not all films should be made in good taste. Provocations, by design, are meant to upend social mores, and though they can sometimes seem like filmed pranks, this book has ideally demonstrated the politically-charged value of their political-incorrectness. Even Neville Stevens said in his report, 'I am not convinced "offence" should be maintained as a central concept in classification,' preferring instead to evaluate potential harm. 'A contemporary classification system should aim to empower consumers to make informed media choices for themselves and those in their care,' he continued. 'Such objectives are also more closely aligned with a system that is more focused on guidance than censorship and is more consistent with a modern consumer-centred media landscape.'

Some readers may still cock an eyebrow at my handwringing over a film classification board that, for its bread and butter, pumps out benign ratings for films like *Uncharted*. (M for 'violence', by the way.) I'll point those doubters to an ABC article from September 2022, titled 'Australia's changing how it regulates the internet — and no-one's paying attention', which notes that the *Online Safety Act 2021*, passed in the dying days of the Morrison government, instructs the technology industry (which includes social media companies, internet service providers and messaging services such as SMS) to develop new codes that will regulate 'harmful online content'. In the words of journalist Ariel Bogle, these codes will 'borrow from an out-of-date classification scheme'. Indeed, the entirety of the internet—nay, each of our socio-technological touchpoints—may soon be rated on the same classifiable elements as any old film or TV show. And therefore, that which is at risk of being refused classification—or 'banned'—expands to every inch of the media we consume.

The *Online Safety Act* gave new enforcement powers to the eSafety Commissioner—the Australian government's official online regulator—allowing them to determine whether online content was Class 1 (which is, or would be Refused Classification) or Class 2 (which is, or would be, X18+ or R18+) without needing to refer content to the board itself; the eSafety Commissioner just needed to refer to the classification guidelines before potentially issuing a removal notice. The Coalition had brought to fulfilment what Labor had attempted a decade earlier. Censorship creep did not, and does not, end.

This was perhaps preceded by the introduction of the *Sharing of Abhorrent Violent Material Act 2019*, designed in response to the viral spread of the Christchurch massacre footage. The Classification Board initially had to classify that shocking livestream as RC just to render its existence illegal; this new bill made it so the eSafety Commissioner could in future issue blocking notices to internet service providers to remove material that promotes, incites, instructs or depicts 'abhorrent violent conduct'. This may be one instance where those on both sides of the censorship debate can come together in agreement, to protest the dissemination of real, violent footage intended to inflame and radicalise in the aid of terrorist agendas. There is also an inbuilt legal defence for journalists, public officials and even artists who wish to use such images—though, in this increasingly censorial nation of ours, that 'defence' is far from a guarantee. (As recently as March of 2023, it was reported that 587 freedom of information requests submitted in 2020 or earlier were yet to be resolved by the Office of the Australian Information Commissioner. Inbuilt avenues to 'legal defence' and 'free access' are perhaps to be taken with a grain of salt in Australia.)

In some instances, the Classification Board is still relied upon to review less extreme footage for enforcement purposes. In April of 2023, they were asked to classify a two-minute title referred to as 'Video in WhatsApp chat group of a video of hotel shooting.' It received an MA-rating for 'footage of actual violence'. Is that classification a success or failure of the system? Truly, I don't know. What I do know is that no one was actually shot or killed during *Ken Park*, *A Serbian Film*, *Salò* …

†

When I started researching and writing this book, following a decade tracking the baffling-seeming decisions of the board and Australian film distributors, I figured I would end up with a text that liberated those movies that had been lost, slashed or spurned. I chose the title *Book of the Banned*—a play on 'Book of the Damned'—to conjure the idea of the 'undead' lurching back to life. However, reflecting back on it now, the book feels more like a graveyard. That which has been lost may never be returned, and the ramifications of those excisions have now exceeded the film industry, given how the tentacles of those who made their names complaining about sex and violence (though mainly sex) are already far-reaching in nearly every facet of Australian life. Part of the reason I took on this project is because so much had been written on the subject in the 1970s, and then a little at the turn of the century, and then barely anything—outside of academia—in the two decades since. (Had those far-reaching ramifications scared everyone away? Was I unwittingly walking into a woodchipper here?) However, censorship in Australia (even the slightly narrower band of film censorship) has not dimmed entirely, and I don't expect it ever will. Ina Bertrand knew this back in 1978: 'So long as there are films that challenge traditional social values, there will be people who want such films suppressed in order to protect society from itself.' She asked, 'Will we ever grow out of censorship altogether? And if we do, will it mean that our society has gone the way of other civilisations whose decadence destroyed them, or will it be because we have finally grown up enough not to need a paternalistic government to tell us what is good for us?' Maybe in this instance, she failed to foresee a third way: Australians thinking we've grown out of censorship because we didn't even realise that our experience of cinema—of media, of the internet—was still being surreptitiously sanitised.

Some censorship mysteries I could never solve: What was cut from Scorsese's *Taxi Driver*, which was classified in 1976 for theatrical release and again for VHS in 1984 and 1985, each instance with a different running time, and twice with a shorter duration than the US theatrical edit? (Did it have anything to do with the *Pillowman*-like copycat crime from 1981, when John Hinckley, seeking the attention of star Jodie Foster, attempted to assassinate President Ronald Reagan, not unlike *Taxi Driver*'s Travis Bickle?) Was the landmark anti-authoritarian comedy *Daisies*, banned by the Czechoslovak Socialist Republic in 1966, ever screened in Australia prior to a Sydney Film Fest retrospective in 2009? (Sources at SFF, MIFF and even the Australian Centre for the Moving Image could find no evidence of its distributors attempting an Aussie showing, or local exhibitors chancing an import.) And seriously, what could have possibly been deemed absolutely unacceptable from the all-star road race comedy *It's a Mad Mad Mad Mad Mad World* that it should have been shown abridged in Australian cinemas?

I also, like Sari Braithwaite, discovered movies, scenes, shots and dialogue that I'd be happy to see remain six feet underground, and wound up even uncovering instances of titles that were being streamed—unclassified—and feeling like I was reporting them to the authorities by asking the services and the board to comment, even if, in the case of *Pen15* and *Violation*, I was a fan. (Stan and AMC declined to provide a response.) I can't help but keep thinking back to *The Human Centipede 2: Full Sequence*, which actually argues (or does it mock the idea?) that people can become ruefully inspired and criminalised by provocative content. I don't subscribe to that theory. But two things can be true: citizens sometimes need to be shielded from criminal footage, and Australia's classification/censorship apparatus has too often been manipulated by politicians for personal reasons only masquerading as 'moral protection'. As Robert Cettl concludes in his book on the subject, *Offensive to a Reasonable Adult*, 'moral judgement upon transgressive discourse' is a recipe for failure.

> Film classification was in 2011 Christian morals policing and nothing more ... In Australia, the principle of 'offence to a reasonable adult' allowed Christian pressure groups to override UN human rights principles regarding free speech and impose their ideology on the nation. Clearly, Australia was not a free democracy, its interest solely dictated by Christian moral pressure.

The thing is, if the bloody politicians didn't get involved, it maybe wouldn't be the worst thing for regular consumers to declare which movies they find 'disgusting'. Catherine Schubert says this on the subject:

> Continued regulation via disgust and anger is an important argument for those seeking to abolish state sanctioned film censorship in Australia. It also demonstrates why they should not seek to abolish disgust and anger as filmic image responses. Such efforts would in any event be futile, as while these emotional responses are primarily taught, they are larger than film itself.

The disgust response was formed in evolution to warn human bodies from the threat of infection. Might that churning gut reaction you feel while watching *The Human Centipede 2* actually be your body in the process of self-classification? As the former chief censor Janet Strickland asked rhetorically, perhaps too long after her own complicated tenure,

> Why is it that we are not allowed to be shocked and offended? Where is it written? It's good to be shocked and offended. It means we can still feel. We are protecting ourselves from being choked, outraged and angered. These are emotions we are not allowed to feel and yet they are very useful emotions. They help to create a value system. If we have nothing that makes us feel shocked, how do we know what our value system is?

At the start of this book I intimated that our national persona was a fallacy; that our self-image of anti-authoritarian independence and larrikinism was a mask for extreme conservatism. Australians had to face it: *we* banned movies too. We feared challenging ideas. We empowered and elected those who proudly modelled a specific interpretation of morality above all others (in fact, we let those extremely questionable figures define morality even when their actions proved to be evidence to the contrary). And we were so willing to believe the false narrative of our world-leading democratic independence that as recently as this decade we let the government put in place some of the world's most regressive controls for how we consume information. Our story of film classification and censorship is the proof of our thirst across the decades for a governmental daddy to tell us what to do. This book has also pointed towards the exceptions to the rule who walk among us, and perhaps you'll say they're evidence Australia retains a sort of bushranging spirit in how we protest these wrongs. But if that idea of Australia was ever accurate, I hope I've also established that we are nonetheless drifting even further away from that imagined ideal of Australia, trending towards puritanical wowserism once more. We're not bushrangers. We're cops.

†

John Waters' seminal ode to bad taste, *Pink Flamingos*, might still today be our best test for what kinds of provocations we'll accept in our movies; like a tuning fork that measures cinematic shock and offence. It follows the drag queen Divine as she seeks to prove her bona fides as the filthiest person walking the planet Earth. She is successful.

In 1997, the OFLC offered an explanation in their annual report as to why they banned *Pink Flamingos* once in 1976, four further times in the early '80s and again for a proposed uncut 25th anniversary screening. (An edited cut was approved in 1977, and the uncut version was eventually granted an 'X' for VHS release in 1984, but that was before the clampdown on X18+ distribution. Today, it is technically unavailable in Australia in uncut form.)

> While the Board recognises that some 23 years on, the film has a dated feel and may not be as shocking to audiences as when it was first released, the Board nonetheless is unanimously of the view that some of the content does still offend against standards generally accepted by reasonable adults to the extent that it should be classified RC.

Nonetheless, that same year, they granted an R-rating to a 105-minute edit that, according to the website refused-classification.com, removed the following scenes: the character Channing masturbating and artificially inseminating a prisoner; Divine's son Crackers raping the character Cookie while putting a live chicken between them; and the incestuous moment in which Divine performs real fellatio on Crackers. (Thankfully, Crackers actor Danny Mills was not also the real Divine's actual son.) The new cut *did* now include a direct-to-camera featurette in which Waters talks about the film's legacy, and he can, at one point, be seen standing cheekily in front of an Australian release poster from 1977 that celebrates the film having finally been cleared for release by the Australian Censorship Board. The poster doesn't mention that it's merely an edited cut.

The board said in 1997 that 'the [edited] film can be accommodated at the "R" level as it does not offend against standards of morality, decency and propriety generally accepted by reasonable adults to the extent that the film should be classified "RC".' This runs counter to the bitterly hilarious and repulsive picture's own intentions. Australia edited *Pink Flamingos* so it did not offend against standards of morality, decency and propriety, and yet, in that same edit, Divine explains her apparent political beliefs to a reporter, which includes advocacy for cannibalism, first-degree murder and eating shit. Filth, she insists, *is* her politics. Unluckily, the board asked for a bit more decency in her filth. Today you can watch the uncut version in Australia by ordering a DVD or Blu-ray from overseas, and by streaming it while using a VPN (or even without a VPN by visiting the bootleg website effedupmovies.com, which is very much what it says on the tin).

Remarkably, *Pink Flamingos*' concluding scene of coprophilia—in which Divine feasts on some dog faeces scooped from the sidewalk—survived Australia's approved cut. But how's this for a contradiction: the board had subsequently refused classification to other films that also depicted coprophilia, urolagnia (which also includes John Howard's dreaded female ejaculation), masochism, sadism and forced paraphilic infantilism (again: men in nappies). And in Western Australia, where this author resides, coprophilia is still spelled out in the local guidelines as a huge no-no. It is in fact illegal in any article (as in: a publication, a film, a computer programme and associated data, a photograph, an object or a sound recording) to describe or depict, in a manner that is likely to cause offence to a reasonable adult, the following:

> (i) the use of violence or coercion to compel any person to participate in, or submit to, sexual conduct; (ii) sexual conduct with or upon the body of a dead person; (iii) the use of urine or excrement in association with degrading or dehumanising conduct or sexual conduct; (iv) bestiality; (v) acts of torture or the infliction of extreme violence or extreme cruelty.

The penalty is $15,000 or imprisonment for 18 months. So I'm really hoping this book can be considered having 'recognised literary, artistic or scientific merit', or I'll be in hotter water than even John Waters. The question is: who will be evaluating this book, and when? What will be the state of Australian permissiveness, or prudishness? Either way, consider me highly nervous.

EPILOGUE

I've spent four years wondering if I'll one day wake up to the news that Australia's government, struck by divine clarity, will suddenly announce the perfect reorganisation of its classification system, and retroactively un-ban *Ken Park*, *A Serbian Film* and everything else this book has attempted to catalogue. Maybe that will have happened sometime between me writing these words and you reading this epilogue. Don't get me wrong: that would be an excellent thing for literally everyone who isn't promoting a contemporary non-fiction book about politicians getting in the way of our gory, sexually explicit art. But I'm not too afraid of this book becoming instantly irrelevant. Losing sleep over the threat of the Australian government unexpectedly doing the smart or right thing feels like a waste of energy.

If I really let my imagination wander, I do entertain the idea that my pursuit of this story might enact some change, even if it's simply by alerting folks to the reality that censorship has indeed factored into their media consumption over the past few decades; that it didn't really disappear sometime in the 1970s despite the best efforts of Don Chipp, Ina Bertrand, Philip Adams, David Stratton, and other anti-censorship champions; and how it's likely to impact the way we navigate the internet going forward. I'll admit I was even masochistically delighted when the Albanese government publicly released Neville Stevens' 2020 review of the Classification System on 30 March 2023, mere days before I tied a ribbon around the final draft of my manuscript. This late-breaking twist necessitated an 11th hour reworking of a chapter about the fact that two consecutive governments—Coalition *and* Labor—had either lost the report between the couch cushions or shoved it so deep down no one else could ever find it. Just six weeks earlier, the assistant secretary of the Classification Branch had refused my Freedom of Information request to access that same report. Then they just went and uploaded it for all and sundry. I wouldn't claim to know how the cogs of government turn, but perhaps it was possible a message had been relayed up the chain that a new book was on the horizon highlighting the failures of the classification system (and how this long dormant and likely scathing review was being hidden from public view). Had my many, *many* media queries about coprophagy finally worn the government down? Did I force their hand? Or was it pure coincidence, after years and years of inaction (because actually, a self-published book that jokes about Kyle MacLachlan's manboobs probably doesn't make it into Anthony Albanese's morning briefing note)? I prefer the version in which the taps of my keyboard boom throughout the corridors of Canberra. Print the legend!

With all this said and done, I just hope readers now appreciate there remains a barrier between what we can see and what we thought we were seeing. Even as I put the finishing touches on this book, I noticed that Ari Aster's bizarthouse 2023 flick *Beau is Afraid* was classified R18+ *twice* by the Board ahead of its cinema release in April. I suspected this was because distributor Roadshow had submitted a second, slightly trimmed cut shortly after the Board returned with its initial classification, in an attempt at seeking a downgraded MA-rating. A spokesperson for the Classification Board instead told me, 'The modifications which include an amendment to the credits and a change in a single line of dialogue at 144 minutes, do not contain any classifiable elements that alter this classification.' So maybe I've been swimming in this morass for too long, and the paranoia is getting to me. Or maybe not. Weeks later, Universal received an R18+ classification for the horror-comedy *Renfield*, starring Nicolas Cage as Dracula and Nicholas Hoult as his servile familiar, Renfield. The following month, a modified version of *Renfield* was resubmitted and classified MA15+. A Classification Board spokesperson confirmed that Universal had cut *Renfield* to gain a less restrictive rating, and it was the censored edit that arrived in our cinemas. Based on the two decision reports for the film, here's some of the content Universal snipped: 'Renfield then implicitly rips the skin off a man's face, with the man's bloodied exposed flesh depicted in a close-up shot,' and 'Renfield then stomps on the man's head, explicitly bursting it and producing a large explosion of textured blood.' Do these excisions materially impact the quality of *Renfield*? Not really. (Well, to be honest, the ridiculous excess of comical gore is kinda all the film has going for it.) Take heart it will be restored for the digital and DVD/Blu-ray release, which has already been classified R18+. But consider all that you've just read in this book. It's 2023 and it's *still happening*. The censors and those who do the censoring may change, but these double-classifications are a shot across the bow to remind us we're not safe from the scissors just yet.

This book was largely written in the shadow of COVID-19. I commenced writing in September 2019 but much work—and some interviews—took place during the frightening, under-enlightened time of 2020, when borders between states were slammed shut and public health advice encouraged us to stay indoors and away from one another. I was happy to comply. But I thought it was interesting, given the topic of the book I was working on while under varying states of lockdown, that we have historically treated controversial movies like public health emergencies too. From the start, in fact, films were considered liable to endanger our lives for being too flammable, while also imperilling our afterlives for being too metaphorically incendiary.

The contrarians among us—myself included—are suspicious of government overreach, especially when it comes to the intimacies of our lives (which I believe includes the consumption and consideration of art). This book is a testament to that. But I'll admit I have been more than willing to submit to strict government control to keep myself and my family safe from the coronavirus pandemic. I try to keep that in mind when I consider the extreme—but earnest—ways in which some have desperately feared the public risk posed by controversial films, because cinema should be a path towards empathy and we'd want those who've discriminated through censorship to take that tact too. The difference is I don't know of anyone who wound up on a ventilator because they watched *The Human Centipede 2*, so be wary of anyone who tries that argument against scandalising cinema in the future.

Perth, Western Australia
31 May, 2023

ACKNOWLEDGEMENTS

The writing and publication of this book would not have been possible without the encouragement and insight of my amazing, genius wife Jenny. I began the process just as she became pregnant with our son Miles, and continued throughout the first three years of his life, and at no point did she waver in her dedication and support. I dedicate this book about extremely gross things to the two of them, which, granted, is kind of a weird present. I also want to thank my wider family for their decades of love and inspiration, mum and dad especially. My parents always cheered me as a writer and dutifully transcribed my stories from an early age. This couldn't have been what they predicted as the ultimate outcome of that positive reinforcement, but I hope they're proud all the same.

I am incredibly grateful to those who agreed to be interviewed, knowing there was no publisher attached and trusting me to handle their quotes responsibly. The first of these was Margaret Pomeranz. I also sincerely thank Amanda Montell, David Elfick, David Roe, David Stratton, Grant Hardie, Janice Loreck, Joe Kapiteyn, Natalie Krikowa, Peter Campbell, Phillip Adams, Radu Jude, Sandra Wollner, Sari Braithwaite, Stuart Richards and Travis Mathews. Special thanks to Margaret Anderson, who sat for several hours of unvarnished and entertaining interviews.

I want to thank my collaborators, who whipped this self-published project into something that is now at least professional-adjacent. Emily Martin of Muse Legal was *Book of the Banned*'s first reader, and provided essential legal guidance (as well as some much appreciated 'lols' in her tracked Word document). Elena Gomez thoroughly edited my manuscript, and you have her to thank for all the parts that are easy to read, and me to blame for the parts that are still confusing. My brilliant cover designer, Hannah Atcheson, helped capture the exact tone of this project at an early stage, which I believe was instrumental in making my Kickstarter campaign a success. If Vaughan Davies is reading this, I want to thank him for typesetting the body text, but I'm going out on a limb and cheering him for what I assume will be excellent work. And thanks also to Emma Daisy, who was so kind and professional during my extremely sweaty 'author's photo' shoot.

I'm humbled by the support of the early champions of this project: Andrew F. Peirce, Ian Hale, James Hall, Lee Zachariah, Richard Sowada, Rochelle Siemienowicz, Susan Midalia, Tom Vincent and Travis Johnson. The following also graciously offered me permission to reprint quotes from their projects, or connected (and vouched for) me with the right people: Bec Wheatley, David Heslin, Dusty Mancinelli and Madeleine Sims-Fewer, Glenn Richards and David Collins, Gregg Araki and Marcus Hu, Idun and Laura Chipp, Ina Bertrand, Ken Jacobs and NACG/The Film-Makers' Cooperative, Malcolm Day, Prano Bailey-Bond and Silver Salt Films, Robbie Swan, Rod Williams, Scott Murray, Stig Bjorkman and the Svenska Filminstitutet/Swedish Film Institute, and Volker Schlöndorff. Additional thanks goes to the stewards of the essential online resource refused-classification.com.

I have to thank The National Library of Australia, Curtin University and Randwick City Library for their resources, as well as Potential Films, Sony Pictures Entertainment, StudioCanal and Umbrella Entertainment for their assistance. I also want to extend my gratitude to the entire team at Luna Palace Cinemas and the Revelation Perth International Film Festival, as well as Alexandra Heller-Nicholas, Chris Taylor, Flick Ford and John Safran for co-signing (and legitimising!) this project with their endorsements.

Hopefully these Acknowledgements have proven that 'self-publication' still requires a cast of hundreds. This is especially true for *Book of the Banned*, which was partly-funded through a Kickstarter campaign in February 2023, when 141 individuals pre-ordered a copy and helped pay for printing costs. Not everyone wanted to be publicly acknowledged, but I sincerely thank them all for their faith in me. Here are just some of those incredible people: Adam Quigley, Adam Trainer, Adrian and Nadia Infirri, Amanda and Steve Cipriani, Andrew Edwards, Andrew French, Andrew Williams, Anthony Morris, Anthony Tran, Audry Olmsted, Axel Carrington, Ben Hammond, Blake Davis, Bonnie Davies, Brandon Bonasera, Brendan Divilly, Brian Nimbalker, Bruce Wilson, Caitlin Paroczai, Carla and Sebastian Miraudo, Carla and Daniel Pastorelli, Charlie Bigwood, Chris Waldock, Clinton Caccamo, Cody Enos, Connor Kiss, Courtney Barnes, Dan Steadman, Daniel Cleary, Daniel Slabicki, Daniel Willis, Danielle Raffaele, Darren Murphy, David Thomas, Dawn Yates, Declan Kelly, Diego Vazquez, Duane Warnecke, Duncan Farr, Dwight Bandy, Eddie Curtis, Edith Firkin, Elizabeth Knuckey, Em Burrows, Evangeline Battalis, Gardner Monks, Geoff Kerrigan, Glenn Dunks, Grace Small, Gregory Corrigan, Iain Potter, Ian Gordon, Jak, James Goodwin, Jane Carracher, Jasmine Hughes, Jeff Miles, Jeffrey J. Ellen, Jemma Morgan, Jeremy Holmes, Jonathan Spiroff, Jonathon Miller, Josh Soutar, Julian Wright, Kailyn Crabbe, Karina Libbey, Katrina O'Mara, Ken Finlayson, Kevin Power, Kieran

Flaherty, Leanne Casellas, Liam Divilly, Libby Caldwell, Libby Noble, Louise Cleary, Madi Fraser, Margaret Cassidy, Mark La Galia, Martin James Robertson, Mary Borsellino, Matt Puccinelli, Matthew McAleer, Meri Fatin, Michael Gibb, Michael Kamen, Michael Schwarz, Michael Snow, Mike Wilson, Natalie Cameron, Peter Lam, Rebecca Harrold, Rhian Todhunter, Richard Gray, Rosie Thompson, Sam McCosh, Samuel Harris, Sara Newton, Sarah Basford Canales, Sarah Lau, Seb Miraudo, Shane Mitchell, Shaun Heenan, Sophie Minissale, Speñcer Montgömérry, Steph K, Stephanie Sutcliffe, Stephen Morgan, Steve Avery, Suzie Worner, Taylah Strano, Tim Fairbanks, Tom Clift, Tom Mann, Tom Reynolds, Tony Hughes-d'Aeth, Tristan Fidler, Vanessa Gudgeon, Wes Evans and Xanthia Sacco. I also want to thank Dave Owen of Rewind VHS for his uniquely charming VHS case add-ons, which were available to buy during the fundraising campaign.

I lastly want to thank The Australian Classification Board and The Australian Classification Review Board. They have been inundated with queries and requests from me not just over the past four years, but for more than a decade. While I appreciate I may have been a (hopefully friendly) thorn in their side during this time, there is no denying that this book only exists due to their prompt replies and contributions. Thank you for responding to my entreaties right up until the end, even when my email signature began promoting an upcoming book with 'dastardly censors' in the title.

NOTES

Introduction:
'Fetishes such as body piercing...': *Guidelines for the Classification of Films 2012* (Cth); 'the strictest of...': Cettl, 2011, p. 4; 'like an old...': *Censor had three snips at Blow-Up*, 1969, p. 2; 'The censor has been gentle...': *Cinema - Strong but never gamey*, 1968, p. 12; 'the average cut...': *Just what does the censor stop us seeing?*, 1953, p. 2; 'If films were an esoteric commodity...': Bertrand, 1978, p. ix.

Chapter 1: How Classification Works (Or Doesn't)
'implies that nothing is banned...': Griffith, 2002, p. 3; 'does not affect the operation...': *Stronger Futures in the Northern Territory (Consequential and Transitional Provisions) Act 2012* (Cth).; '[T]here is a theatre...': O'Grady, 1962, p. 12.

Chapter 2: Meet the Wowsers
'Moral judgments and bannings...': Dutton & Harris, 1970, p. 4; 'a person who is more shocked...': *GENERAL SUMMARY*, 1912, p. 4; 'seemed of a distinctly...': Bertrand, 1978, p. 105; 'The Children's Court...': [Summary of recent Kelly Gang pictures and their effect on youth], 1907, p. 9; 'fulsome in its praise...': Bertrand, 1978, p. 111; 'the story would be horrifying...': Bertrand, 1978, p. 140; 'clearly set out...': Bertrand, 1978, p. 140; 'harmful to public...': *THRILLER FILM BANNED*, 1948, p. 1; 'indecent, suggestive or insufficient...': Bertrand, 1978, p. 129; 'evil effect...': New South Wales, 1936, p. 4172; 'YOU ARE ADVISED...': Bertrand, 1978, p. 95; 'extend the use...': *GOOD FILMS*, 1922, p. 3; 'various misdemeanours...': Commonwealth of Australia, 1927, p. 502; 'the audience...': Commonwealth of Australia, 1928, p. 19; 'Why should dirty American...': Higham, 1965, pp. 18 – 19; 'the most repulsive...': Bertrand, 1978, p. 141; 'horror films are neither...': Dutton & Harris, 1970, p. 54; 'a small minority...': Dutton & Harris, 1970, p. 54; 'There is no doubt...': O'Grady, 1962, p. 13; 'a travesty...': *Just what does the censor stop us seeing?*, 1953, p. 2; 'We don't like...': Higham, 1965, pp. 18 – 19; 'smoothing the pillow...': *"Children of Wasteland" Draws Large Audience*, 1953, p. 2; 'These are the aborigines of Australia...': *Bishop's film dialogue censored*, 1953, p. 1; 'the story of real Australians...': *"Children of Wasteland" Draws Large Audience*, 1953, p. 2; 'for his pains...': O'Grady, 1962, p. 14; '[t]wo of the women...': O'Grady, 1962,

pp. 14 – 15; 'scissors [were] reputedly...': Higham, 1965, p. 17; 'Didn't you find...': Stratton, 2008, p. 113; 'the obvious pleasure...': Dezuanni & Goldsmith, 2015, p. 307; 'the acceptance of Easy Rider...': Bertrand, 1978, p. 181; 'We cannot and should not...': Chipp, 1987, p. 145; 'a scene that depicts...': Chipp, 1987, p. 85; 'I think you've...': Stratton, 2008, p. 184; 'The scene is extremely short...': Tivey, 1970a, p. 47; 'preserve sound moral standard...': Bertrand, 1978, p. 187; 'self-righteous people...': Commonwealth, 1970, p. 1445; '[I]t must be remembered...': Murray, 1974, p. 107; 'left wing communist pornographers...': Strong & Strong, 1971, p. 21; 'all the words...': Dunstan, 1971, p. 17; 'concentrated spate of brutality...': Hall, 1972, p. 42; 'At 104 minutes...': The Australian Classification Board, 2016; 'passionate lovemaking...': Murray, 1978b, p. 201; 'perhaps the most sensational...': Stratton, 1971, p. 40; 'at the setting...': Chipp, 1987, p. 233; 'Is the minister...': New South Wales, 1972, p. 4581; 'The Devils is not...': *British Horror Films*, 2022; 'they use the word...': Stratton, 2008, p. 141.

Chapter 3: The Banned Down Under

'A subversive reference...': *Too Rude for Queensland*, 2017; 'scientific evidence suggests...': McClelland, 1977, p. 330; 'one of the censors...': Media Censorship in Australia, 2013; 'a Satan production...': *Blasphemy, satire, or a bit off: critics can't agree*, 1988, p. 127; 'pornography [to be] totally evil...': Nile, 1974; 'a range of issues...': Government of Queensland, 1990, p. 4; 'struck heavily...': Roberts, 2015; '[Queensland] Films Board of Review...': Government of Queensland, 1990, p. 5; 'the Film Censorship Board does...': Strickland, 1977, p. 208; 'The film has been shown...': Murray, 1982, p. 204; 'Since my time...': Guilliatt & Casimir, 1996; 'a bizarre and frightening...': Bertrand, 1978, p. 197; 'The film they didn't want...': *Australian Films Of The 1970s*, 2020; 'the grotesque, the sexy...': *Australia After Dark*, 2015; 'a furtive gay marriage...': Murray, 1978a, p. 96.

Chapter 4: Are You There Margaret? It's Us, The Police

'not a film...': *Margaret Pomeranz detained by police 2003 - Illegal Ken Park screening - Channel 10 report*, 2003; 'Breathless took my breath away...': Australian Broadcasting Corporation, 2011; 'If teenage actors...': *Ken Park screening, take two: film lovers defiant*, 2003; 'the standards of morality...': The Australian Classification Review Board, 2003; 'singularly uninterested in starvation...': *Chipp off an old block*, 2003; 'Because while Clark...': Kelly, 2006; 'unjust to a friendly power...': Dutton

& Harris, 1970, p. 38; 'Through that door...': Dutton & Harris, 1970, p. 38; 'a big cock...': Dutton & Harris, 1970, p. 40; 'Theatre has been a substitute...': Dutton & Harris, 1970, pp. 50 – 51; 'a barrier of illiterate policemen...': Wells, 1939, p. 45; 'the Classification Review Board only determines...': *Office of Film and Literature Classification*, 2005, p. 82; 'If there are countries...': Cuir, 2007, p. 28; 'graphic as any X-rated movie...': Cockington, 2005, pp. 35 – 36.

Chapter 5: You Can't Say That

'TRICKY LYING TONY...': Gardiner, 2017; 'three audible uses...': The Australian Classification Board, 2019a; 'It is the view...': The Australian Classification Review Board, 2019b; 'If the State decides...': Dutton & Harris, 1970, p. 28; 'to encourage the presentation...': Good Film League of N.S.W., 1926; 'sullies the image...': Commonwealth, 1990, p. 305.

Chapter 6: The 10,000 Days of Sodom

'It thought that the...': *Censorship Of Salò, Or The 120 Days Of Sodom (1975)*, 2021; 'praying for urgent...': Queensland, 1993, p. 3717; 'They told me that...': Commonwealth, 1993, p. 982; 'Not only do I believe...': Commonwealth, 1993, p. 982; 'the producer of Salò...': New South Wales, 1993; 'paedophilia and sexual abuse...': Commonwealth, 1997, p. 7991; 'the age of the young people...': The Australian Classification Board, 1998, p. 147; 'The Classification Board wishes to emphasise...': The Australian Classification Board, 2010a; 'would make Salò visually...': Russo, 2015.

Chapter 7: One of the Most Revolting, Disgusting Pieces of Shit David Stratton Has Ever Seen

'This is a diary...': Kapka, 2014; 'tons and tons of statements...': Edwards, 2020; 'a degree of artistic...': The Australian Classification Board, 2010b; 'With hellacious extremities...': *Censorship Of A Serbian Film (2010)*, 2022; 'There are enough perverts...': Carey, 2011; 'I was first made...': Fenton, 2011; 'the sickest film...': *Censorship Of A Serbian Film (2010)*, 2022; 'pro-life...': Hills, 2012; 'Tankard Reist's opponents...': Baird, 2012; 'director of the women's...': *Pornography: how it is radicalising Australian boys*, 2021; 'Funny how the DVD...': Accent Films [@AccentFilms], 2011a; 'For some it will...': Edwards, 2020; 'To those who have...': Accent Films [@AccentFilms], 2011b; 'The last decision...': Government of South Australia, 2019.

Chapter 8: Festival of Filth

'Dominique Gary plays...': Murray, 1975, p. 230; 'most evil film...': Galvin, 2009; 'as extensive as has ever...': O'Regan, 1985; 'It is not Sada...': Dawson, 1976, p. 110; 'the standards of morality...': Government of Western Australia, 1999a; 'The scene, some 12 minutes...': The Australian Classification Review Board, 1995; 'most censorious measure...': Cochrane, 1999; 'a person who has...': *Classification Act 1995* (Cth); 'it was not a good film...': Dutton & Harris, 1970, p. 69.

Chapter 9: 'People Are Scared of a Hard Penis'

'Classification Board is of the opinion...': The Australian Classification Board, 2017; 'I'll never understand...': Griffin, 2010; 'at the time of submission...': *Directed By Bruce La Bruce*, 2021; 'fuck the censors': Buckmaster, 2010; 'it contains explicit sex scenes...': *Film Censorship: I Want Your Love (2012)*, 2015; 'Is it a fact...': New South Wales, 2012; 'In a PG film...': The Australian Classification Board, 2020c, p. 74; 'Chris [Pontius] stands nude...': The Australian Classification Board, 2022; 'Generally, the Classification...': The Australian Classification Board, 2005, p. 82; 'makes love detumescently...': Ebert, 1969; 'Of all the films...': Comstock, 2006b; 'no erect penises...': Comstock, 2006c; 'fucking criminal...': Wearring, 2008; 'We received, by post...': Comstock, 2006d; 'Still, I suppose...': Stratton, 1971, p. 41; 'All true! All real...': *Censored 1970s American Films - Page 2*, 2022; 'a rare historical record...': *Let Me Die a Woman*, (n.d.).

Chapter 10: Raiding the State-sanctioned Spank Bank

'violent sexual attack...': Tivey, 1970b, p. 38; 'a gypsy mother...': Office of Film and Literature Classification, 1997, p. 411.

Chapter 11: Think of the Children

'Extensive notes...': The Australian Classification Board, 2020a; 'I have now considered...': The Australian Classification Board, 2020b; 'One psychologist...': Quinn, 2020a; 'galling... to witness...': Stratton, 2020; 'The safety and wellbeing...': Melbourne International Film Festival [@MIFFofficial], 2020; 'depiction of how young people...': *Cuties classified MA 15+*, 2020; 'a serious and legitimate...': The Australian Classification Board, 2005; 'I don't think...': Barlow, 2005; 'Being able to get...': *Pedophilia theme sparks film ban call*, 2005; 'I have always thought...': *Censorship Of Mysterious Skin (2004)*, 2021; 'In the Classification Review Board's opinion...': The Australian Classification Review Board, 2005; 'While the state...': *Judge Rules 'Tin Drum' Shows No Child Porn*, 1998; 'Films that have the issue...': Office of Film and Literature Classification, 2005, p. 82.

Chapter 12: No Oral, Please

'For 17 years...': Gallery Global Networks Limited, 2004b; 'necessitated by the negative...': Gallery Global Networks Limited, 2005; 'The Review Board found...': Office of Film and Literature Classification, 2000; 'Under the guidelines...': *Adult Film Censorship: Dreamquest (2000)*, 2011; 'a flexible long...': The Australian Classification Review Board, 2000; 'a strong plot...': The Australian Classification Review Board, 2002; 'The fellatio scene...': Ebert, 1987.

Chapter 13: In the Realm of the Censors

'Good God...': *The sex, the violence, the director and his motive*, 1991; 'act on that maxim...': Christians et al., 2005, p. 15; 'the greatest happiness...': Christians et al., 2005, p. 16; 'a) adults should be...': *National Classification Code 2005* (Cth).; 'It was quite disappointing...': *Production Notes: Bad Luck Banging or Loony Porn*, 2021; 'In the board's opinion...': The Australian Classification Board, 2022; 'To hear that...': Bunbury, 2021; 'While the shootings...': The Australian Classification Board, 2022; 'It's such a complicated area...': Australian Broadcasting Corporation, 2021; 'A former deputy...': Delvecchio, 1996; 'In writing the screenplay...': Elfick, 1997.

Chapter 14: Shudder to Think

'horror films are neither...': Dutton & Harris, 1970, p. 54; 'ultra-violent...': *Censorship Of The Hannibal Lecter (1991-2001) Series*, 2021; 'was more horrible...': Bertrand, 1978, p. 120; 'Suitable only for Adults...': Bertrand, 1978, p. 122; 'Banned in Australia...': *Directed By Ruggero Deodato*, 2011; 'It showed women...': Ward, 1994; 'the filmmaker's claims...': *Film Censorship: M #1*, 2013; 'actually one of the sweetest...': *Canadian Horror Films*, 2021; 'From Oedipus the King...': Miraudo, 2012; 'We were so concerned...': Taylor, 2011; 'Recently we've had a complaint...': Monster Pictures, 2011c; 'the film must be refused classification...': The Australian Classification Review Board, 2011; 'Monster Pictures feels...': *Censorship Of The Human Centipede II (Full Sequence) (2011)*, 2021; 'No it didn't last long...': *Censorship Of The Human Centipede II (Full Sequence) (2011)*, 2021; 'As such, this film...': The Australian Classification Board, 2013; 'an implied sex scene...': The Australian Classification Board, 2021b.

Chapter 15: 'Netflix Classifies Manboobs as Nudity!'
'In Australia, at least...': Murray, 1974, p. 102; 'Developed in partnership...': The Australian Classification Board, 2019b; 'It has been of particular concern...': The Australian Classification Board, 2020c, p. 51; 'It is inequitable...': The Australian Classification Board, 2020c, p. 59; 'The tool requires developers...': Department of Communications and the Arts, 2016.

Chapter 16: A Collective Failure of Nerve
'to update Australia's classification...': *Have your say on classification regulation*, 2020; 'The former government...': The Australian Classification Board, 2022; 'the need to take...': Commonwealth of Australia, 2020; '88% of respondents...': Department of Infrastructure, Transport, Regional Development, Communications and the Arts, 2022, p. iii; 'The National Classification Scheme...': Commonwealth of Australia, 2011, p. ix; '[Dylan] spits on his...': The Australian Classification Board, 2021a; 'depiction of the sexual...': The Australian Classification Board, 2022; 'professionally produced...': Commonwealth of Australia, 2020, p. 9; 'fines or other civil penalties...': Commonwealth of Australia, 2020, p. 60; 'achieving the requirements...': Commonwealth of Australia, 2020, p. 49; 'To continue high...': Commonwealth of Australia, 2020, p. 11; 'The number of titles...': *Age Ratings*, 2023; 'produce classification decisions...': *Classification (Publications, Films and Computer Games) (Spherex Classification Tool) Approval 2022* (Cth).; 'some outstandingly unpleasant sequences...': Mudge 2019; 'Violence: rough or injurious...': Ross, 2011; 'no films have been...': Schubert, 2017, p. 261; 'I can't think...' FitzSimons, 2022; 'not the sort of junk...': *Film Censorship: M #3*, 2013; 'Censorship had and has...': Dutton & Harris, 1970, pp. 79 – 80; 'happy clapper...': Marr, 2008; 'unprecedented powers...': *Insufficient safeguards in new surveillance law*, 2021; 'Creeping censorship...': Dutton & Harris, 1970, p. 81; 'The question, however...': Strong & Strong, 1971, p. 20; 'suicide, incitement...': Commonwealth of Australia, 2020, p. 11; 'I am not convinced...': Commonwealth of Australia, 2020, p. 34; 'borrow from an out-of-date...': Bogle, 2022; 'So long as there...': Bertrand, 1978, p. 198; 'Film classification was in 2011...': Cettl, 2011, pp. 829 - 830; 'Continued regulation via disgust...': Schubert, 2017, p. 280; 'Why is it that we...': Guilliatt & Casimir, 1996; 'the use of violence...': *Classification (Publications, Films and Computer Games) Enforcement Act 1996* (WA).

Epilogue:
'Renfield then implicitly rips...': The Australian Classification Board, 2023.

BIBLIOGRAPHY

A tip for festival organisers: get your films banned. (2012, November 5). Retrieved May 2023, from Crikey: https://www.crikey.com.au/2012/11/05/a-handy-tip-for-festival-organisers-get-your-films-banned/

Accent Films [@AccentFilms]. (2011a, September 19). *Funny how the DVD store owner who complained about the film to SA AG has never returned the DVD screener [Tweet]*. Retrieved May 2023, from Twitter: https://twitter.com/AccentFilms/status/115680596558225408

Accent Films [@AccentFilms]. (2011b, September 19). *To those who have already purchased the DVD, we THINK you are safe but, nowadays, we cannot rule a house [Tweet]*. Retrieved May 2023, from Twitter: https://twitter.com/AccentFilms/status/115683564976214016

Actors make the most of their parts. (2008, April 23). Retrieved May 2023, from The Sydney Morning Herald: https://www.smh.com.au/entertainment/actors-make-the-most-of-their-parts-20080423-gdsan9.html

Adult Film Censorship: Dreamquest (2000). (2011, September 16). Retrieved May 2023, from Refused Classification: https://web.archive.org/web/20170512130355/http://www.refused-classification.com/censorship/adult-films/dreamquest.html

Age Ratings. (2023, January 10). Retrieved May 2023, from Spherex: https://www.spherex.com/localized-age-ratings

Alvin's purple patches removed for Television. (1973, December 20). Retrieved May 2023, from The Age: https://news.google.com/newspapers?nid=1300&dat=19731220&id=JJ0QAAAAIBAJ&sjid=05ADAAAAIBAJ&pg=5957,4791413

Andrews, K. (1996, June 26). *Pain and shame of a violent culture*. Retrieved May 2023, from The Australian Financial Review: https://www.afr.com/politics/pain-and-shame-of-a-violent-culture-19960626-k6yer

Arrests over Hail Mary. (1986, June 10). Retrieved May 2023, from The Canberra Times/ACM: http://nla.gov.au/nla.news-article118124045

Australia After Dark. (2015, April 17). Retrieved May 2023, from GuideDoc: https://guidedoc.tv/documentary/australia-after-dark-documentary-film/

Australian Broadcasting Corporation. (2002, December 18). *Screen Sex*. Retrieved May 2023, from ABC News: https://www.abc.net.au/radionational/programs/breakfast/screen-sex/3529430

Australian Broadcasting Corporation. (2011, May 4). *Breathless: The Classic*. Retrieved May 2023, from At the Movies with David and Margaret: https://web.archive.org/web/20170830175154/http://www.abc.net.au/atthemovies/txt/s3198267.htm

Australian Broadcasting Corporation. (2020). *ABC Submission to the Review of Australian classification regulation*. Retrieved May 2023, from Department of Infrastructure, Transport, Regional Development and Communications: https://www.infrastructure.gov.au/sites/default/files/submissions/abc_1.pdf

Australian Broadcasting Corporation. (2021, October 6). *Nitram: is it wrong to make a movie about a mass shooter - and should you go and see it?* Retrieved May 2023, from ABC Radio Perth: https://www.abc.net.au/perth/programs/mornings/ethics-of-nitram/13572754

The Australian Classification Board. (2005, April 19). *Decision Report: Mysterious Skin*. Department of Infrastructure, Transport, Regional Development, Communications and the Arts.

The Australian Classification Board. (2010a, April 14). *Classification Board classifies a modified version of Salo o le 120 Giornate di Sodoma R 18+ (Restricted)*. Retrieved May 2023, from Australian Classification: https://web.archive.org/web/20100920034435/http://classification.gov.au/www/cob/rwpattach.nsf/VAP/(9A5D88DBA63D32A661E6369859739356)~Media+release+-+Salo+-+April+2010.pdf/$file/Media+release+-+Salo+-+April+2010.pdf

The Australian Classification Board. (2010b, November 25). *Decision Report: Srpski Film / A Serbian Film*. Department of Infrastructure, Transport, Regional Development, Communications and the Arts.

The Australian Classification Board. (2011, September 1). *Classification Board Annual Report 2010/2011*. Retrieved May 2023, from Australian Classification: https://webarchive.nla.gov.au/wayback/20191107004031/http://www.classification.gov.au/About/AnnualReports/Pages/Annual-reports-2010-11-classo-board.aspx

The Australian Classification Board. (2013, February 27). *Decision Report: Father's Day*. Department of Infrastructure, Transport, Regional Development, Communications and the Arts.

The Australian Classification Board. (2016, July 12). *Decision Report: McCabe & Mrs. Miller*. Department of Infrastructure, Transport, Regional Development, Communications and the Arts.

The Australian Classification Board. (2017, October 19). *Classification of the film Tom of Finland and allegations that the Classification Board is "homophobic"*. Retrieved May 2023, from Australian Classification: https://www.classification.gov.au/about-us/media-and-news/media-releases/classification-film-tom-finland-and-allegations-classification-board-homophobic

The Australian Classification Board. (2019a, August 7). *Decision Report: The Australian Dream*. Department of Infrastructure, Transport, Regional Development, Communications and the Arts.

The Australian Classification Board. (2019b, November 15). *Australia leading the way with Netflix on classification*. Retrieved May 2023, from Australian Classification: https://www.classification.gov.au/about-us/media-and-news/news/australia-leading-way-netflix-classification

The Australian Classification Board. (2020a, June 30). *Application for Exemption or Declaration*. Retrieved May 2023, from Department of Infrastructure, Transport, Regional Development, Communications and the Arts: https://www.infrastructure.gov.au/sites/default/files/migrated/department/ips/files/log/foi-21-036-docs-for-release.pdf

The Australian Classification Board. (2020b, July 3). *Decision on application for section 6H declaration in relation to the Melbourne International Film Festival (MIFF) 68½*. Retrieved May 2023, from Department of Infrastructure, Transport, Regional Development, Communications and the Arts: https://www.infrastructure.gov.au/sites/default/files/migrated/department/ips/files/log/foi-21-036-docs-for-release.pdf

The Australian Classification Board. (2020c, February). *Review of Australian Classification Regulation - Classification Board Submission*. Retrieved May 2023, from Department of Infrastructure, Transport, Regional Development, Communications and the Arts: https://www.infrastructure.gov.au/sites/default/files/submissions/classification-board.pdf

The Australian Classification Board. (2021a, August 6). *Decision Report: Violation*. Department of Infrastructure, Transport, Regional Development, Communications and the Arts.

The Australian Classification Board. (2021b, November 15). *TITANE*. Retrieved May 2023, from Australian Classification: https://www.classification.gov.au/titles/titane

The Australian Classification Board. (2022, October). *Classification Board and Classification Review Board Annual Reports 2021–22*. Retrieved May 2023, from Australian Classification: https://www.classification.gov.au/about-us/research-and-publications/classification-board-and-classification-review-board-annual-reports-2021-22

The Australian Classification Board. (2023, April 14). *Decision Report: Renfield*. Department of Infrastructure, Transport, Regional Development, Communications and the Arts.

The Australian Classification Review Board. (1995, December 22). *Decision Report: Dead Man*. Department of Infrastructure, Transport, Regional Development, Communications and the Arts.

The Australian Classification Review Board. (2000, December 8). *33rd Meeting - 9-10, 17th November 2000*. Retrieved May 2023, from Australian Classification: https://web.archive.org/web/20070904213001/http://www.classification.gov.au/resource.html?resource=99&filename=99.pdf

The Australian Classification Review Board. (2002, May 10). *Decision Report: Baise-Moi*. Department of Infrastructure, Transport, Regional Development, Communications and the Arts. Retrieved May 2023, from Australian Classification: https://web.archive.org/web/20070904213207/http://www.classification.gov.au/resource.html?resource=92&filename=92.pdf

The Australian Classification Review Board. (2003, June 6). *Decision Report: Ken Park*. Department of Infrastructure, Transport, Regional Development, Communications and the Arts. Retrieved May 2023, from Australian Classification: https://web.archive.org/web/20070904212911/http://www.classification.gov.au/resource.html?resource=230&filename=230.pdf

The Australian Classification Review Board. (2005, August 1). *Decision Report: Mysterious Skin*. Department of Infrastructure, Transport, Regional Development, Communications and the Arts. Retrieved May 2023, from Australian Classification: https://web.archive.org/web/20070904214823/http://www.classification.gov.au/resource.html?resource=597&filename=597.pdf

The Australian Classification Review Board. (2011, November 28). *The Human Centipede II (Full Sequence) classified RC upon review*. Department of Infrastructure, Transport, Regional Development, Communications and the Arts. Retrieved May 2023, from Australian Classification: https://www.classification.gov.au/sites/default/files/2019-09/crb-decision-28november2011-human-centipede-ii-full-sequence.docx

The Australian Classification Review Board. (2019, May 21). *Rocketman classified M*. Retrieved May 2023, from Australian Classification: https://www.classification.gov.au/about-us/media-and-news/media-releases/rocketman-classified-m

Australian Films Of The 1970s. (2020, October 14). Retrieved May 2023, from Refused Classification: https://www.refused-classification.com/censorship/film-1/australian/#night-of-fear

Australia's talking pig gets the chop from Chinese film censors. (1996, April 8). Retrieved May 2023, from The Irish Times: https://www.irishtimes.com/news/australia-s-talking-pig-gets-the-chop-from-chinese-film-censors-1.38405

Baird, J. (2012, January 21). *Plenty of room under the feminism umbrella*. Retrieved May 2023, from The Sydney Morning Herald: https://www.smh.com.au/politics/federal/plenty-of-room-under-the-feminism-umbrella-20120120-1qahb.html The use of this work has been licensed by Copyright Agency except as permitted by the Copyright Act, you must not re-use this work without the permission of the copyright owner or Copyright Agency.

Barlow, K. (2005, July 19). *US censorship debate brews*. Retrieved May 2023, from ABC PM: https://web.archive.org/web/20230127222557/https://www.abc.net.au/pm/content/2005/s1417856.htm

Barnes, B., & Deb, S. (2017, March 3). *An Alabama Drive-In Bans 'Beauty and the Beast' Over Gay Character*. Retrieved May 2023, from The New York Times: https://www.nytimes.com/2017/03/03/movies/beauty-and-the-beast-ban-alabama-drive-in-gay-character.html

Barnett, D. (2010, June 16). *A return to wowserism in the name of politics*. Retrieved May 2023, from ABC News: https://www.abc.net.au/news/2010-06-16/34994

Bell, G. (1984, May 1). Long knives flash at the film censorship board. *The Bulletin, 104* (5414), pp. 20-21. Retrieved May 2023, from Are Media Pty Limited / aremediasyndication.com.au / 'The Bulletin': http://nla.gov.au/nla.obj-1764861775

Bertrand, I. (1978). *Film Censorship in Australia*. St Lucia, QLD: University of Queensland Press.

Bertrand, I. (1989). *Cinema in Australia: A Documentary History*. Kensington, NSW: NSW Press.

Bishop's film dialogue censored. (1953, April 30). Retrieved May 2023, from The Courier-Mail: https://trove.nla.gov.au/newspaper/article/50559822

Blasphemy, satire, or a bit off: critics can't agree. (1988, September 30). Retrieved May 2023, from The Sydney Morning Herald: https://smharchives.smedia.com.au/Olive/APA/freesearch/get/image.ashx?kind=preview&href=SMH%2F1988%2F09%2F30&page=1&ext=png

Bogle, A. (2022, September 21). *Australia's changing how it regulates the internet — and no-one's paying attention*. Retrieved May 2023, from ABC News: https://www.abc.net.au/news/science/2022-09-21/internet-online-safety-act-industry-codes/101456902

Bridge, J. A., Greenhouse, J. B., Ruch, D., Stevens, J., Ackerman, J., Sheftall, A. H., Horowitz, L. M., Kelleher, K. J., & Campo, J. V. (2019). *Association Between the Release of Netflix's 13 Reasons Why and Suicide Rates in the United States: An Interrupted Time Series Analysis*. Journal of the American Academy of Child & Adolescent Psychiatry. Retrieved May 2023, from Journal of the American Academy of Child & Adolescent Psychiatry: https://www.jaacap.org/article/S0890-8567(19)30288-6/fulltext

British Board of Film Classification. (2021, October 13). *Bad Luck Banging Or Loony Porn*. Retrieved May 2023, from BBFC: https://www.bbfc.co.uk/release/bad-luck-banging-or-loony-porn-film-qxnzzxq6vlgtmtawmdayndy

British Horror Films. (2022, February 10). Retrieved May 2023, from Refused Classification: https://www.refused-classification.com/censorship/film-1/british-horror/

Buckmaster, L. (2010, August 30). *Cops didn't show, but maybe they should have: gay zombie porno sickens*. Retrieved May 2023, from Crikey: https://www.crikey.com.au/2010/08/30/cops-didnt-show-but-maybe-they-should-have-gay-zombie-prno-sickens/

Buckmaster, L. (2017, October 17). *Donkey sex OK, but gay sex is not? Australia's film classification board is homophobic*. Retrieved May 2023, from Flicks: https://www.flicks.com.au/features/donkey-sex-ok-but-gay-sex-is-not-why-australias-film-classification-board-is-homophobic/

Buckmaster, Luke [@lukebuckmaster]. (2021, January 31). *Tom of Finland is coming to @StanAustralia on Feb 6. The classification board was upset about something I wrote for [Tweet]*. Retrieved May 2023, from Twitter: https://twitter.com/lukebuckmaster/status/1355818063615016963

Bunbury, S. (2021, July 16). *Director addresses controversy about Port Arthur massacre movie*. Retrieved May 2023, from The Sydney Morning Herald: https://www.smh.com.au/culture/movies/director-addresses-controversy-about-port-arthur-massacre-movie-20210715-p58a3k.html The use of this work has been licensed by Copyright Agency except as permitted by the Copyright Act, you must not re-use this work without the permission of the copyright owner or Copyright Agency.

Burgess, K. (2019, September 4). *AFP raids on ABC, Newscorp journalist cost taxpayers*. Retrieved May 2023, from The Canberra Times: https://www.canberratimes.com.au/story/6355512/pezzullo-praised-police-over-journalist-raids/

Camfield v. City of Oklahoma City, 248 F.3d 1214 (10th Circuit - City of Oklahoma May 4, 2001).

Canadian Horror Films. (2021, August 24). Retrieved May 2023, from Refused Classification: https://www.refused-classification.com/ccnsorship/film-1/canadian-horror/

Carey, A. (2011, July 2). *Political parable or perversion?* Retrieved May 2023, from The Sydney Morning Herald: https://www.smh.com.au/entertainment/movies/political-parable-or-perversion-20110701-1gv0n.html

Carroll, W. (2017, May 21). *Is Nil by Mouth the bleakest kitchen-sink drama ever made?* Retrieved May 2023, from Little White Lies: https://lwlies.com/articles/nil-by-mouth-gary-oldman-kitchen-sink-drama/

Censor had three snips at Blow-Up. (1969, August 20). Retrieved May 2023, from Papua New Guinea Post-Courier: https://trove.nla.gov.au/newspaper/article/251520289

Censored 1970s American Films - Page 2. (2022, January 28). Retrieved May 2023, from Refused Classification: https://www.refused-classification.com/censorship/film-1/american-03/

Censorship Of A Serbian Film (2010). (2022, July 8). Retrieved May 2023, from Refused Classification: https://www.refused-classification.com/censorship/film-1/a-serbian-film/

Censorship Of Mysterious Skin (2004). (2021, August 5). Retrieved May 2023, from Refused Classification: https://www.refused-classification.com/censorship/film-1/mysterious-skin/

Censorship Of Salò, Or The 120 Days Of Sodom (1975). (2021, August 5). Retrieved May 2023, from Refused Classification: https://www.refused-classification.com/censorship/film-1/salo-or-the-120-days-of-sodom/

Censorship Of The Hannibal Lecter (1991-2001) Series. (2021, August 5). Retrieved May 2023, from Refused Classification: https://www.refused-classification.com/censorship/film-1/hannibal-lecter/

Censorship Of The Human Centipede II (Full Sequence) (2011). (2021, August 5). Retrieved May 2023, from Refused Classification: https://www.refused-classification.com/censorship/film-1/human-centipede-2-full-sequence/#

Cettl, R. (2011). *Offensive to a Reasonable Adult*. Adelaide, SA: Transgressor.

Children and the cinema. (1921, July 9). Retrieved May 2023, from The Sydney Morning Herald: http://nla.gov.au/nla.news-article15948822

"Children of Wasteland" Draws Large Audience. (1953, June 17). Retrieved May 2023, from Townsville Daily Bulletin: https://trove.nla.gov.au/newspaper/article/62502232

China praises Lee despite Mountain ban. (2006, March 8). Retrieved May 2023, from The Guardian: https://www.theguardian.com/film/2006/mar/07/awardsandprizes.china

Chipp, D. (1987). *Chipp*. North Ryde, NSW: Methuen Haynes.

Chipp off an old block. (2003, November 26). Retrieved May 2023, from The Age: https://www.theage.com.au/national/chipp-off-an-old-block-20031126-gdwt6o.html The use of this work has been licensed by Copyright Agency except as permitted by the Copyright Act, you must not re-use this work without the permission of the copyright owner or Copyright Agency.

Christians, C. G., Rotzoll, K. B., Fackler, M., McKee, K. B., & Woods, Jr., R. H. (2005). *Media Ethics: Cases and Moral Reasoning (Seventh Edition)*. New York: Routledge.

Cinema - Strong but never gamey. (1968, August 6). Retrieved May 2023, from The Canberra Times: http://nla.gov.au/nla.news-page11663519

Classification Act 1995 (Cth). https://www.legislation.gov.au/Series/C2004A04863 Sourced from the Federal Register of Legislation at 7 May 2023. For the latest information on Australian Government law please go to https://www.legislation.gov.au CC BY 4.0 https://creativecommons.org/licenses/by/4.0/legalcode

Classification (Publications, Films and Computer Games) Enforcement Act 1996 (WA) https://www.legislation.wa.gov.au/legislation/statutes.nsf/law_a114.html Based on content from the Western Australian Legislation website at 7 May 2023. For the latest information on Western Australian legislation, visit www.legislation.wa.gov.au CC BY 4.0 https://creativecommons.org/licenses/by/4.0/legalcode

Classification (Publications, Films and Computer Games) (Spherex Classification Tool) Approval 2022 (Cth). (2023, January). Retrieved May 2023, from Australian Classification: https://www.classification.gov.au/sites/default/files/documents/classification-publications-films-and-computer-games-spherex-classification-tool-approval-2022.pdf

Cochrane, N. (1999, October 12). Internet censorship bill draws industry warning. *The Age*. The use of this work has been licensed by Copyright Agency except as permitted by the Copyright Act, you must not re-use this work without the permission of the copyright owner or Copyright Agency.

Cockington, J. (2005). *Banned: tales from the bizarre history of Australian obscenity*. Sydney, NSW: ABC Books for the Australian Broadcasting Corporation.

Collective Shout. (2011, September 15). *Calls for A Serbian Film to be banned for depictions of child rape and extreme sexual violence against women*. Retrieved May 2023, from Collective Shout: https://www.collectiveshout.org/calls_for_a_serbian_film_to_be_banned_for_depictions_of_child_rape_and_extreme_sexual_violence_against_women

Collective Shout. (2011, September 24). *Win! 'A Serbian Film' refused classification upon review*. Retrieved May 2023, from Collective Shout: https://www.collectiveshout.org/win_a_serbian_film_refused_classification_upon_review

Commonwealth. *Parliamentary debates*. Estimates Committees. 26 February 1998. 27. https://parlinfo.aph.gov.au/parlInfo/search/display/display.w3p;query=Id:committees/estimate/g0000128.sgm/0022

Commonwealth. *Parliamentary debates*. House of Representatives. 22 April 1970. 1445. https://parlinfo.aph.gov.au/parlInfo/search/display/display.w3p;query=Id%3A%22hansard80%2Fhansardr80%2F1970-04-22%2F0050%22

Commonwealth. *Parliamentary debates*. House of Representatives. 22 September 1997. 7991. https://parlinfo.aph.gov.au/parlInfo/search/display/display.w3p;query=Id%3A%22chamber%2Fhansardr%2F1997-09-22%2F0018%22 CC BY-NC-ND 3.0 AU. Reproduced with permission.

Commonwealth. *Parliamentary debates*. Senate. 6 September 1993. 982. https://parlinfo.aph.gov.au/parlInfo/search/display/display.w3p;query=Id%3A%22chamber%2Fhansards%2F1993-09-06%2F0096%22 CC BY-NC-ND 3.0 AU. Reproduced with permission.

Commonwealth. *Parliamentary debates*. Senate. 10 May 1990. 305. https://parlinfo.aph.gov.au/parlInfo/search/display/display.w3p;query=Id%3A%22chamber%2Fhansards%2F1990-05-10%2F0119%22

Commonwealth. *Parliamentary debates*. Senate. 28 February 2001. 22246. https://parlinfo.aph.gov.au/parlInfo/search/display/display.w3p;query=Id%3A%22chamber%2Fhansards%2F2001-02-28%2F0126%22

Commonwealth. *Parliamentary debates*. Senate Committees. 22 April 2016. 1. https://parlinfo.aph.gov.au/parlInfo/search/display/display.w3p;query=Id%3A%22committees%2Fcommsen%2F74b0779c-2bcc-4e4a-a804-5572b0ab1f8f%2F0001%22

Commonwealth of Australia. (1927). *Royal Commission on the Moving Picture Industry: Minutes of Evidence*. Canberra: Government Printer.

Commonwealth of Australia. (1928). *Report of the Royal Commission on the Moving Picture Industry in Australia*. Canberra: Government Printer. Retrieved May 2023, from National Library of Australia: http://nla.gov.au/nla.obj-52787365

Commonwealth of Australia. (1991, June 30). *Censorship Procedure [1991] ALRC 55*. Retrieved May 2023, from Australian Law Reform Commission: http://www.austlii.edu.au/au/other/lawreform/ALRC/1991/55.html

Commonwealth of Australia. (2011, June). *Review of the National Classification Scheme: achieving the right balance*. Retrieved May 2023, from National Library of Australia: https://nla.gov.au/nla.obj-788427540

Commonwealth of Australia. (2012, February). *Classification-Content Regulation and Convergent Media (ALRC Report 118)*. Retrieved May 2023, from Australian Law Reform Commission: https://www.alrc.gov.au/publication/classification-content-regulation-and-convergent-media-alrc-report-118/

Commonwealth of Australia. (2020, May). *Review of Australian classification regulation - Report*. Retrieved May 2023, from Department of Infrastructure, Transport, Regional Development, Communications and the Arts: https://www.infrastructure.gov.au/sites/default/files/documents/review-of-australian-classification-regulation--may2020.pdf CC BY 4.0 https://creativecommons.org/licenses/by/4.0/legalcode

Comstock, T. (2006a, July 11). *A Criminal Intent to Arouse*. Retrieved May 2023, from Comstock Films: https://web.archive.org/web/20060825061934/http://www.comstockfilms.com/blog/tony/2006/07/11/a-criminal-intent-to-arouse/

Comstock, T. (2006b, August 22). *DAMON AND HUNTER: The Film the Australian Government Doesn't Want You to See*. Retrieved May 2023, from Comstock Films: https://web.archive.org/web/20071215174741/http://www.comstockfilms.com/blog/tony/2006/08/20/damon-and-hunter-the-film-the-australian-government-doesnt-want-you-to-see/

Comstock, T. (2006c, August 23). *Removed by Order of the Australian Office of Film and Literature Classification*. Retrieved May 2023, from Comstock Films: https://web.archive.org/web/20060903220018/http://www.comstockfilms.com/blog/tony/2006/08/23/removed-by-order-of-the-australian-office-of-film-and-literature-classification/

Comstock, T. (2006d, August 28). *Curiouser and Curiouser: OFLC Requests Permission to Use DAMON AND HUNTER for Training Purposes*. Retrieved May 2023, from Comstock Films: https://web.archive.org/web/20071215112251/http://www.comstockfilms.com/blog/tony/2006/08/28/curiouser-and-curiouser-oflc-requests-permission-to-use-damon-and-hunter-for-training-purposes/

Comstock, T. (2006e, August 29). *Defaming the OFLC?!?* Retrieved May 2023, from Comstock Films: https://web.archive.org/web/20071215174630/http://www.comstockfilms.com/blog/tony/2006/08/29/defaming-the-oflc/

Comstock, T. (2006f, August 30). *Will DAMON AND HUNTER play at QueerDOC?* Retrieved May 2023, from Comstock Films: https://web.archive.org/web/20071215174603/http://www.comstockfilms.com/blog/tony/2006/08/30/will-damon-and-hunter-play-at-queerdoc/

Comstock, T. (2011). *Tony Comstock's KA an of Silence*. Retrieved May 2023, from Tony Comstock's KA an of Silence: http://www.tonycomstock.com

Crawley, K. (2010). *The Farce of Law: Performing and Policing Norm and Ahmed in 1969*. Retrieved May 2023, from University of Wollongong Australia: https://ro.uow.edu.au/cgi/viewcontent.cgi?article=1265&context=ltc

Crowe v Graham, 121 CLR 375 (High Court of Australia March 8, 1968).

Cuir, R. (2007, April). Larry Clark: Eye of the Storm (un oeil dans la tempête). *Artpress* (No. 333), pp. 22 - 29. Retrieved May 2023 from Art Press: https://www.artpress.com/wp-content/uploads/2014/12/3159.pdf

Cuties classified MA 15+. (2020, October 23). Retrieved May 2023, from Australian Classification: https://www.classification.gov.au/about-us/media-and-news/news/cuties-classified-ma-15

Dawson, J. (1976, September). Forms and Feelings Under the Rising Sun: Nagisa Oshima. *Cinema Papers* (10), pp. 107-110. Retrieved May 2023, from Cinema Papers: https://archivesonline.uow.edu.au/nodes/view/5019#idx32857

Delvecchio, J. (1996, August 22). *Crime film reopens old wounds*. The Sydney Morning Herald. The use of this work has been licensed by Copyright Agency except as permitted by the Copyright Act, you must not re-use this work without the permission of the copyright owner or Copyright Agency.

Department of Communications and the Arts. (2016, August). *Pilot of the International Age Rating Coalition (IARC) Classification Tool - Final Report*. Retrieved May 2023, from Department of Infrastructure, Transport, Regional Development, Communications and the Arts: https://www.infrastructure.gov.au/sites/default/files/documents/foi-25-1920-pilot-international-age-rating-coalition-classification-tool.pdf

Department of Communications and the Arts. (2019, December). *Terms of Reference - Review of Australian classification regulation*. Retrieved May 2023, from Department of Infrastructure, Transport, Regional Development, Communications and the Arts: https://www.infrastructure.gov.au/sites/default/files/terms-of-reference-review-of-australian-classification-regulation.pdf

Department of Infrastructure, Transport, Regional Development, Communications and the Arts. (2022, May 27). *Report on classification usage and attitudes research 27 May 2022*. Retrieved May 2023, from Australian Classification: https://www.classification.gov.au/sites/default/files/documents/5270_ditrdc_classification_usage_publication_report_finalv2.pdf

Dezuanni, M., & Goldsmith, B. (2015). Disciplining the screen through education: the Royal Commission into the Moving Picture Industry in Australia. *Studies in Australasian Cinema, 9* (3), 298 - 311. Retrieved May 2023, from Queensland University of Technology: https://eprints.qut.edu.au/87495/3/87495a.pdf Reprinted by permission of Taylor & Francis Ltd, http://www.tandfonline.com

Directed By Bruce La Bruce. (2021, August 24). Retrieved May 2023, from Refused Classification: https://www.refused-classification.com/censorship/film-1/bruce-la-bruce/

Directed By Ruggero Deodato. (2022, December 30). Retrieved May 2023, from Refused Classification: https://www.refused-classification.com/censorship/film-1/ruggero-deodato/#cannibal-holocaust

Dunstan, K. (1971, November 27). Batman's Melbourne - Now it's hard to be caught with a kids' movie. *The Bulletin, 093* (4783), p. 17. Retrieved May 2023, from Are Media Pty Limited / aremediasyndication.com.au / 'The Bulletin': http://nla.gov.au/nla.obj-1413439620

Dutton, G., & Harris, M. (1970). *Australia's Censorship Crisis*. Melbourne, VIC: Sun Books.

Ebert, R. (1969, September 23). *I Am Curious (Yellow)*. Retrieved May 2023, from Roger Ebert: https://www.rogerebert.com/reviews/i-am-curious-yellow-1969

Ebert, R. (1987, July 10). *Devil in the Flesh*. Retrieved May 2023, from Roger Ebert: https://www.rogerebert.com/reviews/devil-in-the-flesh-1987

Edwards, J. (2020, September 29). *A Sitdown with Director Srdan Spasojević of 'A Serbian Film'*. Retrieved May 2023, from Monsters Madness and Magic: https://www.monstersmadnessandmagic.com/written-interviews/a-sitdown-with-director-srdan-spasojevis-of-a-serbian-film

Elfick, D. (1997, February 4). Violence in Film. *Violence, Crime and the Entertainment Media*. Sydney: Australian Institute of Criminology. Retrieved May 2023, from National Library of Australia: https://webarchive.nla.gov.au/awa/20010320130000/http://www.aic.gov.au/conferences/violence/elfick.pdf

Exorcist Ban Overturned. (2001, April 15). Retrieved May 2023, from The Catholic Leader: https://catholicleader.com.au/news/exorcist-ban-overturned_37383/

Farnsworth, S., & Byrne, E. (2020, June 23). *George Pell High Court ruling on appeal against child sex abuse convictions to be handed down in virtual vacuum*. Retrieved May 2023, from ABC News: https://www.abc.net.au/news/2020-04-06/george-pell-high-court-appeal-decision/12126288

Fenton, A. (2011, August 18). *State Government bans 'depraved' horror movie A Serbian Film*. Retrieved May 2023, from The Advertiser: https://www.adelaidenow.com.au/news/south-australia/state-government-bans-depraved-horror-movie-a-serbian-film/news-story/328dbb0a02b45b76880071958f3c00a0

Film Censorship: I Want Your Love (2012). (2015, September 26). Retrieved May 2023, from Refused Classification: https://web.archive.org/web/20201014063514/https://www.refused-classification.com/censorship/films/i-want-your-love-2012.html

Film Censorship: M #1. (2013, July 6). Retrieved May 2023, from Refused Classification: https://web.archive.org/web/20201014062852/https://www.refused-classification.com/censorship/films/m.html#man-behind-the-sun

Film Censorship: M #3. (2013, July 6). Retrieved May 2023, from Refused Classification: https://web.archive.org/web/20201014062905/https://www.refused-classification.com/censorship/films/m-3.html

Filmmaker defends the 'real' Ken Park. (2003, June 16). Retrieved May 2023, from The Sydney Morning Herald: https://www.smh.com.au/entertainment/movies/filmmaker-defends-the-real-ken-park-20030616-gdgxq7.html

FitzSimons, P. (2022, October 23). *Fred Nile confesses: I'm sorry I prayed for rain on the Mardi Gras parade*. Retrieved May 2023, from The Sydney Morning Herald: https://www.smh.com.au/national/nsw/fred-nile-confesses-i-m-sorry-i-prayed-for-rain-on-the-mardi-gras-parade-20221020-p5brjx.html. The use of this work has been licensed by Copyright Agency except as permitted by the Copyright Act, you must not re-use this work without the permission of the copyright owner or Copyright Agency.

Flynn, D. (2020, September 20). *Classification Board turns blind eye to paedophile grooming film 'Cuties'*. Retrieved May 2023, from Australian Christian Lobby: https://www.acl.org.au/mr_netflixcuties

Forbes, M. (1986, June 10). *FILM FESTIVAL OPENS AMIDST CONTROVERSY*. Retrieved May 2023, from Tharunka: https://trove.nla.gov.au/newspaper/article/228650448

Fred Nile finds a new home among Seniors. (2022, May 19). Retrieved May 2023, from The Guardian: https://www.theguardian.com/australia-news/2022/may/19/fred-nile-finds-a-new-home-among-seniors

Gabbatt, A. (2016, September 15). *Cannibal horror film too Raw for viewers as paramedics are called*. Retrieved May 2023, from The Guardian: https://www.theguardian.com/film/2016/sep/14/cannibal-horror-film-raw-toronto-film-festival

Gallery Global Networks Limited. (2003a, April 2). *Gallery Global Announces Major Distribution Deal of Playboy Programming*. Retrieved May 2023, from Iguana2: https://newswire.iguana2.com/af5f4d73c1a54a33/ims.asx/XX292410/IMS_Major_distribution_deal_of_Playboy_programming

BIBLIOGRAPHY † 263

Gallery Global Networks Limited. (2003b, July 30). *GCN: Adult Channel Video Ent. Subscription Service Online*. Retrieved May 2023, from Iguana2: https://newswire.iguana2.com/af5f4d73c1a54a33/ims.asx/XX301933/IMS_GCN:_Adult_Channel_Video_Ent._Subscription_Service_Online

Gallery Global Networks Limited. (2004a, July 19). *Gallery Global Networks Announces Launch of Adult Movie Rental Business www.thedvdcompany.com*. Retrieved May 2023, from Iguana2: https://newswire.iguana2.com/af5f4d73c1a54a33/ims.asx/XX335737/IMS_Launch_of_Adult_Movie_Rental_Business

Gallery Global Networks Limited. (2004b, October 28). *Annual Report 2003*. Retrieved May 2023, from Iguana2: https://newswire.iguana2.com/af5f4d73c1a54a33/ims.asx/XX310577/IMS_Annual_Report

Gallery Global Networks Limited. (2005, November 30). *Chairman's Address*. Retrieved May 2023, from Iguana2: https://newswire.iguana2.com/af5f4d73c1a54a33/ims.asx/XX392710/IMS_Chairmans_AGM_Address_to_Shareholders

Galvin, P. (2009, June 10). *Pure Shit Review*. Retrieved May 2023, from SBS: https://www.sbs.com.au/movies/review/pure-shit-review

Game IARC Censorship Timeline. (2022, August 4). Retrieved May 2023, from Refused Classification: https://www.refused-classification.com/censorship-timelines/game-iarc/

Gardiner, S. (2017, August 29). *Activist Danny Lim has offensive behaviour conviction quashed over Tony Abbott sign*. Retrieved May 2023, from The Sydney Morning Herald: https://www.smh.com.au/national/nsw/activist-danny-lim-has-offensive-behaviour-conviction-quashed-over-tony-abbott-sign-20170829-gy6ft4.html

GENERAL SUMMARY. (1912, January 11). Retrieved May 2023, from Camperdown Chronicle: http://nla.gov.au/nla.news-article25121633

Ginnane, A. I. (1974, December). Film censorship can still be heavy. *Cinema Papers* (4), p. 313. Retrieved May 2023, from Cinema Papers: https://issuu.com/libuow/docs/cpdec74

Good Film League of N.S.W. (1926, July 1). *Good film bulletin the official organ of the Good Film League of N.S.W*. Artarmon, NSW.

GOOD FILMS. (1922, September 20). Retrieved May 2023, from The Newcastle Sun: http://nla.gov.au/nla.news-article162774992

Government of Queensland (1990, August 27). Cabinet Minutes, Subject: Classification of Films and Literature Bill. Retrieved from Queensland Government: https://www.archivessearch.qld.gov.au/api/download_file/DR54289

Government of South Australia. (2019, October 30). *Classification Council get the axe*. Retrieved May 2023, from Attorney-General's Department: https://web.archive.org/web/20200318201617/https://www.agd.sa.gov.au/newsroom/classification-council-get-axe

Government of Western Australia. (1999a, March 10). *The film 'Sick: The Life and Death of Bob Flanagan, Supermasochist' censored*. Retrieved May 2023, from Government of Western Australia: https://www.mediastatements.wa.gov.au/Pages/Court/1999/03/The-film-%27Sick-The-Life-and-Death-of-Bob-Flanagan,-Supermasochist%27censored.aspx

Government of Western Australia. (1999b, March 16). *Censored film to be screened at REVelation Film Festival*. Retrieved May 2023, from Government of Western Australia: https://www.mediastatements.wa.gov.au/Pages/Court/1999/03/Censored-film-to-be-screened-at-REVelation-Film-Festival.aspx

Griffin, M. (2010, July 21). *Zombie porn director 'delighted' by ban*. Retrieved May 2023, from The Sydney Morning Herald: https://www.smh.com.au/entertainment/movies/zombie-porn-director-delighted-by-ban-20100721-10k8z.html. The use of this work has been licensed by Copyright Agency except as permitted by the Copyright Act, you must not re-use this work without the permission of the copyright owner or Copyright Agency.

Griffith, G. (2002). *Censorship in Australia: Regulating the Internet and other recent developments*. Sydney: NSW Parliamentary Library Research Service. Retrieved May 2023, from Parliament of New South Wales: https://www.parliament.nsw.gov.au/researchpapers/Documents/censorship-in-australia-regulating-the-internet-/04-02.pdf

Gross, T. (2015, November 11). *Shonda Rhimes On Running 3 Hit Shows And The Limits Of Network TV*. Retrieved May 2023, from NPR: https://www.npr.org/2015/11/11/455594842/shonda-rhimes-on-running-three-hit-shows-and-the-limits-of-network-tv

Guidelines for the Classification of Films 2012 (Cth). https://www.legislation.gov.au/Details/F2012L02541 Sourced from the Federal Register of Legislation at 7 May 2023. For the latest information on Australian Government law please go to https://www.legislation.gov.au CC BY 4.0 https://creativecommons.org/licenses/by/4.0/legalcode

Guilliatt, R., & Casimir, J. (1996, July 6). *The return of the wowsers*. Retrieved May 2023, from The Sydney Morning Herald: http://web.archive.org/web/19970113054119/www.smh.com.au/daily/content/Jul/6/features/960706-features.html The use of this work has been licensed by Copyright Agency except as permitted by the Copyright Act, you must not re-use this work without the permission of the copyright owner or Copyright Agency.

Hall, S. (1972, February 19). Ultra-violence: the new wave. *The Bulletin, 094* (4794), pp. 42-43. Retrieved May 2023, from Are Media Pty Limited / aremediasyndication.com.au / 'The Bulletin': http://nla.gov.au/nla.obj-1328840022

Hall, S. (1973, June 2). Festival films not so esoteric. *The Bulletin, 095* (4857), p. 52. Retrieved May 2023, from Are Media Pty Limited / aremediasyndication.com.au / 'The Bulletin': http://nla.gov.au/nla.obj-1413736511

Have your say on classification regulation. (2020, January 8). Retrieved May 2023, from Australian Classification: https://www.classification.gov.au/about-us/media-and-news/news/have-your-say-classification-regulation

Hernandez, E., Kaufman, A., & Brooks, B. (2001, July 24). *DAILY NEWS: Solondz Changes New Film; Outfest Winners; Jackson Heads to USA*. Retrieved May 2023, from Indiewire: https://www.indiewire.com/news/general-news/daily-news-solondz-changes-new-film-outfest-winners-jackson-heads-to-usa-80851/

Heron, A. (2008, November 23). *Cahiers du cinéma's 100 Greatest Films*. Retrieved May 2023, from FILMdetail: https://www.filmdetail.com/2008/11/23/cahiers-du-cinemas-100-greatest-films/

Higham, C. (1965, November 20). Faces on the Cutting Room Floor: Film censorship: the unnecessary secrets. *The Bulletin, 087* (4473), pp. 17-19. Retrieved from Are Media Pty Limited / aremediasyndication.com.au / 'The Bulletin': http://nla.gov.au/nla.obj-686668537

Hills, R. (2012, January 8). *Who's afraid of Melinda Tankard Reist?* Retrieved May 2023, from The Sydney Morning Herald: https://www.smh.com.au/lifestyle/whos-afraid-of-melinda-tankard-reist-20120110-1psdx.html

Hooten, F. (2008). It Droppeth as the Gentle Rain: The Birth of Australian Experimental Film. *Metro Magazine* (159), 138-141.

Insufficient safeguards in new surveillance law. (2021, August 25). Retrieved May 2023, from Human Rights Law Centre: https://www.hrlc.org.au/news/2021/8/25/insufficient-safeguards-in-new-surveillance-law

Ireland, D. (2005, August 4). *Restoring Pasolini*. Retrieved May 2023, from LA Weekly: https://www.laweekly.com/restoring-pasolini/

Johnson, T. (2018, February 21). *Oscar Nominated Film Censored For Australian Audiences*. Retrieved May 2023, from FilmInk: https://www.filmink.com.au/oscar-nominated-film-censored-australian-audiences/

Judge Rules 'Tin Drum' Shows No Child Porn. (1998, October 21). Retrieved May 2023, from The Oklahoman: https://www.oklahoman.com/article/2630316/judge-rules-tin-drum-shows-no-child-porn

Just what does the censor stop us seeing? (1953, July 21). Retrieved May 2023, from The West Australian: http://nla.gov.au/nla.news-article49221807

Kalina, P. (2010, July 21). *Gay zombie porn gets festival flick*. Retrieved May 2023, from The Sydney Morning Herald: https://www.smh.com.au/entertainment/movies/gay-zombie-porn-gets-festival-flick-20100720-10jls.html

Kapka, A. (2014, December 07). *Understanding A Serbian Film: The Effects of Censorship and File-sharing on Critical Reception and Perceptions of Serbian National Identity in the UK*. Retrieved May 2023, from Frames Cinema Journal: https://framescinemajournal.com/article/understanding-a-serbian-film-the-effects-of-censorship-and-file-sharing-on-critical-reception-and-perceptions-of-serbian-national-identity-in-the-uk/

Kelly, C. (2006, June 30). *The MySpace Director*. Retrieved May 2023, from Slate: https://slate.com/news-and-politics/2006/06/larry-clark-the-myspace-director.html

Ken Park screening, take two: film lovers defiant. (2003, July 5). Retrieved May 2023, from The Sydney Morning Herald: https://www.smh.com.au/entertainment/movies/ken-park-screening-take-two-film-lovers-defiant-20030705-gdh1ki.html

Knaus, C. (2023, March 21). *Australia's FOI backlog: 587 cases remain unresolved more than three years on*. Retrieved May 2023, from The Guardian: https://www.theguardian.com/australia-news/2023/mar/21/australia-foi-freedom-of-information-backlog-587-cases-unresolved-more-than-three-years

Knegt, P. (2010, October 25). *John Waters Brings "Sodom" To The TIFF Bell Lightbox*. Retrieved May 2023, from Indiewire: https://www.indiewire.com/2010/10/john-waters-brings-sodom-to-the-tiff-bell-lightbox-244592/

Knegt, P. (2012, March 4). *James Franco Stands Up For Sex In Film After Travis Mathews' 'I Want Your Love' Is Banned In Australia*. Retrieved May 2023, from Indiewire: https://www.indiewire.com/2013/03/james-franco-stands-up-for-sex-in-film-after-travis-mathews-i-want-your-love-is-banned-in-australia-40402/

Knott, M. (2014, February 27). *Australia bans award-winning Swedish film Children's Island over child porn concerns*. Retrieved May 2023, from The Sydney Morning Herald: https://www.smh.com.au/entertainment/movies/australia-bans-awardwinning-swedish-film-childrens-island-over-child-porn-concerns-20140227-33lxx.html

Koslowski, M. (2018, June 14). *Director Who Wrote Homophobic Rant "Unresigns" As Head Of Melbourne Underground Film Festival*. Retrieved May 2023, from Junkee: https://junkee.com/richard-wolstencroft-muff/163328

Koziol, M. (2019, September 8). *Bongs, bare bottoms and bad language: behind the scenes with Australia's chief censor*. Retrieved May 2023, from The Sydney Morning Herald: https://www.smh.com.au/national/bongs-bare-bottoms-and-bad-language-behind-the-scenes-with-australia-s-chief-censor-20190904-p52nwd.html

Lattman, P. (2007, September 27). *The Origins of Justice Stewart's "I Know It When I See It"*. Retrieved May 2023, from The Wall Street Journal: https://www.wsj.com/articles/BL-LB-4338

Lease, D. (1997, August). *The Tin Drum Controversy*. Retrieved May 2023, from Eclectica Magazine: https://www.eclectica.org/v1n11/lease_tindrum.html

Leston, R. (2022, January 19). *Which John Wick Movie Has The Highest Kill Count?* Retrieved May 2023, from SlashFilm: https://www.slashfilm.com/739031/which-john-wick-movie-has-the-highest-kill-count/

Let Me Die a Woman. (n.d.). Retrieved May 2023, from Criterion Channel: https://www.criterionchannel.com/let-me-die-a-woman

Lies (Gojitmal) (1999). (2003, March 27). Retrieved May 2023, from Michael D's Region 4 DVD Video Info Page: http://www.michaeldvd.com.au/Reviews/Reviews.asp?ID=2736

Linklater, A. (2001, June 23). *Dangerous liaisons*. Retrieved May 2023, from The Guardian: https://www.theguardian.com/film/2001/jun/22/features.features11

Maddox, M. (2005). *God Under Howard: The Rise of the Religious Right in Australian Politics*. Sydney, NSW: Allen & Unwin.

Margaret Pomeranz detained by police 2003 – Illegal Ken Park screening – Channel 10 report. (2003, July 3). Retrieved May 2023, from YouTube: https://www.youtube.com/watch?v=WIFOzn5MsLk

Marr, D. (2008, April 26). *Carve up in political kitchen*. The Sydney Morning Herald. The use of this work has been licensed by Copyright Agency except as permitted by the Copyright Act, you must not re-use this work without the permission of the copyright owner or Copyright Agency.

Massey, M. (1988, September 23). *The Latest Temptation Is To Ask What All The Fuss Is About*. Retrieved May 2023, from Australian Financial Review: https://www.afr.com/politics/the-latest-temptation-is-to-ask-what-all-the-fuss-is-about-19880923-jl5cz

Mayrhofer, D. (1989, February). *Media Briefs July – December 1988*. Media International Australia. Retrieved May 2023, from Sage Journals: https://journals.sagepub.com/doi/abs/10.1177/1329878X8905100124?journalCode=miaa

McCarthy, J. (1997, December). *Oklahoma and The Tin Drum*. Retrieved May 2023, from The Ethical Spectacle: https://www.spectacle.org/997/mcarth.html

McClelland, G. (1977). Des Draydon: interview. *Cinema Papers* (12), p. 330. Retrieved May 2023, from Cinema Papers: https://issuu.com/libuow/docs/cinemapaper1977aprno012

Media Censorship in Australia. (2013, August 27). *The following article was submitted directly to McOz and it is being posted with the permission of the author [Status update]*. Retrieved May 2023, from Facebook: https://www.facebook.com/MediaCensorshipInAustralia/posts/426539010788645

Media Censorship in Australia. (2021, October 22). Today, Friday 22 Oct 2021, is the 30th anniversary of my 22 Oct 1991 Customs bust in Brisbane. As you [Status update]. Retrieved May 2023, from Facebook: https://www.facebook.com/MediaCensorshipInAustralia/posts/pfbid02WpmZKHnpWTBdsZtzTAi8XkNpMK8X4gXF93ckHus3SW5TuJgzQbD2Q7Qq1xpi53yFl

Melbourne International Film Festival [@MIFFofficial]. (2020, July 31). *The safety and wellbeing of the MIFF community and broader Australian public is of paramount concern to the festival [Tweet]*. Retrieved May 2023, from Twitter: https://twitter.com/miffofficial/status/1288942442918682625

Miller, D., & Kaufman, A. (2018, January 11). *Five women accuse actor James Franco of inappropriate or sexually exploitative behavior*. Retrieved May 2023, from The Los Angeles Times: https://www.latimes.com/business/hollywood/la-fi-ct-james-franco-allegations-20180111-htmlstory.html

Miraudo, S. (2009a, June 19). *The Hangover censorship controversy answered!* Retrieved May 2023, from Quickflix: https://qfxblog.wordpress.com/2009/06/19/the-hangover-censorship-controversy-answered/

Miraudo, S. (2009b, June 30). *Australia gets censored cut of Bruno!* Retrieved May 2023, from Quickflix: https://qfxblog.wordpress.com/2009/06/30/australia-gets-censored-cut-of-bruno/

Miraudo, S. (2012, February 21). *Life's a gas – The Human Centipede 2: Full Sequence review*. Retrieved May 2023, from Quickflix: https://qfxblog.wordpress.com/2012/02/21/lifes-a-gas-the-human-centipede-2-full-sequence-review/

Miraudo, S. (2014, February 17). *Return of the Mick – Wolf Creek 2 review*. Retrieved May 2023, from Quickflix: https://qfxblog.wordpress.com/2014/02/17/return-of-the-mick-wolf-creek-2-review/

Miraudo, S. (2019a, March 7). *How Did They Film the Kissing in "Pen15"?* Retrieved May 2023, from Student Edge: https://studentedge.org/article/how-did-they-film-the-make-out-scene-in-pen15

Miraudo, S. (2019b, August 8). *Adam Goodes Doco "The Australian Dream" Has Been Rated MA15+, Restricting Reach to Young People*. Retrieved May 2023, from Student Edge: https://studentedge.org/article/adam-goodes-doco-the-australian-dream-has-been-rated-ma15-restricting-access-to-young-people

Miraudo, S. (2020, June 9). *Why Did Netflix Raise the Rating for "Moonlight" from M to MA15+ in Australia?* Retrieved May 2023, from Student Edge: https://studentedge.org/article/why-did-netflix-raise-the-classification-rating-for-moonlight-in-australia

Monster Pictures. (2011a, November 6). *POOH FOUND IN FOYER - is it yours? Yes that's right folks I just spoke to a very dismayed Jordan Bastian [Status update]*. Retrieved May 2023, from Facebook: https://www.facebook.com/monsterpictures/photos/a.224558637581149/268013976568948/?__cft__[0]=AZWfHIRvfJgl32bl1Ho2xutRHjIBQPaKbFzL7OML ZLhmqBBtM5MRbhDjag_4ON7QS0lyYhUnLczYvKn5jmO9HcHsz_Xy_rwvY5_XPF2sfKhlAePpisvBjK10pe9Hn4MVQeVNFKzVGVdbcCutoAoKbVjZ&__tn__=%

Monster Pictures. (2011b, December 13). *Great news Monster Maniacs - THE HUMAN CENTIPEDE 2: FULL SEQUENCE has been cleared by the Director of the Australian Government [Status update]*. Retrieved May 2023, from Facebook: https://www.facebook.com/monsterpictures/photos/a.224558637581149/286250704745275

Monster Pictures. (2011c, December 21). *THE HUMAN CENTIPEDE 2: Perth Western Australia Sellout screening*. Retrieved May 2023, from YouTube: https://www.youtube.com/watch?v=7xwchiEProI

Moran, R. (2021, November 8). *It has film festival audiences fainting in the aisles. But how bad is Titane?* Retrieved May 2023, from The Sydney Morning Herald: https://www.smh.com.au/culture/movies/it-has-film-festival-audiences-fainting-in-the-aisles-but-how-bad-is-titane-20211108-p596ud.html

Moses, A. (2009, April 1). *Conroy backtracks on internet censorship policy*. Retrieved May 2023, from The Sydney Morning Herald: https://www.smh.com.au/technology/conroy-backtracks-on-internet-censorship-policy-20090401-gdtgbo.html

Mudge, J. (2019, January 3). *Dr. Lamb*. Retrieved May 2023, from Eastern Kicks: https://www.easternkicks.com/reviews/dr-lamb/

Mumford, G. (2019, July 16). *Netflix cuts controversial suicide scene from 13 Reasons Why*. Retrieved May 2023, from The Guardian: https://www.theguardian.com/tv-and-radio/2019/jul/16/netflix-cuts-controversial-suicide-scene-from-13-reasons-why

Murray, S. (1974). The censor speaks. *Cinema Papers* (2), pp. 102-109. Retrieved May 2023, from Cinema Papers: https://archivesonline.uow.edu.au/nodes/view/5011#idx32005

Murray, S. (1975). 4th International Perth Film Festival. *Cinema Papers* (10), pp. 227-230. Retrieved May 2023, from Cinema Papers: https://archivesonline.uow.edu.au/nodes/view/5016#idx32558

Murray, S. (1978a). John Lamond. *Cinema Papers* (18), p. 96. Retrieved May 2023, from Cinema Papers: https://archivesonline.uow.edu.au/nodes/view/5028?keywords=Cinema%20Papers%201978&highlights=eyIwIjoiY2luZW1hIiwiMSI6InBhcGVycyIsIjIiOiIxOTc4LiIsIjQiOiJwYXBlcnMsIiwiOCI6IihjaW5lbWEiLCIxMiI6IjE5NzgiLCIxMyI6InBhZ2VzIn0=&lsk=70188c65b2c0b0d18f6e248b4cb06d49#

Murray, S. (1978b). The Quarter. *Cinema Papers* (15), pp. 200-201. Retrieved May 2023, from Cinema Papers: https://issuu.com/libuow/docs/cinemapaper1978janno015

Murray, S. (1982). Strickland strikes. *Cinema Papers* (38), p. 204. Retrieved May 2023, from Cinema Papers: https://archivesonline.uow.edu.au/nodes/view/5048

National Classification Code 2005 (Cth). https://www.legislation.gov.au/Details/F2013C00006 Sourced from the Federal Register of Legislation at 7 May 2023. For the latest information on Australian Government law please go to https://www.legislation.gov.au CC BY 4.0 https://creativecommons.org/licenses/by/4.0/legalcode

Netflix [@NetflixTudum]. (2018, November 28). *Life of Brian was banned in certain parts of Britain, Norway, the United States, and Ireland for 28 years because [Tweet]*. Retrieved May 2023, from Twitter: https://twitter.com/netflixfilm/status/1067500453892505600

New South Wales. *Parliamentary debates*. Legislative council. 2 June 1936. 4172. https://api.parliament.nsw.gov.au/api/hansard/search/daily/searchablepdf/HANSARD-290296563-8433

New South Wales. *Parliamentary debates*. Legislative council. 7 September 1993. https://www.parliament.nsw.gov.au/Hansard/Pages/HansardResult.aspx#/docid/HANSARD-1820781676-69091

New South Wales. *Parliamentary debates*. Legislative council. 21 February 2012. 4581. https://www.parliament.nsw.gov.au/permalink?id=HANSARD-1820781676-46167

New South Wales. *Parliamentary debates*. Legislative council. 29 February 1972. 4581. https://api.parliament.nsw.gov.au/api/hansard/search/daily/searchablepdf/HANSARD-290296563-418

Nicole Kidman's BIRTH: shocking double standards. (2005, April 29). Retrieved May 2023, from John Mark Ministries: http://www.jmm.org.au/articles/14853.htm

Nile, F. (1974, August 29). Statement. *Catholic Weekly.*

NITRAM. (2021). Retrieved May 2023, from State Cinema: https://web.archive.org/web/20211102080041/https://statecinema.com.au/movie/nitram

O'Faircheallaigh, C., Graham , P., & Warburton, J. (1991). *Service delivery and public sector marketing.* South Melbourne, VIC: Macmillan.

Office of Film and Literature Classification. (1997, October 1). *Annual Report [of the] Classification Board and Classification Review Board 1996/1997.* Retrieved May 2023, from Australian Classification: https://nla.gov.au/nla.obj-1186375587/view?sectionId=nla.obj-1291555859&partId=nla.obj-1188690627#page/n131/mode/1up

Office of Film and Literature Classification. (1998, October 2). *Annual Report [of the] Classification Board and Classification Review Board 1997/1998.* Retrieved May 2023, from National Library of Australia: http://nla.gov.au/nla.obj-2312918404

Office of Film and Literature Classification. (2000, January 28). *Annual report [of the] Classification Board and Classification Review Board 1999/2000.* Retrieved May 2023, from National Library of Australia: http://nla.gov.au/nla.obj-1363875347

Office of Film and Literature Classification. (2005, October 17). *Annual report [of the] Classification Board and Classification Review Board 2004/2005.* Retrieved May 2023, from National Library of Australia: http://nla.gov.au/nla.obj-906356340

O'Grady, D. (1962, June 16). Paid to have a dirty mind? *The Bulletin, 084* (4296), pp. 12-15. Retrieved May 2023, from Are Media Pty Limited / aremediasyndication.com.au / 'The Bulletin': https://nla.gov.au/nla.obj-673080968

O'Regan, T. (1985). Film societies and festivals in WA. In T. &. O'Regan, *The Moving Image: Film and Television in Western Australia 1896 - 1985.* Perth, WA, Australia: History and Film Association of W.A.

Online Safety Bill 2021 (Cth) s. 9. https://parlinfo.aph.gov.au/parlInfo/search/display/display.w3p;query=Id%3A%22legislation%2Fbills%2Fr6680_aspassed%2F0009%22

The 100 Greatest Movies of All Time. (2022, December 21). Retrieved May 2023, from Variety: https://variety.com/lists/best-movies-of-all-time/pixote-1980/

Other People's Letters - Wowser. (1941, July 12). Retrieved May 2023, from ABC weekly: http://nla.gov.au/nla.obj-1322277203

Parker, J. (1997, August 8). *'Tin Drum' Film Lawsuit Moved To U.S. Court.* Retrieved May 2023, from The Oklahoman: https://www.oklahoman.com/story/news/1997/08/08/tin-drum-film-lawsuit-moved-to-us-court/62306700007/

Pedophilia theme sparks film ban call. (2005, July 19). Retrieved May 2023, from The Sydney Morning Herald: https://www.smh.com.au/entertainment/movies/pedophilia-theme-sparks-film-ban-call-20050719-gdlpjx.html The use of this work has been licensed by Copyright Agency except as permitted by the Copyright Act, you must not re-use this work without the permission of the copyright owner or Copyright Agency.

Pell, G. (2011, December 11). *Sensible decision*. Retrieved May 2023, from Catholic Archdiocese of Sydney: https://web.archive.org/web/20121101120309/http://www.sydneycatholic.org/people/archbishop/stc/2011/20111211_137.shtml

Pornography: how it is radicalising Australian boys. (2021, March 17). Retrieved May 2023, from Radio National: https://www.abc.net.au/radionational/programs/religionandethicsreport/pornography:-how-it-is-radicalising-australian-boy/13256350

Port Arthur massacre footage posted on internet. (2011, July 28). Retrieved May 2023, from ABC News: https://www.abc.net.au/news/2011-07-28/port-arthur-youtube-video/2813556

Production Notes: Bad Luck Banging or Loony Porn. (2021). Retrieved May 2023, from Magnolia Pictures: https://static1.squarespace.com/static/576454e629687fb39bd1f977/t/618943e89d1fc76bc5d41890/1636385768955/BADLUCKBANGINGfinalnotes.pdf

Qin, A. (2016, November 1). *To Many in China, Bai Ling's Role in Documentary Is a Step Too Far*. Retrieved May 2023, from The New York Times: https://www.nytimes.com/2016/11/02/world/asia/china-bai-ling-long-march.html

Queensland. *Parliamentary debates*. Legislative assembly. 24 August 1993. 3717. https://documents.parliament.qld.gov.au/events/han/1993/930824HA.PDF

Quinn, K. (2010, November 11). *Zombie-porn: festival director's home raided by police*. Retrieved May 2023, from The Sydney Morning Herald: https://www.smh.com.au/entertainment/movies/zombieporn-festival-directors-home-raided-by-police-20101111-17omu.html

Quinn, K. (2011, February 24). *Gay zombie porn movie saga finally settles*. Retrieved May 2023, from The Sydney Morning Herald: https://www.smh.com.au/entertainment/movies/gay-zombie-porn-movie-saga-finally-settles-20110224-1b5zj.html

Quinn, K. (2020a, July 30). *Melbourne International Film Festival dumps android child sex film*. Retrieved May 2023, from The Age: https://www.theage.com.au/culture/movies/melbourne-international-film-festival-dumps-android-child-sex-film-20200725-p55fdr.html

Quinn, K. (2020b, August 20). *Melbourne International Film Festival (online) - Karl Quinn responds to Tom Ryan and David Stratton about MIFF's decision to pull THE TROUBLE WITH BEING BORN from its program and reports on his interview with the director Sandra Wollner*. Retrieved May 2023, from Film Alert 101: https://filmalert101.blogspot.com/2020/08/melbourne-international-film-festival_20.html

Rice, A. (1999, July 15). *Eyes Digitally Shut*. Retrieved May 2023, from Wired: https://www.wired.com/1999/07/eyes-digitally-shut/

Richie, D. (2009, April 30). *In the Realm of the Senses: Some Notes on Oshima and Pornography*. Retrieved May 2023, from Criterion: https://www.criterion.com/current/posts/1108-in-the-realm-of-the-senses-some-notes-on-oshima-and-pornography

Roach, V. (2014, February 18). *Wolf Creek 2 downgraded to teenager-friendly rating*. Retrieved May 2023, from News.com.au: https://www.news.com.au/entertainment/movies/wolf-creek-2-downgraded-to-teenagerfriendly-rating/news-story/a90070c969f217224aa5568f4014f9f9

Roberts, M. (2015, May 28). *Australian Films Centre Stage at the 62nd Sydney Film Festival*. Retrieved May 2023, from Rochford Street Reviews: https://rochfordstreetreview.com/2015/05/28/australian-films-centre-stage-at-the-62nd-sydney-film-festival/

Roohizadegan, Ashley [@theCriticAR]. (2022, October 8). *I was scrolling through old photos, and I found this gem. Anyone know why there are two classifications on the cover? [Tweet]*. Retrieved May 2023, from Twitter: https://twitter.com/theCriticAR/status/1578670174236180480

Rose, T. (2022, September 7). *'Lack of consent': push for Australian film classifications to note 'concerning' scenes*. Retrieved May 2023, from The Guardian: https://www.theguardian.com/australia-news/2022/sep/07/lack-of-consent-push-for-australian-film-classifications-to-note-concerning-scenes

Ross, N. (2011, June 29). *Secrets of obscenity: the classification riddle*. Retrieved May 2023, from ABC News: https://www.abc.net.au/news/2011-06-29/secrets-of-obscenity-the-classification-riddle/2776656

Rowan-Legg, S. (2012, February 22). *Charges against Sitges Festival & director Ángel Sala dropped*. Retrieved May 2023, from Screen Anarchy: https://screenanarchy.com/2012/02/charges-against-sitges-festival-director-angel-sala-dropped.html

Russo, P. (2015, December). *Beyond Perverse Allegiance: The Problem of Viewers' Engagement in Pier Paolo Pasolini's Salò or The 120 Days of Sodom*. Retrieved May 2023, from Senses of Cinema: https://www.sensesofcinema.com/2015/pier-paolo-pasolini/viewers-engagement-in-salo/

Ryan Gosling fired from film after ice cream binge. (2010, December 3). Retrieved May 2023, from Reuters: https://www.reuters.com/article/us-gosling-idUSTRE6B20MT20101203

Ryan, R. J. (2016). *Arts-Media Censorship: Doing the Right Thing the Wrong Way*. Macquarie University, Department of Media, Music, Communication and Cultural Studies. Retrieved May 2023, from Macquarie University: https://doi.org/10.25949/19444034.v1

Sandeman, J. (2021, June 10). *BREAKING NEWS: CHRISTIAN DEMOCRATIC PARTY IN RECEIVERSHIP*. Retrieved May 2023, from Eternity News: https://www.eternitynews.com.au/australia/breaking-news-christian-democratic-party-in-recievership/

Schubert, C. (2017). *Film Classification and Censorship in Australia: a filmic image response perspective*. Adelaide: Flinders University. Retrieved May 2023, from Flinders University: https://flex.flinders.edu.au/file/43cb39b1-41f9-4bf8-a87a-425cc44d6856/1/ThesisSchubert2017OA.pdf

Seniors United Party of Australia. (2022, January 30). *Policies of The Seniors United Party Of Australia*. Retrieved May 2023, from Seniors United Party of Australia: https://web.archive.org/web/20220311113952/https://www.seniorsunitedparty.com.au/policies-of-the-seniors-party-of-australia/

The sex, the violence, the director and his motive. (1991, July 12). Retrieved May 2023, from The Sydney Morning Herald: https://smharchives.smedia.com.au The use of this work has been licensed by Copyright Agency except as permitted by the Copyright Act, you must not re-use this work without the permission of the copyright owner or Copyright Agency.

Sharon Austen Limited. (2001, February 26). *Final Terms of Acquisition of Divolution Agreed*. Retrieved May 2023, from Iguana2: https://newswire.iguana2.com/af5f4d73c1a54a33/ims.asx/XX229325/IMS_Final_Terms_of_Acquisition_of_Divolution_Agreed

Sharon Austen Limited. (2002, June 6). *"SHARON AUSTEN LIMITED" CUTS OUT THE MIDDLE MAN AND GOES LONG ON SEX TOYS*. Retrieved May 2023, from Iguana2: https://newswire.iguana2.com/af5f4d73c1a54a33/ims.asx/XX266915/IMS_Exclusive_Deal_with_Erostar_Erotic_Novelities

Sheldon, M. (2015, July 31). *Viridiana (1961)*. Retrieved May 2023, from Classic Art Films: http://www.classicartfilms.com/viridinia-1961

Shoard, C. (2011, May 21). *Jafar Panahi not in Cannes for This Is Not a Film premiere*. Retrieved May 2023, from The Guardian: https://www.theguardian.com/film/2011/may/21/jafar-panahi-cannes-not-film-premiere

Siegel, T. (2018, August 3). *Disney's 'Christopher Robin' Won't Get China Release Amid Pooh Crackdown (Exclusive)*. Retrieved May 2023, from The Hollywood Reporter: https://www.hollywoodreporter.com/heat-vision/christopher-robin-refused-china-release-winnie-pooh-crackdown-1131907

Silva, J. d. (2006, October 24). *Obscenity and Article 175 of the Japanese Penal Code: A Short Introduction to Japanese Censorship*. Retrieved May 2023, from EigaNove: http://eiga9.altervista.org/articulos/obscenity.html

Silva, K. (2015, October 1). *Hardcore porn, explosives and violent novels: The books banned in Queensland*. Retrieved May 2023, from Brisbane Times: https://www.brisbanetimes.com.au/national/queensland/hardcore-porn-explosives-and-violent-novels-the-books-banned-in-queensland-20151001-gjzgyg.html

Silverton, P. (2009). *Filthy English: The How, Why, When, And What Of Everday Swearing*. Edinburgh: Portobello Books.

Smith, N. M. (2011, October 25). *We Interview the Director of "A Serbian Film," Now on DVD (And Yes, the Movie Deserves Its Rep)*. Retrieved May 2023, from Indiewire: https://www.indiewire.com/2011/10/we-interview-the-director-of-a-serbian-film-now-on-dvd-and-yes-the-movie-deserves-its-rep-51495/

Social Media Powerful Weapon in Fight Against Sexploitation of Girls. (2011, December 7). Retrieved May 2023, from Catholic Archdiocese of Sydney: https://web.archive.org/web/20120109035428/http://www.sydneycatholic.org/news/latest_news/2011/2011127_122.shtml

Stratton, D. (1971, November 13). What we'll see when the children aren't looking. *The Bulletin, 093* (4781), pp. 39-41. Retrieved from Are Media Pty Limited / aremediasyndication.com.au / 'The Bulletin': https://nla.gov.au/nla.obj-1413438516/view?sectionId=nla.obj-1641595810

Stratton, D. (2008). *I Peed on Fellini*. North Sydney: Random House Australia Pty Ltd.

Stratton, D. (2020, August 12). *Melbourne International Film Festival (online) - David Stratton has some thoughts about MIFF's decision to withdraw THE TROUBLE WITH BEING BORN (Sandra Wollner, Austria, 2020) from its program*. Retrieved May 2023, from Film Alert 101: http://filmalert101.blogspot.com/2020/08/melbourne-international-film-festival_12.html

Strickland, J. (1977). How Australian film censorship works. *Cinema Papers* (11), pp. 206-208. Retrieved May 2023, from Cinema Papers: https://issuu.com/libuow/docs/cinemapaper1977janno011

Strickland, J. (1992, December). Censorship in the 1990s. (P. Mallam, Ed.) *Communications Law Bulletin, 12* (3), p. 10.

Strong, R., & Strong, J. (1971). *Mr. Chipp and the Porno-Push*. Melbourne: Minton Publishing Co.

Stronger Futures in the Northern Territory (Consequential and Transitional Provisions) Act 2012 (Cth). https://www.legislation.gov.au/Details/C2013C00553 Sourced from the Federal Register of Legislation at 7 May 2023. For the latest information on Australian Government law please go to https://www.legislation.gov.au CC BY 4.0 https://creativecommons.org/licenses/by/4.0/legalcode

[Summary of recent Kelly Gang pictures and their effect on youth]. (1907, May 2). *The Bulletin, 028* (1420), p. 8. Retrieved May 2023, from Are Media Pty Limited / aremediasyndication.com.au / 'The Bulletin': http://nla.gov.au/nla.obj-691067474

't' titles. (n.d.). Retrieved May 2023, from The Chopping List: http://users.tpg.com.au/boschy69/chopping/titles_t.html#Twister

Tadros, E. (2022, November 7). *New tool cuts wait for US TV shows from up to 20 days to 24 hours*. Retrieved May 2023, from Australian Financial Review: https://www.afr.com/companies/media-and-marketing/new-tool-cuts-wait-for-us-tv-shows-from-up-to-20-days-to-24-hours-20221106-p5bvwp

Tankard Reist, M. (2021, March 9). *Why "consent" doesn't stand a chance against porn culture*. Retrieved May 2023, from ABC News: https://www.abc.net.au/religion/consent-education-does-not-stand-a-chance-against-pornography/13231364

Taylor, A. (2011, August 21). *Film banned in Britain approved here*. Retrieved May 2023, from The Sydney Morning Herald: https://www.smh.com.au/entertainment/movies/film-banned-in-britain-approved-here-20110820-1j3vp.html The use of this work has been licensed by Copyright Agency except as permitted by the Copyright Act, you must not re-use this work without the permission of the copyright owner or Copyright Agency.

THRILLER FILM BANNED. (1948, August 6). Retrieved May 2023, from The Advertiser: https://trove.nla.gov.au/newspaper/article/43777661

Tivey, B. (1970a, June 27). Banned films for special people. *The Bulletin, 092* (4710), p. 47. Retrieved May 2023, from Are Media Pty Limited / aremediasyndication.com.au / 'The Bulletin': http://nla.gov.au/nla.obj-1162049357

Tivey, B. (1970b, August 1). Better than the book. *The Bulletin, 092* (4715), pp. 38-39. Retrieved May 2023, from Are Media Pty Limited / aremediasyndication.com.au / 'The Bulletin': http://nla.gov.au/nla.obj-1178051276

Too Rude for Queensland. (2017, August 14). Retrieved May 2023, from State Library of Queensland: https://www.slq.qld.gov.au/discover/exhibitions/past-exhibitions/freedom-then-freedom-now/too-rude-queensland

Tremonti, A. M. (2004, April 19). *Whole Show Blow-by-Blow*. Retrieved May 2023, from The Current: https://web.archive.org/web/20040807111304/http://www.cbc.ca/thecurrent/2004/200404/20040419.html

The Trouble with Being Born (2020). Retrieved May 2023, from Box Office Mojo: https://www.boxofficemojo.com/title/tt9220966/?ref_=bo_se_r_1

Vnuk, H. (2003). *Snatched: Sex and Censorship in Australia*. Milsons Point, NSW: Random House.

Ward, K. (1994, July). *John Dickie: Incensored*. Retrieved May 2023, from Tabula Rasa: http://www.tabula-rasa.info/Horror/JohnDickie.html

Wearring, M. (2008, April 20). *Damon and Hunter do it*. Retrieved May 2023, from Star Observer: https://www.starobserver.com.au/news/national-news/new-south-wales-news/damon-and-hunter-do-it/10092

Wells, H. (1939). *Travels of a Republican Radical in Search of Hot Water*. Harmondsworth: Penguin Books Limited.

What the M?! (2021, September 13). Retrieved May 2023, from Te Mana Whakaatu - Classification Office: https://www.classificationoffice.govt.nz/news/blog-posts/what-the-m/

White, A. (2017, November 27). *Heironymus Merkin: the surreal sex musical that doomed Anthony Newley's marriage to Joan Collins*. Retrieved May 2023, from The Telegraph: https://www.telegraph.co.uk/films/0/heironymus-merkin-surreal-sex-musical-destroyed-anthony-newleys/

Whitmore, H. (1965, May 8). Wholesome or Prissy? *The Bulletin, 087* (4445), pp. 24-26. Retrieved May 2023, from Are Media Pty Limited / aremediasyndication.com.au / 'The Bulletin': https://nla.gov.au/nla.obj-682855594

Williams, R. (2012, December 6). *Once Banned in Queensland, Australia*. Retrieved May 2023, from Letterboxed: https://letterboxd.com/bosch/list/once-banned-in-queensland-australia/

Willsher, K. (2020, May 13). *'La Covid': coronavirus acronym is feminine, Académie Française says*. Retrieved May 2023, from The Guardian: https://www.theguardian.com/world/2020/may/13/le-la-covid-coronavirus-acronym-feminine-academie-francaise-france

Wood, M. (2006, May 22). *Viridiana: The Human Comedy*. Retrieved May 2023, from The Crtierion Collection: https://www.criterion.com/current/posts/423

Zyber, J. (2015, November 2). *Mulholland Drive*. Retrieved May 2023, from High-Def Digest: https://bluray.highdefdigest.com/23834/mulhollanddrcriterion.html

Photo Credit: Emma Daisy

Simon Miraudo is a Western Australian writer, broadcaster and film critic. He is the General Manager of RTRFM, which is an independent, non-profit community radio station that provides an alternative voice for WA through innovative music and talks programming, with a strong focus on the arts, culture, social justice, politics and the environment. Simon has presented a film review segment on RTRFM since 2010, and has covered films extensively for the ABC and The Guardian, among other outlets. You can find more than 1,400 of his film reviews on Rotten Tomatoes, where he is a verified contributor. He lives in Perth with his wife, Jenny, and son, Miles.

www.ingramcontent.com/pod-product-compliance
Lightning Source LLC
Chambersburg PA
CBHW020331010526
44107CB00054B/2077